The
College Success
Reader

D0878742

As part of Houghton Mifflin's ongoing commitment to the
environment, this text has been printed on recycled paper.

The College Success Reader

Robert Holkeboer
Eastern Michigan University

Thomas Hoeksema
New Mexico State University

HOUGHTON MIFFLIN COMPANY
Boston   New York

Director of Student Success Programs: Barbara A. Heinssen
Associate Editor: Melissa Plumb
Associate Project Editor: Tamela Ambush
Editorial Assistant: Jodi O'Rourke
Senior Production/Design Coordinator: Sarah Ambrose
Senior Manufacturing Coordinator: Florence Cadran

Cover design: Rebecca Fagan
Cover photograph: © Tom Collicott/Graphistock

Copyright © 1998 by Houghton Mifflin Company. All rights reserved.

No part of this work may be reproduced or transmitted in any form or by any means, electronic or mechanical, including photocopying and recording, or by any information storage or retrieval system without the prior written permission of the copyright owner unless such copying is expressly permitted by federal copyright law. With the exception of non-profit transcription in Braille, Houghton Mifflin is not authorized to grant permission for further uses of copyrighted selections reprinted in this text without the permission of their owners. Permission must be obtained from the individual copyright owners as identified herein. Address requests for permission to make copies of Houghton Mifflin material to College Permissions, Houghton Mifflin Company, 222 Berkeley Street, Boston, MA 02116-3764.

Printed in the U.S.A.

Library of Congress Catalog Card Number: 97-72488

Student Book ISBN: 0-395-85706-6

123456789-DOH-01 00 99 98 97

MEMORIAL LIBRARY
STATE UNIVERSITY COLLEGE
CORTLAND, NEW YORK 13045

Contents

To the Instructor

Why The College Success Reader?

Why Adopt *The College Success Reader?*

The College Success Reader is a lively, eclectic volume of essays about college life and learning that can be used as a primary text in a variety of college classroom settings, especially those that emphasize the basic skills of reading, writing, and critical thinking. Its emphasis on introducing college students to the richness, complexity, and challenge of the college experience makes the text easily adaptable to the college success classroom as well.

The authors range from well-known writers such as Malcolm X, Adrienne Rich, and Anna Quindlen to an ordinary college student such as Christopher Lee, who despite a severe learning disability, managed to graduate from college and write a book about his heroic effort to succeed. The essays and apparatus are designed to stimulate animated small-group discussion among first-year college students who must find their own perspective on such difficult issues as academic honesty, balancing academic responsibilities with the need for personal growth, competition for grades, diversity, gender roles, and responsible sexuality.

Because the text is for and about first-year college students, college students played a substantial role in its overall concept, design, and evaluation. The essays were selected or approved on the basis of student interest and level of engagement.

The contents are grouped into five broad subject areas:

- Part 1, "The Motivation to Learn," opens with the success stories of Malcolm X and Christopher Lee and continues with motivational essays addressed to career-minded students, women, and adult learners.
- Part 2, "Learning to Learn," addresses some important academic issues, such as the value of liberal arts requirements, the lecture system, time management, how to prepare for and write essay exams, and academic integrity.
- Part 3, "Campus Culture," treats the nonacademic side of college life: student attitudes, binge drinking, fraternity and sorority life, intercollegiate athletics, and service learning.

- Part 4, "Sex and Relationships," deals with perception and communication issues between men and women and includes discussions of date rape, gender differences, and gender bias.
- Part 5, "Living with Diversity," treats multicultural issues such as ethnic and racial self-segregation and cultural stereotypes. It concludes with an upbeat essay by Diane Cole, "Don't Just Stand There," which offers practical suggestions on how ordinary college students can challenge prejudice and reduce racial hatred on their own campuses.

The College Success Reader offers many advantages for the instructor who is looking for an academically substantial reader that addresses issues of immediate concern to students and stimulates genuine student interest and response.

- It provides user-friendly apparatus—easy for instructors to teach from and enjoyable for students to use.
- It emphasizes the importance of careful reading, critical thinking, and audience-directed writing.
- Its editorial apparatus encourages active, cooperative learning in small groups.
- It challenges students intellectually rather than condescending to them.
- It treats students as adults who are responsible for their academic and personal success in college.
- It provides a realistic portrayal of college life.

The College Success Reader offers first-year college students the opportunity to read, think, speak, and write about the new institutional culture they have entered. As they wrestle with significant issues, students will be sharpening their skills in reading, reasoning, writing, and team building. Equally important, they will be making meaningful connections between their academic lives and real-world issues.

Topical Coverage

The College Success Reader contains twenty-eight essays on topics of interest and importance to college students.

- The purposes of attending college and the motivation to learn
- Liberal arts requirements, time management, and academic integrity
- Campus environmental activism
- Fraternity and sorority life
- Alcohol and substance abuse
- Sexual responsibility and safety

- Gender roles and stereotypes
- The diversity of American culture

Instructors are encouraged to assign only the readings that work best for them and to supplement the assigned readings with course pack materials tailored to each particular course.

Text Features

The College Success Reader is supported by editorial elements designed to foster an interactive, team-based approach to learning.

- The text opens with two extended essays by the authors directed at the college student who is seeking a competitive edge in the twenty-first-century job market. "Active Reading" and "Active Writing" explain why effective reading, thinking, and writing skills are valued by employers and include practical suggestions for improving these essential skills.
- Each part begins with an introduction, which offers a wider perspective on the part topic and briefly introduces the essays in that part. The Introduction is followed by a prewriting activity called "Write Before You Read," in which students reflect on what they already know about the topic before they begin reading. Each part contains five or six thematically related essays of varying length and complexity.
- Each essay begins with a preview introducing the essay topic and author. At the end of each essay are three activities designed to ensure active reading and clear writing about the essay topic. "Dialogue" consists of three questions intended to unpack the essay and stimulate class discussion. "Writing Topics" offers a full range of standard college-composition writing strategies, from free-written journal entries to formal, extended essays. Finally, "Interaction" is a focused group activity that encourages critical thinking, active communication, and team building.
- Each part concludes with an exercise called "Reflections," which asks students to review the attitudes they described in the prewriting exercise and indicate how those attitudes have changed as a result of reading the essays in the part. This is followed by an optional writing assignment, which usually requires an extended formal essay dealing with some aspect of the part topic.

We are grateful not only to the authors and publishers of the essays for sharing their copyrighted work but also to the students and educators who reviewed the manuscript and made thoughtful suggestions for improvement. These include our student panel of reviewers from Eastern Michigan University—John Proffitt, Michael Rodman, and Jan Habarth; Dr. Christopher Burnham and Dr. Stuart Brown from New Mexico State University; Sally Firmin, Baylor University, Texas, Mary L. Hummel, University of Michigan, and Alexandra Jepson Rodgers, Florida State University. Finally, we want to thank Bill Webber, former director of Student Success Programs at Houghton Mifflin, and his outstanding production staff: Tamela Ambush, Jodi O'Rourke, Sarah Ambrose and Florence Cadran. Any errors that have survived this comprehensive review are entirely the responsibility of the authors.

R.H.
T.H.

To the Student

Active Reading

Each year for the past twenty-five years, the verbal skills of American students, as measured by standardized tests taken by high school seniors, have declined. Television and video games are usually blamed for the problem, but there are other causes as well.

- Schools have de-emphasized grammar and syntax, assigning less reading and writing and relying more heavily on short-answer and fill-in-the-blank writing assignments that are easier to grade.
- Most college-prep programs no longer require a foreign language, and almost none require Latin, which helps students understand the building blocks of language and from which nearly half of all English words are derived.
- Schools are relying more heavily on visual media, especially user-friendly computer programs and video games that ask only for keystroke responses to verbal cues.

This all adds up to passive learning, which is the least effective kind. Reading, writing, and reciting are active processes; they take more effort but produce better results.

Although colleges are assigning less reading and writing than in years past, you can still expect to do a good deal of both during your college career, especially as you begin work in your major field. Students who put off taking required composition and literature courses until later in their college careers are making a big mistake, since the skills taught in these courses are applicable to virtually every course in the college curriculum. At the same time, students who take composition and literature immediately with the idea of getting them out of the way also are making a mistake. Reading and writing are skills that need to be continually honed; without constant practice, they rapidly deteriorate.

If you want to become an educated, successful person, you will need to become a habitual reader. If you have other time-consuming habits (watching TV, playing video games, shopping), consider making this rule for yourself: I will spend at least as much time reading in a day as I spend watching TV (or shopping or shooting hoops). A good corollary to this rule is: I will do my reading first and the less demanding activity afterward, as a reward.

Reading for Information

Much of the reading you will do in college and after you graduate will be for the sole purpose of acquiring information—rapidly processing factual information in textbooks, newspapers, journals, reports, manuals, and reference works. You might start your nonfiction habit by reading a good daily newspaper each morning (*New York Times, Wall Street Journal*), a weekly newsmagazine (*Time, U.S. News & World Report*), or a monthly magazine (*Harper's, The Atlantic, Psychology Today, Consumer Reports*).

Practice Active Reading

Since factual writing—especially in college textbooks—can sometimes be tedious, you'll need to make a special effort to involve yourself in the material. The best way to do this is to practice the active reading principles known as SQ3R.

1. **Survey.** Quickly preview the material. Examine the title, headings, and subheadings. What are the main ideas? How is the information organized?

2. **Question.** Transform the title, headings, and subheadings (main ideas) into questions. What questions can you expect to find answers to here?

3. **Read.** Read rapidly with a single purpose: to find answers to your questions. Raise (and answer) additional questions as you go along.

4. **Recite.** Stop periodically to look away from the text to see if you can recite (preferably aloud) the answers to your questions. Write the answers on a separate sheet of paper without referring to the text.

5. **Review.** When you finish, go over the entire text again, looking away from the text as much as possible, until you can recall it accurately.

Try to notice when your attention wanders. After one minute? Five minutes? Fifteen minutes? Break up your reading into time periods that coincide with your ability to concentrate. Stop whenever your attention wavers and do a quick body check: Am I alert? Am I getting tired? Has my mind been wandering? Am I getting too relaxed? Fatigue and boredom are reasons to take a break, not to quit. Take a brief time-out to psych yourself up for the next reading stint.

During your break, reject all negative thoughts (I'm bored. My mind is a sieve. This is dull stuff. I'm tired. This is too difficult. I don't understand. I wish I were doing something else.). Replace them with positive thoughts (I'm on a roll! My mind is a steel trap! I won't stop until I master this material!).

Always read with a pencil in hand and stay active as you read by marking up your text. This will personalize the text for you and help you internalize and remember the information. Following are some suggestions for marking up your text:

1. Write the *topic* of the text (answer to the question, What is this text *about?*) at the top of the page and draw a box around it in the text.
2. Look for a *definition* of the topic (usually this will occur early in the text). Underline it and write "DEF" in the column next to the definition.
3. Write "EX" in the column next to any *examples* or *illustrations*.
4. What are the major points the author is making? Number them in the text and circle the numbers.
5. Put a question mark in the column next to anything you don't understand.
6. Put an exclamation point in the column next to anything you think is interesting or important.
7. Relate the passage to your own life or to something you already know (the design of your ninth-grade science fair project, for example) by writing a brief note in the column. Draw a happy face or write "ME" next to it to identify it as your own idea.
8. Double-underline *major* ideas or definitions.
9. Single-underline *secondary* ideas or definitions.

Now imagine yourself being tested on your reading. If you were testing someone else on their reading of the text, what are some questions you might ask? Write out answers to your own questions.

Above all, try to see connections between what you're reading and what you already know. When you can find a connection between new knowledge and old knowledge, the new material will be more meaningful, and you will be more likely to remember it.

Read Rapidly

When you're reading for pleasure, speed is pointless: rushing through a great poem is like wolfing down a gourmet meal. But if your purpose is to obtain and retain information, the faster you read and the more you remember, the better.

According to speed-reading expert Robert Zorn, the average adult reads about 200 words per minute (wpm). The average college student reads about 350 wpm (or one page per minute). Most readers, whatever their speed, comprehend about half of what they read. Since the quantity of reading declines after a person leaves school, college students read significantly faster than college graduates. Reading speed is a direct factor of constant practice.

With sustained practice and effort, it is possible to double or triple your reading speed in a matter of weeks while maintaining or even increasing your comprehension, and without spending money on instruction.

1. Increase your vocabulary by ten words a week. A larger vocabulary will enable you to read more difficult material faster. Running into words we don't understand slows us down.
2. Use a moving object as you read. The eye follows a moving object. As you read, move a pencil or three-by-five-inch index card down the page. Gradually increase the speed. Remember: your mind controls both your reading speed and the speed of your pencil. You must force the pencil to move slightly faster than the eye wants to move.
3. Reduce or eliminate regressions. A regression entails going back and rereading. According to Zorn, each regression costs you about fifty wpm. To eliminate regressions, Zorn suggests making a *reading window*. Take a three-by-five-inch index card and cut out a horizontal slit measuring two and a half inches by one-quarter inch. The card will block out extraneous material that diverts the eye and causes regressions.
4. Notice and eliminate body motion. Kinesthetic learners (people who habitually move their bodies while learning) are the slowest readers. Have someone watch you when you study: do you jiggle or rock to and fro? Notice it, concentrate on it, and stop it.
5. Notice and eliminate vocalizing. Aural or auditory learners talk, mumble, whisper, or hum to themselves as they read. Since people can read much faster than they can speak, vocalizing slows us down. (Zorn points out that George Washington was both a kinesthetic and an auditory learner—he read aloud on horseback!) Some auditory learners need noise—background music, for example—to learn; others need absolute quiet. What you need to eliminate is not necessarily background noise, but the tendency to move your lips and tongue and to hear the words as you read.
6. Use your eyes only. Visual learners are the fastest readers. Try to block out the stimulation of any other sense as you read.

7. Read in chunks. Rather than focusing / your eyes / on a single word / at a time, / try to / take in two or three words / (or a single thought unit) / at a time. Gradually increase the size of the chunks / to a whole line of print. At the end of a line, practice a *down-and-back* eye sweep. (The opposite, a *back-and-down* eye sweep, takes you back over the line you just read—a time-wasting regression.) Eventually, this zigzag eye motion will allow you to take in larger and larger chunks of print.

As you practice the techniques of rapid reading, you will find your comprehension declining at first. As you get better at it, your comprehension will soon be back to normal and then will begin to increase as your concentration improves.

There is certainly no harm in working with one of the many speed-reading aids available on the market—videos, computer software, tachistoscopes, eye-span trainers, and pace accelerators. Whether you use sophisticated training aids, take a speed-reading course, or practice the above principles on your own, you will need patience and many hours of concentrated effort. As with all the strategies and techniques for becoming a better student, you'll get the best results if you devise a plan and stick to it.

Expect to achieve modest gains from a concentrated speed-reading program, but remember that real learning is not just a matter of accumulating information. It is also a matter of processing that information, relating one idea to another and to your own life, applying information to the solution of a problem, thinking imaginatively, and making value judgments. Above all, learning brings pleasure and satisfaction, which speed-readers—grimly intent on acquiring data, repressing all sensual responses to a text, and setting new speed records—blithely ignore. Real learning occurs not while you are rapidly scanning a text, but when you look away and think about what you read.

Reading for Pleasure

Aside from acquiring useful information, there are other purposes for, and benefits to be gained from, habitual reading. In the fifth century B.C., the Chinese philosopher Confucius (a contemporary of the Greek playwright Sophocles) cited a few of the pleasures of reading good literature.

- Reading "lifts the will," inspiring us to do things we thought were impossible.
- It "sharpens the vision," helping us see clearly what was formerly blurred.

- It helps us "make distinctions and resent evil." Good literature clarifies our values and helps us not only to see the choices available to us but also to choose the right ones.
- It "confirms us in civic and domestic virtue." In books we meet more people than we could ever meet in life. By measuring ourselves alongside them, we acquire a sense of our place in society and become more sensitive to the problems and needs of others.
- It "teaches the names of many birds, animals, plants, and trees." While reading for pleasure, we are also acquiring valuable information from authors who have devoted many hours of study to their topics.

Wide reading gives a person a sense of command over the world and a sense of self-possession. Occasionally, you will have the good fortune to find just the right book at the right time, a book that speaks directly to you and changes your life. Although this happy event is largely a matter of serendipity, the chances of its happening will increase the more you read.

Wide reading is important to learning because to learn something new we need a context or background for learning. Learning feeds on itself. The more you know, the more you are able to learn. We can't possibly live long enough, travel enough, experience enough, or meet enough people to learn all we need to know. Reading gives us an efficient and economical means of expanding the context of our lives. We may not have the time or money to travel to Tibet, but we can read a book about Tibet. We may never meet a General Motors executive, but we can read books about executive wheeling and dealing in the auto industry. We certainly will not wish personal tragedy upon ourselves, but we can prepare ourselves for it by imaginatively experiencing the suffering of others.

Reading is an acquired discipline and a lifelong habit. Your college schedule will leave you with precious little time for leisure reading. One way to form the habit is to keep a good book on your night table at all times and read yourself to sleep, even if it's only five or ten minutes a night.

Choose reading material that is slightly challenging but still interesting. Just as children eventually cease to enjoy cotton candy, your taste in books will gradually become more sophisticated and your standards more demanding.

Following are some guidelines for selecting leisure reading:

- Try not to restrict yourself to one kind of reading material—Agatha Christie mysteries, sci-fi, self-help books, romances. Keep an open mind and try new authors and genres. Try books written by and about the opposite sex. Read books about cultures that are alien to you. If you mostly read novels, try an occasional volume of history or biography. In other words, vary your reading diet.

- An exciting plot is just one of the many possible virtues of a novel. Learn to enjoy fiction for other reasons—style and character development, for example. Good stories don't always have happy endings. Look instead for an appropriate or satisfying ending.

- Seek out reading material that challenges your beliefs. When you find your values challenged, be grateful for the opportunity to reexamine your values and clarify them even further.

- Read the classics. (Mark Twain defined a classic as a book everybody wishes they had read but nobody has.) Classics are great books not because experts say they are, but because they have entertained, instructed, and permanently changed the lives of people for generations. They stay fresh and can be reread profitably. They grow on you.

The Reading Habit

Habits—both good ones and bad ones—are the result of repetitive behavior over time. Following are some ways to develop a reading habit:

- Students spend a lot of time waiting in line—in the cafeteria, at registration, outside a professor's office, waiting for a ride. Since there's always a chance you might get stuck somewhere with nothing to do, get in the habit of carrying a small paperback in your purse or backpack. Nobel Prize–winning poet T. S. Eliot memorized all three volumes of Dante's *Divine Comedy*—and learned Italian in the process—while waiting for the Harvard Square bus!

- Keep a list of the books you've read with the date you completed them, along with a brief personal reaction—what you thought of the book, what you learned. You'll take great personal satisfaction in watching this list grow over time.

- Read with a pencil and your vocabulary notebook close at hand. Underline passages that strike you as beautifully composed or that contain ideas you want to remember. Write your own ideas in the column. Circle words you don't understand and add them to your vocabulary list. Try to be an active reader even when you're only reading for pleasure.

Building Your Vocabulary

The English language contains more than 600,000 words. According to linguist William Safire, a well-educated person has a reading and writing vocabulary of only about 20,000 words but uses only 2,000 of them when speaking. Twenty-five percent of our spoken vocabulary consists of only ten words. (*I* ranks first; *you* ranks second.) Our vocabulary increases by hundreds of words a year while we are in school; after we leave, it increases by only twenty-five to fifty words a year—proof that constant and active reading and learning are the keys to building a strong vocabulary.

The reason for developing a strong vocabulary is not because we need more words for ordinary conversation. Nor is it to impress people. The real reason is that words are tools for thinking about and understanding the world. One research study of successful Americans in all walks of life indicated a direct correlation between vocabulary range and salary within a profession. Language gives us power and mastery over our environment. When you add a new word to your vocabulary, you acquire a new idea, a new way of seeing, a new avenue of thought. In your other courses, you are being introduced to the mysteries of an academic discipline primarily by being introduced to its essential vocabulary.

Words are the tools by which humans think. Some students say, "I know what I mean, but I just can't express it." Although this is sometimes true of feelings and ineffable experiences (love or moments of spiritual insight), it is rarely true of ideas. If we don't have the words, we don't have the idea.

The best way to increase your vocabulary is to read actively. When you encounter a word that you'd like to add to your vocabulary, circle it and, at the first opportunity, write it in a notebook used only for that purpose. Write down both the word and the context in which it appeared. Look it up in a good dictionary (most paperback dictionaries are inadequate because they don't give alternative meanings and word origins) and record the definition. Note the etymology (how the word evolved) and other meanings. Note how the word is pronounced; say it out loud. At your first opportunity, use the new word in a conversation or in a paper you're writing. Actually using the word yourself is a crucial step toward making the word your own.

Be on the lookout for new words. Make it a private, active hobby. As you look for new vocabulary words, be selective. Pick words you've heard before but whose meaning is unclear to you (vocabulary experts call these "frontier words"). Sometimes you'll hear a new word in a lecture and then see it again in your reading a day or two later. Those are good words to zero in on. Pick words that sound interesting to you and that you think might be useful to you. Unless they're related to your major interest, avoid technical terms that you may never see again and will probably never use. Limit your vocabulary-building program to about ten words a week. Review all your words once a week (use three-by-five-inch flash cards if you like) or have someone test you on them.

Buy a small notebook that you will use exclusively for vocabulary building. Over the next week, find ten new words that you want to add to your vocabulary. For each word, write down the following information:

1. The word itself (in capital letters)
2. The pronunciation of the word (unless it's obvious)
3. The preferred (first) dictionary definition
4. The etymology (only if it's interesting or helpful for you)
5. The context in which you heard or read the word

Bring your notebook to class a week from now and show your instructor or share with your group your first ten words. After that, keep it up—ten words a week.

Always relate a word to an idea that has meaning to you. It's a waste of time to memorize definitions in a vacuum. If you acquire new words at the same rate as you acquire new ideas, you'll find that both your rate of learning and your rate of vocabulary building will gradually accelerate. A new idea introduces you to ten new words. A new word opens up ten new ideas.

Keeping a Journal

In many college success courses, students are required to keep a journal. You could begin your journal by writing about your reading habits, using the following questions as a guide:

1. Are you a fast or slow reader? Do you think your reading comprehension would improve or decline if you forced yourself to read faster?
2. Sometimes people read just for pleasure and sometimes just for information. Do the two forms of reading call for different strategies and techniques? For example, do you read faster or slower when reading for information?
3. Describe a book you read recently for pleasure. What did you like about it?
4. Can you list five books that you read during the past year and briefly describe their contents? List five more that you've heard something about and would like to read. Why do these books interest you?
5. How would you describe your vocabulary? What conscious steps have you taken, if any, to improve it? How would a stronger vocabulary benefit you?

Journal writing should be free and easy. Don't censor yourself too much or worry about spelling and grammar. Write as fast as you can think.

Summary

Although habitual readers are sometimes stereotyped as antisocial, ivory tower types, reading is actually a social activity. Words are the primary tools by which human beings communicate with each other.

Active, habitual readers acquire powerful tools for living. The ability to read rapidly with good comprehension is not only essential to success in college but also indispensable in today's job market. Habitual readers tend to be good writers and clear thinkers with a good understanding of human nature. Reading for information teaches us to analyze and synthesize, to think critically and creatively, and to express ourselves clearly. Reading imaginative literature gives us a better understanding of human nature as we encounter a gallery of characters we will never have the opportunity to meet in life. A happy byproduct of the reading habit is a powerful vocabulary—a common characteristic of successful people.

To the Student

Active Writing

A poll of Fortune 500 employers asked the question, What is the major weakness in the college graduates you consider for employment? The answer was virtually unanimous: they don't know how to write!

Developing strong writing skills will give you an edge in today's job market because good writers tend to be clear thinkers. Writing well requires imagination, critical-thinking and problem-solving skills, careful organization, and an understanding of people and their needs—just what employers are looking for.

Writing Strategies

You'll be given many writing assignments in college, in various styles and formats. Among these will be the following:

- Personal essays two to five pages in length
- Terse lab reports in the sciences
- Formal and informal class journals
- Reviews and reaction papers
- Critical essays of five to ten pages that ask you to make and defend value judgments about other works
- Term papers of ten to twenty pages that require careful library research and in-depth analysis of narrowly defined subjects

When you're given a writing assignment, the first question to ask is, What is the *purpose* of this writing task? What am I expected to accomplish?

A second, related question is, Who is my *audience*? What do they already know, and what do they need to know about my topic?

Following are some frequently assigned writing strategies, along with some goals and strategies for accomplishing them:

1. Informing

GOAL: *Inform* your reader about something (car radios, oil-spill cleanup techniques, schizophrenia).

Strategies: Pick a subject you already know something about. Answer the questions an average person might ask. If the topic is complicated, use examples and illustrations. Organize your material so that everything is crystal clear. Avoid preaching. Stick to the facts. Concentrate on organization and clarity.

2. Defining

GOAL: *Distinguish an item from all other items* in its class.

Strategies: Start by identifying the general classification the item falls under: human beings, for example, are distinguished from other animals by genus (*Homo*), species (*sapiens*), family (*Hominidae*), order (primates), and class (mammals). Next, distinguish the item from other similar items. Socialism, for example, is a social system, but what kind exactly? How does it differ from, say, a free-enterprise system? How is it different from related movements and systems such as anarchism and communism? How did the Marxist/Leninist version of socialism differ from other socialist systems in the past? Another helpful way of defining an abstract term is to *give examples,* as we have done here.

3. Comparing and Contrasting

GOAL: Help your reader to understand two related terms by showing *similarities and differences* between them.

Strategies: Start by making two lists—one of similarities and one of differences. Cross out the similarities and differences that are trivial. Concentrate on the ones that help your reader to reach a better understanding of the two terms.

4. Persuading

GOAL: Make your reader *do* something (vote, recycle, take up aerobics).

Strategies: Establish your credibility as someone better informed than, though not morally superior to, your reader. Assume that your reader is a well-intentioned person who, if properly informed, will do the right thing. Keep the tone of your writing positive and upbeat. Show the advantages of the recommended action.

5. Convincing

GOAL: *Influence your reader's thinking* on a controversial issue.

Strategies: Convincing differs from persuading by appealing to reason and logic rather than emotion. To persuade is to change someone's beliefs; to convince is to change his or her thinking. Your challenge is to convince your reader that your position, though not the only one, is the best one to take on the issue. Imagine a reader who is somewhat informed about the issue but has not yet taken a firm stand or has taken what you believe to be an uninformed stand. Use logic and evidence to make your points. Try to be balanced and fair. Openly admit the advantages of opposing views, then show that, on balance, your view is the best one.

6. Critiquing a work of art, film, literature, music, or dance

GOAL: Evaluate the work and *make judgments* about its aesthetic worth.

Strategies: Begin by thinking about what makes a work of art good or bad. Clarify your aesthetic standards at the outset: on what basis are you judging the work? Assume a reader who is somewhat familiar with the work you are discussing; it's unnecessary to summarize the plot of a novel, for example. Ask three questions: (1) What was the author (artist, composer) trying to do? (2) How well was it done? (3) Was it worth doing? Since criticism is highly subjective, your writing will be evaluated not so much on the correctness of your position as on how well you support it by reference to the work of art itself and to clearly defined values and standards.

7. Expressing

GOAL: *Express* your feelings or narrate a personal experience.

Strategies: Assume a reader who will respect the subjective nature of your writing and treat it in confidence. A good personal essay provides a truthful rendering of events and emotions. It promotes a reaction of familiar empathy and helps the reader to achieve a better understanding of human experience. The emphasis is not so much on what you say but on how you say it. Pay close attention to diction (choice of words), sentence and paragraph construction, and style. Clarity and simplicity work best; steer clear of flowery language and purple prose.

Choosing a Topic

If your topic is assigned and you are not given a list of topics from which to choose, try to find an angle to the topic that interests you. Usually these topics are open-ended; they offer a wide range of possible approaches. If you are given a choice, choose a topic you care about. In either case, it's essential that you be excited by your topic. If you care about your topic, your writing will actually improve.

Brainstorming is a useful first step in choosing a topic. Brainstorming is a method of free association. Rapidly jot down ideas, good or bad, as they come to you, without making value judgments or censoring yourself. A darkened computer screen is a good way to brainstorm by yourself: when you finally turn up the light, you'll be amazed at how much you've written. If the topic is wide-open, brainstorm items you're interested in, for example:

baseball   cancer research   Japanese flower arranging

the Middle East   gangsta rap

my uncle   TV sitcoms of the 1960s   the flute

conflict resolution   teaching preschoolers

If you've been asked to write about, say, a controversial issue in the news, brainstorm all the issues you can think of:

prison management   the professionalization of college sports

ground water pollution   health management organizations

tax abatement for new sports stadiums   the Palestinian issue

capital punishment   abortion rights

baseball   new treatments for drug addiction

Cross out the items that you know the least about and that interest you least:

~~*prison management*~~   *the professionalization of college sports*

~~*ground water pollution*~~   ~~*health management organizations*~~

tax abatement for new sports stadiums   ~~*the Palestinian issue*~~

~~*capital punishment*~~   ~~*abortion rights*~~

baseball   new treatments for drug addiction

Brainstorm everything you know about the topics that remain, for example:

Baseball. *Card collecting . . . memories of Tiger Stadium . . . history of the game . . . Cal Ripken's streak . . . salaries out of sight . . . free agency . . . Curt Flood . . . Little League (mean coach) . . . playing in the rain . . . pitching mechanics . . . shoulder injury . . . rehab . . . pitching machine . . . ability to bunt . . . once saw Ken Griffey, Jr. in Kmart . . . how to choose a bat . . . TV coverage of last year's World Series . . .*

If your instructor has not specified a writing strategy (persuade, explain, argue, express), almost any of your brainstorming ideas could be the seed of an essay. If you are limited to a certain writing strategy, go back over your list and see which items would be most appropriate. In the baseball example above, you could

- *persuade* someone to take up card collecting;
- *explain* how pitching machines work;
- *argue* that free agency has hurt the game;
- *express* how you felt as a Little Leaguer.

Narrowing Your Topic

The next step—and it's an important one—is to narrow your topic sufficiently to allow you to say something meaningful about it in the available space. This will require some research: what has been said about the topic? If you can't find enough background material—all the books are checked out or there just isn't any—now is the time to switch topics. But usually the problem is the reverse: there's too much material to process in a short time.

Start by getting a rapid, broad overview of your topic. Overviews can be found in encyclopedias and specialized dictionaries (in the library reference room), book introductions, or the first few pages of a recent scholarly article in which the author summarizes the research to date.

Then select an aspect of the topic that interests you. You can't summarize the current state of cancer research in one paragraph, but you might be able to summarize the results of a recent experiment at Duke University. Restrict your subsequent research to one small corner of a large topic.

Narrow topics are actually easier to write about than broad ones, where you may get bogged down in what Samuel Johnson called "the grandeur of generality." Your instructor can help you narrow your topic. Always clear your topic with your instructor as early as possible, even if it's not required.

Following is an example of a topic gradually narrowed down from general to specific:

1. Motion pictures
2. The early days of motion pictures
3. The evolution of the motion-picture projector
4. The kinetoscope
5. Thomas Edison's role in the invention of the kinetoscope

Stating a Thesis

Many first-year college students think a topic and a thesis are the same thing. They're not. A topic is your subject—what you're writing about. A thesis is what you have to say about your subject.

If you have a topic but no thesis, your essay will resemble a child's report on Argentina: a rambling, disorganized string of unrelated facts. A thesis gives your paper focus; it is the central organizing principle.

If your topic is the Oedipus complex, your thesis might be "Sigmund Freud discovered the Oedipus complex partly from his reading of Sophocles and Shakespeare and partly through self-analysis." A topic is usually expressed in a word or phrase; a thesis is expressed in a complete sentence.

A good thesis should be a true statement supported by ample evidence. But the mere fact that it is true and amply supported is not enough. A good thesis also must be insightful and significant. Compare these two thesis statements:

A. *There are both similarities and differences between Henry Ford and William Crapo Durant.*
B. *Although they were both brilliant engineers and creative entrepreneurs, Henry Ford's deep conservatism and insistence on private ownership paved the way for successful competition by General Motors, the brainchild of the more imaginative and flexible genius William Crapo Durant.*

The first statement is true but reveals nothing about either Ford or Durant. The second gives us some insight into the two automotive pioneers and the nature of the competition between Ford Motor Company and General Motors.

A good way to start forming a thesis is to ask whatever questions occur to you about your topic: How did motion pictures get started? Why is movement in silent pictures so jerky? Why do the actors wear that garish makeup? What inventions enabled sound and color to be introduced into motion pictures? You'll find the answers to your questions by doing research. The answers, reduced to the bare essentials, constitute your thesis sentence.

Writing the Paper

Arrange your note cards in the order of your outline. Write from the cards. Avoid the temptation to say everything. Be economical. Each of your note cards represents a lot of work, so it will hurt when you throw one out, but your paper will be better for it. If possible, use a word processor, which will make revising and editing much easier. When working on your rough draft, don't get it right, get it written. You can revise later.

Try to complete a rough draft at least a week before your paper is due. Then set it aside for a few days to "let the cake cool." When you come back, you'll see things you didn't see before.

As you prepare your final draft, try to eliminate unnecessary words by pretending that you're being charged a dollar for each word you use: see how much money you can save by trimming. Also look for vague, wordy expressions that don't say what you really mean. Use your thesaurus to find a more precise, economical equivalent. Write simply and clearly. Say what you have to say and then quit.

Proofreading. Turning in a paper without proofreading it is like going on a date without checking your appearance in the mirror: you'll never notice the jam on your face, but your date will.

When you've finished your final draft, go over it once for spelling (use a spell checker or look up words you're unsure of in a dictionary), grammar, punctuation, and mechanics. Then go over it a second time for style, organization, logic, and overall flow. It's OK to get a friend (preferably a senior English major) to look it over. An outsider will see things you missed. It's also OK to make minor corrections on the draft you're handing in.

Try to have all papers, especially long research papers, turned in before exam week so that you can devote your time exclusively to studying.

Here are a few final tips on writing a paper:

- It's OK to skim dictionaries, encyclopedias, commercial study guides, and college textbooks as preliminary reading for background, but these entries are too brief and superficial to constitute meaningful research.
- When you're taking notes in the library, whenever time permits write out your best ideas in complete sentences as they might eventually appear in your paper. You'll thank yourself later when you sit down to write because, without realizing it, you'll actually have written a major portion of your paper while taking notes.
- Try to hook your reader in the opening line. Avoid trite beginnings such as "Webster defines ——— as . . ." or obvious truisms such as "Cigarettes are a serious health hazard." Notice opening lines that catch your interest in your own reading and try to imitate them. Avoid beginning or ending your paper with a quote; save the first and last words for yourself.

- Your own ideas—not the words of others—should dominate your paper. Use quotations to add interest and support your points. Quote only when the source says it better than you could or when the source is a respected authority. If it's just information, put it in your own words while still identifying the source. If the information is common knowledge (such as the distance from Paris to Berlin), you don't have to cite the source.
- The physical appearance of your paper can make a big difference (sometimes as much as a full letter grade).
- Always keep a copy of your paper.
- When your paper is returned, look at the comments as well as the grade. Make a list of things to look out for and improve on in your next writing assignment.

Always	*Never*
Word-process and laser-print your paper.	Use sticky erasable paper.
Use good-quality white paper.	Use paper clips or binders.
Double-space your paper.	Use paper torn out of a spiral notebook.
Proofread carefully.	Fold your paper.
Include a title page.	
Check your title page for misspellings.	
Put your name on the title page.	
Add a blank page at the end for comments.	
Staple at upper left.	

Keyboarding and Word-Processing Skills

A recent graduate from one of the nation's top law schools was asked what advice she would give a first-year college student. "Learn to type" was her instant response.

Basic keyboarding skills are essential for today's college student. You will be required to complete a great many papers outside of class. Most instructors prefer that written work be word-processed; some require it. Studies show that word-processed work is graded significantly higher than handwritten papers. Moreover, keyboarding is fast becoming an essential job skill in almost every area of employment.

Rapid and accurate keyboarding also is important because the more you learn, the faster your mind works. If you're writing everything out longhand or using the two-finger hunt-and-peck method, you'll find your hand trailing behind your brain. Fast, accurate keyboarding will free up time for other tasks and things you enjoy.

The key to rapid keyboarding is not looking at the keyboard. As soon as you're able to find all the characters without looking, you can practice on your own without tutorial help. If you've never learned to keyboard, enroll in a course at your community college, adult vocational school, or recreation center. An alternative method is to use an educational software program. The computing center on your campus is sure to have a selection of typing tutorial software. These programs are self-paced and provide instant feedback on speed and accuracy. They also recognize the keystrokes that are difficult for you and automatically provide exercises to increase your fluency with the difficult letters.

The many advantages of word processors have rendered the typewriter obsolete. Word processors and computers allow you to add, delete, and rearrange text. They give you an instant word and page count. You can keep your desk free by storing all your schoolwork on a hard drive. You can insert attractively produced charts, graphs, and other graphics into your text. You can print in a wide variety of fonts and easily italicize or boldface text for emphasis.

Word processors have a liberating effect on writing, partly because your work is private until you choose to print it out but also because it's so easy to make corrections. Knowing that you can always delete text you don't like with a single keystroke frees you to say anything that comes to mind. If you can't think of the right word, you can just type XXXXXX and move on, tucking the word in later. Spell checkers and other specialized software enable you to notice and correct mistakes of spelling, grammar, organization, and style.

Many college English departments have invested in computer writing labs because computers have been shown to have a dramatic positive effect on student writing. Researchers at the City University of New York studied 1,695 college students representing a wide range of academic ability. They found that, without exception, every student who used computers showed some improvement in writing ability, with the most dramatic improvements occurring among the most able and least able students.

Though most often used for word processing, computers can help you in other ways, too. You can use specialized software to arrange your notes; outline your papers; plan your schedule; write a speech; design banners, posters, brochures, and newsletters; improve your math skills; and budget your money. With an access port or modem, you can access your library's on-line catalog and tap the vast wealth of information on the Internet.

A Word About Plagiarism

A would-be author once sent a book manuscript to the eighteenth-century literary giant Samuel Johnson. He asked Johnson to read it and give his opinion on it. The great writer returned the book with a short note. "Your manuscript," he wrote, "is both good and original. But the part that is original is not good and the part that is good is not original."

Plagiarism—sometimes called intellectual shoplifting—is passing off someone else's ideas as your own in a speech or essay. There's nothing wrong with borrowing ideas; good writers do it all the time. But as Hollywood screenwriter Wilson Mizner put it, "Copy from one, it's plagiarism; copy from many, it's research."

The way to give credit is to cite, or document, your sources. When plagiarism is unintentional (copying a passage word for word without acknowledging the source), it may be the result of haste, carelessness, or ignorance. Whether in a speech or a paper, you must cite the source whenever you quote directly or paraphrase (put someone else's ideas in your own words). The only exception to this rule is common knowledge—information that is generally known and widely available, such as the population of the United States. If you're not sure whether something is common knowledge, go ahead and document it to be on the safe side.

When you're taking notes from your reading, be careful to put all direct quotes in quotation marks. If you're paraphrasing a long passage, read it over until you have the gist; then look away from the source and express the idea in your own words. Look at the source again to make sure your paraphrase is accurate and contains no phrases verbatim from the original. Remember, even if you paraphrase, you must cite your source.

Besides being unethical, plagiarism is foolish because it is almost always detected. Experienced instructors can tell immediately whether a paper has been plagiarized. First, they have had many years of exposure to student writing and have a reliable sense of the range of writing ability normally found among college students. Second, they obtain writing samples from essay tests and in-class writing assignments and can detect significant stylistic differences in plagiarized work. Third, they have done many years of research and are intimately acquainted with the published work in their field, especially the commercial study guides such as *Cliffs Notes* that are widely available in college bookstores. There have even been cases of students plagiarizing from an instructor's own publications. Finally, instructors have access to computer programs that detect plagiarism and identify research papers purchased from "paper mills" (companies that sell research papers for profit).

The penalty for plagiarism, as for cheating, is up to the instructor. The most merciful will require that the writing assignment be done over, often on a different and more difficult topic, but the plagiarist may be given a failing grade for the paper or the course and, in serious or repeated cases, be suspended from college. Outside the academic setting, the original author may sue the plagiarist for a large settlement.

Summary

Effective writing is important in almost all professional careers. That's why virtually all your college courses will require some kind of writing. Successful writing involves understanding the purpose of the writing task and the needs of your imaginary reader. Choose topics that interest you and narrow your topic by formulating a precise thesis. Plan ahead for major writing chores such as a research paper and break the work into a series of steps—bibliography, reading, note taking, outlining, writing, revising, and proofreading. You'll write faster and better if you use a word processor—and get help with your spelling, too. And always make sure your work is your own; when you borrow someone else's ideas, give credit where credit is due.

The
College Success
Reader

Part I

The Motivation to Learn

INTRODUCTION

As an enrolled student at one of 3,500 postsecondary institutions in the United States, you are one of 17 million adults who have decided to continue their education beyond high school.

Most of these students are motivated, at least in part, by the prospect of better jobs and a more prosperous lifestyle. Unemployment rates in 1994 for twenty-five- to twenty-nine-year-olds were 3 percent for college graduates and 9 percent for individuals with a high school diploma or less.[1] And the material advantages of a college degree are substantial, even after you subtract the rising costs of tuition and the years of foregone wages while attending college. According to the U.S. Census Bureau, a thirty-year-old male high school graduate earned an average of $20,000[2] in 1993, while his college-graduate counterpart earned $34,000. Males with degrees beyond the baccalaureate averaged $48,653.

There's no doubt about it: college helps you make a better living. But it also helps you make a better life. Taking pleasure in the sensations and laws of the natural world, understanding current events in the light of the past, developing a strong set of personal values, being able to read books and people with equal facility, practicing the skills of communication—all these lifelong pursuits and more are required in college.

Students who are motivated only by the desire for a career are sometimes impatient with general studies requirements and yawn their way through them, with predictable results. General studies courses are the building blocks for the courses you will take in your major, courses specifically designed to prepare you for a career.

The desire for a lucrative job is not in itself a sufficient motivation to persist and succeed in college. The motivation to succeed must be found deep within oneself. Higher learning must be seen as having intrinsic value—not as a means to an end, but as the only thing that will satisfy the universal human need for knowledge, beauty, and understanding.

It was this need that motivated Malcolm X to educate himself painstakingly in prison—an education that lifted him above a dead-end life of petty crime to become a leader of people. What drove him was a desire for mastery—over himself, his environment, and those who had enforced on him a life of subservience. In this part, we have included the passage from his autobiography in which he describes his efforts to over-

---

1. "The Cost of Higher Education," U.S. Department of Education pamphlet #6, National Center for Education Statistics (1995), p. 15.

2. This figure has fallen from $28,000 in 1979, suggesting that a college degree—once a luxury— is fast becoming a necessity.

come illiteracy and gain access to the mysteries of knowledge as they were found in books.

The second essay in this part is an account of the struggle by Christopher Lee, a heavily recruited athlete at the University of Georgia, to overcome a learning disability so severe that the simple task of writing a check was a potential source of embarrassment. Writing, he said, was his "worst nightmare." But with the help of his writing teacher, Rosemary Jackson, and with a strenuous personal effort, he was able not only to graduate from college but also to write and publish a book about his experiences.

All first-time college students, regardless of their age, feel a mixture of fear and exhilaration. Fear of academic failure can throttle our best efforts, and it's only a little comforting to be told that such fear is irrational or that others are feeling the same thing. In "To Err Is Human," the distinguished physician Lewis Thomas offers some consolation by reminding us that error is an endearing human trait that often leads to satisfying insights and breakthrough discoveries. Failure, he says, is the flip side of success and necessary to it. It is by making wrong choices that we stumble at last upon the right ones.

The next essay in this part, "Claiming an Education," is not really an essay at all but a fall convocation address by poet Adrienne Rich given at Douglass College, Rich's alma mater. She challenges the students at Douglass, a college for women, to treat their education as a contract between teacher and student. As in any contract, students must expect to give as much as they get. She urges students to *claim* their education—that is, to actively take it as their rightful due.

"Take This Fish and Look at It" is a classic account by the famous entomologist Samuel Scudder of his first few days in college, when he fell under the spell of a demanding but compassionate instructor, Louis Agassiz, a scientist who virtually created the discipline of natural history. Agassiz taught his students not to be satisfied with surface appearances but to look deeply, ask questions, and resist the easy answer.

Part 1 concludes with college instructor Marcia Yudkin's description of her first encounter with the special needs of adult learners, "I Thought I Was a Terrific Teacher Until One Day. . . ." Confronted by imminent and open rebellion against the teaching methods she had used successfully in the past, Yudkin was forced to reevaluate her assumptions about college students and make radical changes in her teaching methods. For adult learners, she soon discovered, success in college is literally a matter of survival.

The motivation to succeed in college is different for each student, but every successful college student has one thing in common: a powerful, sustaining desire to learn.

Write Before You Read

A. After you've read the introduction, take a few minutes to survey the contents of this part. Then write three questions you expect will be answered in the course of your reading.

1. _____

_____

2. _____

_____

3. _____

_____

B. Briefly reflect on each of the following topics. Then write freely and rapidly about what you already know about the topic, relevant experiences you have had, and any opinions you have formed about it.

1. What motivates you to learn _____

_____

_____

_____

_____

_____

2. Your greatest fears about college _____

_____

_____

_____

_____

_____

3. What you hope to get from your college experience _____

_____

_____

_____

_____

_____

Learning to Read
Malcolm X

PREVIEW

By the time of his assassination in 1965, Malcolm X had become a national hero to hundreds of thousands of African Americans for his leadership role in the civil rights movement. But until his autobiography was published shortly after his death, even many of his followers were unaware that he had once been virtually illiterate. Convicted of robbery in 1946, Malcolm was sentenced to seven years in Norfolk Prison Colony, where he fell under the spell of the Black Muslims and their leader, Elijah Muhammad. Inspired by his new awareness of the systematic disenfranchisement of African Americans, Malcolm acquired a hunger to learn more about the history of his people and their struggle. In the following passage from his autobiography, cowritten with Roots *author Alex Haley, he describes his painstaking efforts in prison to teach himself to read and write.*

It was because of my letters that I happened to stumble upon starting to acquire some kind of a homemade education.

I became increasingly frustrated at not being able to express what I wanted to convey in letters that I wrote, especially to Mr. Elijah Muhammad. In the street, I had been the most articulate hustler out there—I had commanded attention when I said something. But now, trying to write simple English, I not only wasn't articulate, I wasn't even functional. How would I sound writing in slang, the way I would *say* it, something such as, "Look, daddy, let me pull your coat about a cat, Elijah Muhammad—"

Many who today hear me somewhere in person, or on television, or those who read something I've said, will think I went to school far beyond the eighth grade. This impression is due entirely to my prison studies.

It had really begun back in the Charlestown Prison, when Bimbi first made me feel envy of his stock of knowledge. Bimbi had always taken charge of any conversations he was in, and I had tried to emulate him. But every book I picked up had few sentences which didn't contain any-

---

SOURCE: From *The Autobiography of Malcolm X* by Malcolm X with the assistance of Alex Haley. Copyright © 1964 by Alex Haley and Malcolm X. Copyright © 1965 by Alex Haley and Betty Shabazz. Reprinted by permission of Random House, Inc. Reprinted without footnotes.

where from one to nearly all of the words that might as well have been in Chinese. When I just skipped those words, of course, I really ended up with little idea of what the book said. So I had come to the Norfolk Prison Colony still going through only book-reading motions. Pretty soon, I would have quit even these motions, unless I had received the motivation that I did.

I saw that the best thing I could do was get hold of a dictionary—to study, to learn some words. I was lucky enough to reason also that I should try to improve my penmanship. It was sad. I couldn't even write in a straight line. It was both ideas together that moved me to request a dictionary along with some tablets and pencils from the Norfolk Prison Colony school.

I spent two days just riffling uncertainly through the dictionary's pages. I'd never realized so many words existed! I didn't know *which* words I needed to learn. Finally, just to start some kind of action, I began copying.

In my slow, painstaking, ragged handwriting, I copied into my tablet everything printed on that first page, down to the punctuation marks.

I believe it took me a day. Then, aloud, I read back, to myself, everything I'd written on the tablet. Over and over, aloud, to myself, I read my own handwriting.

I woke up the next morning, thinking about those words—immensely proud to realize that not only had I written so much at one time, but I'd written words that I never knew were in the world. Moreover, with a little effort, I also could remember what many of these words meant. I reviewed the words whose meanings I didn't remember. Funny thing, from the dictionary first page right now, that "aardvark" springs to my mind. The dictionary had a picture of it, a long-tailed, long-eared, burrowing African mammal, which lives off termites caught by sticking out its tongue as an anteater does for ants.

I was so fascinated that I went on—I copied the dictionary's next page. And the same experience came when I studied that. With every succeeding page, I also learned of people and places and events from history. Actually the dictionary is like a miniature encyclopedia. Finally the dictionary's A section had filled a whole tablet—and I went on into the B's. That was the way I started copying what eventually became the entire dictionary. It went a lot faster after so much practice helped me to pick up handwriting speed. Between what I wrote in my tablet, and writing letters, during the rest of my time in prison I would guess I wrote a million words.

I suppose it was inevitable that as my word-base broadened, I could for the first time pick up a book and read and now begin to understand what the book was saying. Anyone who has read a great deal can imagine the new world that opened. Let me tell you something: from then until I left that prison, in every free moment I had, if I was not reading in the library, I was reading on my bunk. You couldn't have gotten me out of books with a wedge. Between Mr. Muhammad's teachings, my correspondence, my visitors, . . . and my reading of books, months passed without my even thinking about being imprisoned. In fact, up to then, I never had been so truly free in my life.

The Norfolk Prison Colony's library was in the school building. A variety of classes was taught there by instructors who came from such places as Harvard and Boston universities. The weekly debates between inmate teams were also held in the school building. You would be astonished to know how worked up convict debaters and audiences would get over subjects like "Should Babies Be Fed Milk?"

Available on the prison library's shelves were books on just about every general subject. Much of the big private collection that Parkhurst had willed to the prison was still in crates and boxes in the back of the library—thousands of old books. Some of them looked ancient: covers faded, old-time parchment-looking binding. Parkhurst . . . seemed to have been principally interested in history and religion. He had the money and the special interest to have a lot of books that you wouldn't have in a general circulation. Any college library would have been lucky to get that collection.

As you can imagine, especially in a prison where there was heavy emphasis on rehabilitation, an inmate was smiled upon if he demonstrated an unusually intense interest in books. There was a sizable number of well-read inmates, especially the popular debaters. Some were said by many to be practically walking encyclopedias. They were almost celebrities. No university would ask any student to devour literature as I did when this new world opened to me, of being able to read and *understand*.

I read more in my room than in the library itself. An inmate who was known to read a lot could check out more than the permitted maximum number of books. I preferred reading in the total isolation of my own room.

When I had progressed to really serious reading, every night at about ten P.M. I would be outraged with the "lights out." It always seemed to catch me right in the middle of something engrossing.

Fortunately, right outside my door was a corridor light that cast a glow into my room. The glow was enough to read by, once my eyes adjusted to it. So when "lights out" came, I would sit on the floor where I could continue reading in that glow.

At one-hour intervals the night guards paced past every room. Each time I heard the approaching footsteps, I jumped into bed and feigned sleep. And as soon as the guard passed, I got back out of bed onto the floor area of that light-glow, where I would read for another fifty-eight minutes—until the guard approached again. That went on until three or four every morning. Three or four hours of sleep a night was enough for me. Often in the years in the streets I had slept less than that.

The teachings of Mr. Muhammad stressed how history had been "whitened"—when white men had written history books, the black man simply had been left out. Mr. Muhammad couldn't have said anything that would have struck me much harder. I had never forgotten how when my class, me and all of those whites, had studied seventh-grade United States history back in Mason, the history of the Negro had been covered in one paragraph, and the teacher had gotten a big laugh with his joke, "Negroes' feet are so big that when they walk, they leave a hole in the ground."

This is one reason why Mr. Muhammad's teachings spread so swiftly all over the United States, among *all* Negroes, whether or not they became followers of Mr. Muhammad. The teachings ring true—to every Negro. You can hardly show me a black adult in America—or a white one, for that matter—who knows from the history books anything like the truth about the black man's role. In my own case, once I heard of the "glorious history of the black man," I took special pains to hunt in the library for books that would inform me on details about black history.

I can remember accurately the very first set of books that really impressed me. I have since bought that set of books and I have it at home for my children to read as they grow up. It's called *Wonders of the World.* It's full of pictures of archeological finds, statues that depict, usually, non-European people.

I found books like Will Durant's *Story of Civilization.* I read H. G. Wells' *Outline of History. Souls of Black Folk* by W. E. B. Du Bois gave me a glimpse into the black people's history before they came to this country. Carter G. Woodson's *Negro History* opened my eyes about black empires before the black slave was brought to the United States, and the early Negro struggles for freedom.

J. A. Rogers' three volumes of *Sex and Race* told about race-mixing before Christ's time; and Aesop being a black man who told fables; about Egypt's Pharaohs; about the great Coptic Christian Empires; about Ethiopia, the earth's oldest continuous black civilization, as China is the oldest continuous civilization.

Mr. Muhammad's teaching about how the white man had been created led me to *Findings in Genetics* by Gregor Mendel. (The dictionary's

G section was where I had learned what "genetics" meant.) I really studied this book by the Austrian monk. Reading it over and over, especially certain sections, helped me to understand that if you started with a black man, a white man could be produced; but starting with a white man, you never could reproduce a black man—because the white chromosome is recessive. And since no one disputes that there was but one Original Man, the conclusion is clear.

During the last year or so, in the *New York Times*, Arnold Toynbee used the word "bleached" in describing the white man. His words were: "White (i.e., bleached) human beings of North European origin. . . ." Toynbee also referred to the European geographic area as only a peninsula of Asia. He said there is no such thing as Europe. And if you look at the globe, you will see for yourself that America is only an extension of Asia. (But at the same time Toynbee is among those who have helped to bleach history. He has written that Africa was the only continent that produced no history. He won't write that again. Every day now, the truth is coming to light.)

I never will forget how shocked I was when I began reading about slavery's total horror. It made such an impact upon me that it later became one of my favorite subjects when I became a minister of Mr. Muhammad's. The world's most monstrous crime, the sin and the blood on the white man's hands, are almost impossible to believe. Books like the one by Frederick Olmsted opened my eyes to the horrors suffered when the slave was landed in the United States. The European woman, Fanny Kemble, who had married a Southern white slaveowner, described how human beings were degraded. Of course I read *Uncle Tom's Cabin*. In fact, I believe that's the only novel I have ever read since I started serious reading.

Parkhurst's collection also contained some bound pamphlets of the Abolitionist Anti-Slavery Society of New England. I read descriptions of atrocities, saw those illustrations of black slave women tied up and flogged with whips; of black mothers watching their babies being dragged off, never to be seen by their mothers again; of dogs after slaves, and of the fugitive slave catchers, evil white men with whips and clubs and chains and guns. I read about the slave preacher Nat Turner, who put the fear of God into the white slavemaster. Nat Turner wasn't going around preaching pie-in-the-sky and "non-violent" freedom for the black man. There in Virginia one night in 1831, Nat and seven other slaves started out at his master's home and through the night they went from one plantation "big house" to the next, killing, until by the next morning 57 white people were dead and Nat had about 70 slaves following him. White people, terrified for their lives, fled from their homes, locked themselves up in public buildings, hid in the woods, and some even left the state. A small army of soldiers took two months to catch and hang Nat Turner. Somewhere I have read where Nat Turner's example is said to have inspired John Brown to invade Virginia and attack Harper's Ferry nearly thirty years later, with thirteen white men and five Negroes.

I read Herodotus, "the father of History," or, rather, I read about him. And I read the histories of various nations, which opened my eyes gradually, then wider and wider, to how the whole world's white men had indeed acted like devils, pillaging and raping and bleeding and draining the whole world's nonwhite people. I remember, for instance, books such as Will Durant's *The Story of Oriental Civilization*, and Mahatma Gandhi's accounts of the struggle to drive the British out of India.

Book after book showed me how the white men had brought upon the world's black, brown, red, and yellow peoples every variety of the sufferings of exploitation. I saw how since the sixteenth century the so-called "Christian trader" white man began to ply the seas in his lust for Asian and African empires, and plunder, and power. I read, I saw, how the white man never has gone among the nonwhite peoples bearing the Cross in the true manner and spirit of Christ's teachings—meek, humble, and Christlike.

I perceived, as I read, how the collective white man had been actually nothing but a piratical opportunist who used Faustian machinations to make his own Christianity his initial wedge in criminal conquests. First, always "religiously," he branded "heathen" and "pagan" labels upon ancient nonwhite cultures and civilizations. The stage thus set, he then turned upon his nonwhite victims his weapons of war.

I read how, entering India—half a *billion* deeply religious brown people—the British white man, by 1759, through promises, trickery, and manipulations, controlled much of India through Great Britain's East India Company. The parasitical British administration kept tentacling out to half of the subcontinent. In 1857, some of the desperate people of India finally mutinied—and, excepting the African slave trade, nowhere has history recorded any more unnecessary bestial and ruthless human carnage than the British suppression of the nonwhite Indian people.

Over 115 million African blacks—close to the 1930's population of the United States—were murdered or enslaved during the slave trade. And I read how when the slave market was glutted, the cannibalistic white powers of Europe next carved up, as their colonies, the richest areas of the black continent. And Europe's chancelleries for the next century played a chess game of naked exploitation and power from Cape Horn to Cairo.

Ten guards and the warden couldn't have torn me out of those books. Not even Elijah Muhammad could have been more eloquent than those books were in providing indisputable proof that the collective white man had acted like a devil in virtually every contact he had with the world's collective nonwhite man. I listen today to the radio, and watch television, and read the headlines about the collective white man's fear and tension concerning China. When the white man professes ignorance about why the Chinese hate him so, my mind can't help flashing back to what I read, there in prison, about how the blood forebears of this same white man raped China at a time when China was trusting and helpless. Those original white "Christian traders" sent into China millions of pounds of opium. By 1839, so many of the Chinese were addicts that China's desperate government destroyed twenty thousand chests of opium. The first Opium War was promptly declared by the white man. Imagine! Declaring *war* upon someone who objects to being narcotized! The Chinese were severely beaten, with Chinese-invented gunpowder.

The Treaty of Nanking made China pay the British white man for the destroyed opium; forced open China's major ports to British trade; forced China to abandon Hong Kong; fixed China's import tariffs so low that cheap British articles soon flooded in, maiming China's industrial development.

After a second Opium War, the Tientsin Treaties legalized the ravaging opium trade, legalized a British-French-American control of China's customs. China tried delaying that Treaty's ratification; Peking was looted and burned.

"Kill the foreign white devils!" was the 1901 Chinese war cry in the Boxer Rebellion. Losing again, this time the Chinese were driven from Peking's choicest areas. The vicious, arrogant white man put up the famous signs, "Chinese and dogs not allowed."

Red China after World War II closed its doors to the Western white world. Massive Chinese agricultural, scientific, and industrial efforts are described inside a book that *Life* magazine recently published. Some observers inside Red China have reported that the world never has known such a hate-white campaign as is now going on in this nonwhite country where, present birth-rates continuing, in fifty more years Chinese will be half the earth's population. And it seems that some Chinese chickens will soon come home to roost, with China's recent successful nuclear tests.

Let us face reality. We can see in the United Nations a new world order being shaped, along color lines—an alliance among the nonwhite nations. America's U.N. ambassador Adlai Stevenson complained not long ago that in the United Nations "a skin game" was being played. He was right. He was facing reality. A "skin game" *is* being played. But Ambassador Stevenson sounded like Jesse James accusing the marshal of carrying a gun. Because who in the world's history ever has played a worse "skin game" than the white man?

Mr. Muhammad, to whom I was writing daily, had no idea of what a new world had opened up to me through my efforts to document his teaching in books.

When I discovered philosophy, I tried to touch all the landmarks of philosophical development. Gradually, I read most of the old philosophers, Occidental and Oriental. The Oriental philosophers were the ones I came to prefer; finally, my impression was that most Occidental philosophy had largely been borrowed from the Oriental thinkers. Socrates, for instance, traveled in Egypt. Some sources even say that Socrates was initiated into some of the Egyptian mysteries. Obviously Socrates got some of his wisdom among the East's wise men.

I have often reflected upon the new vistas that reading opened to me. I knew right there in prison that reading had changed forever the course of my life. As I see it today, the ability to read awoke inside me some long dormant craving to be mentally alive. I certainly wasn't seeking any degree, the way a college confers a status symbol upon its students. My homemade education gave me, with every additional book that I read, a little bit more sensitivity to the deafness, dumbness, and blindness that was afflicting the black race in America. Not long ago, an English writer telephoned me from London, asking questions. One was, "What's your alma mater?" I told him, "Books." You will never catch me with a free fifteen minutes in which I'm not studying something I feel might be able to help the black man.

Yesterday I spoke in London, and both ways on the plane across the Atlantic I was studying a document about how the United Nations proposes to insure the human rights of the oppressed minorities of the world. The American black man is the world's most shameful case of minority oppression. What makes the black man think of himself as only an internal United States issue is just a catch-phrase, two words, "civil rights." How is the black man going to get "civil rights" before first he wins his *human* rights? If the American black man will start thinking about his *human* rights, and then start thinking of himself as part of one of the world's great peoples, he will see he has a case for the United Nations.

I can't think of a better case! Four hundred years of black blood and sweat invested here in America, and the white man still has the black man begging for what every immigrant fresh off the ship can take for granted the minute he walks down the gangplank.

But I'm digressing. I told the Englishman that my alma mater was

14

books, a good library. Every time I catch a plane, I have with me a book that I want to read—and that's a lot of books these days. If I weren't out here every day battling the white man, I could spend the rest of my life reading, just satisfying my curiosity—because you can hardly mention anything I'm not curious about. I don't think anybody ever got more out of going to prison than I did. In fact, prison enabled me to study far more intensively than I would have if my life had gone differently and I had attended some college. I imagine that one of the biggest troubles with colleges is there are too many distractions, too much panty-raiding, fraternities, and boola-boola and all of that. Where else but in a prison could I have attacked my ignorance by being able to study intensely sometimes as much as fifteen hours a day?

DIALOGUE

1. What was Malcolm X's initial motivation for teaching himself to read and write? How did his motivation change over time?
2. Think of a time in your life when you were strongly motivated to learn something. Share your experience with your group. What did you want to learn? What made you interested in the subject? How did you go about educating yourself, and where did you turn for help? Did you make some early mistakes? What did you learn from them? Are you still interested in the subject today? Why or why not?
3. General education courses are sometimes referred to as liberal arts because they are intended to liberate the human spirit. What does knowledge liberate us from? In what ways did Malcolm find knowledge liberating?

WRITING TOPICS

1. Choose at random a page from the dictionary and duplicate Malcolm's experience by copying ten complete entries. Prepare a statement that comments on this exercise. What new knowledge or information did you gain? Were you as engaged by the exercise as Malcolm was?
2. Clarify the distinction Malcolm makes between *human rights* and *civil rights*. Does the distinction apply to minorities and nonminorities alike? Explain.
3. Malcolm states that "the ability to read awoke inside me some long dormant craving to be mentally alive." Describe your earliest memories of reading. Do you read for pleasure or only what is assigned? How have you grown as a person through reading?

INTERACTION

Divide into two groups. Group 1 should discuss the following statement and prepare arguments that support the statement's premise:

There are many benefits and virtues to Malcolm X's homemade and nontraditional self-styled education.

Group 2 should discuss the statement below and prepare arguments in support of the statement's premise:

There are limitations and dangers inherent in Malcolm X's unsystematic and agenda-driven self-education.

Then share your arguments with each other.

Writing: My Worst Nightmare
Christopher Lee and Rosemary Jackson

PREVIEW

Despite severe learning disabilities, Christopher Lee was admitted on a swimming scholarship to the University of Georgia, where he was placed in an intensive basic skills program. To be admitted to regular classes, he had to demonstrate college-level competency in reading, writing, and math. Lee soon realized that the tricks he had used to survive in school ("faking it") would not work at the University of Georgia. He would either have to overcome his disabilities or abandon his dream of earning a college degree.

Five years later, Lee graduated and, with help from his tutor, Rosemary Jackson, wrote a book about his struggle called Faking It: A Look into the Mind of a Creative Learner. *This book, written by a person who once had difficulty with such ordinary tasks as writing a check or taking a driving test, is a moving testament to individual courage and a message of hope for thousands of college students who struggle to learn.*

My first memory of learning to write was in the second grade when we started learning to write in cursive. I know I must have struggled through learning to print because I still have trouble keeping my "b's" and "d's" and "n's" and "u's" straight. However, like many other difficult or embarrassing things in my life, I have managed to bury those memories too deep to recall. I feel that it is important to try to describe what writing is like for me because writing is one of my biggest handicaps.

It is important to remember that all learning disabilities are different and that other people with learning disabilities may have difficulty writing for entirely different reasons. My unique learning abilities affect my ability to both see and hear the letters correctly, and my language disabilities affect my ability to express my thoughts.

Thoughts of writing give me a very uneasy feeling. When I am writ-

---

SOURCE: "Writing My Worst Nightmare." Reprinted by permission of Christopher Lee and Rosemary Jackson: *Faking It: A Look Into The Mind Of a Creative Learner* (Boynton/Cook Publishers, A subsidiary of Reed Elsevier Inc., Portsmouth, NH, 1992).

ing, everything is uncertain. I never know if anything I'm writing is correct; stopping and starting, I am constantly trying to figure out how to form the next letter or to decide what the next letter should be. Certain words are particularly difficult. For instance, I can never spell "girl" right. I go back and forth—is it "girl" or "gril?" Neither looks right. I see everything as being jagged. The rules of punctuation and spelling have never made sense. Words never seem to be spelled the way I hear them, and they never look the same way twice.

It is difficult to explain what goes on in my head when I am trying to write because language itself is an obstacle for me. When I am trying to spell a word, it's as if there are twenty-six letters spinning around in my head, each letter having its own box. The boxes contain sounds. The letters are trying to find their boxes by finding their sounds. I don't really see them but I feel like they're up there looking for a place to settle. Only a few of the letters in my head have dropped out of the flurry into their proper boxes. For instance, the letter "b" has come to be easier to understand than other letters; therefore, I assume I have found the box containing the sound for "b." There are times when I still have trouble forming the letter because I confuse it with "d," but the sound-symbol connection has been made. I am aware that I have found this box because, without hesitation, I can name some words that start with "b." I cannot do this with many letters.

The boxes in my head are not in any kind of order. The letters are flying above the boxes searching for some sort of order. All these boxes are screaming out sounds, and I cannot pull the letters down to match the sounds. I have been trying to match these boxes with their sounds for almost twenty years. It becomes very frustrating when communication depends so much on knowing these twenty-six little letters.

When I am writing I try to match the sounds with the letters the best I can. Even if I have all the time in the world I never seem to be able to match enough letters with sounds to write a word. After concentrating so hard on trying to match the letters to the boxes, I eventually force the letters into a word. The end result is that I am never sure if I have written the word correctly. After so many years of forcing the fit, the boxes are all out of shape, making it easier to place the wrong letters within. At the same time, I have to concentrate on what the final spelling looks like so I can store it in my memory. I have to remember *my* spelling so I will know the word when I come back to it. Concentration is the key here. I am concentrating so much on just finding the correct letters and figuring out how to form the letter so that I will recognize it later, that to put my ideas into some kind of coherent order is almost impossible. I feel very lucky when I have a teacher who is organized enough to put important notes on the board during a lecture. Then I simple have to worry about transferring the letters correctly onto my paper; I worry about trying to decipher what they say another time.

I did not learn how to write until I learned how to use a computer. This sounds ironic, but in my past writing was spelling, and since I could not spell, I could not write. When I discovered a word processing system with a spelling check, I finally understood that writing involved putting thoughts and ideas into some kind of written form. Knowing that the computer would catch my spelling errors, I began to ignore my spelling. Then I began to look at writing as content. This did not happen until I was a freshman in college. Before learning to use a computer, I saw writing as a bunch of spelling words that I had to reproduce in horizontal fashion. Writing was simply a horizontal spelling test.

The computer helped me to discover that there was more to writing than just spelling. First of all, the computer was something new and different and was a relief from pencil and paper. All my life pencil and paper had been a nightmare. When I picked up a pencil and paper to write, my stomach would automatically tighten, and my nightmare would begin. The computer helped me view writing in a different way. It helped me to shed my fear of the pencil and paper. Sitting down in front of a computer was not nearly as frightening to me as sitting down with a pencil and paper. For this reason, I immediately saw the computer as a sign of hope. I had never been able to put down the right words with a pencil, but sitting at a keyboard seemed to free my mind. A pencil was like a piece of dead wood in my hands, and trying to make this stick form letters always seemed awkward and difficult. When using a keyboard, however, the letters seemed to come out through my fingertips. The writing seemed to be closer to my brain.

Not only did the computer allow me to view writing with a sense of excitement, it also allowed me to see the written symbols in a neat, organized fashion. For years I had trained my handwriting to be messy and as unreadable as possible so I could hide all my mistakes. This was a con job. When my teachers selected papers to read in class, I was sure they wouldn't read mine because they couldn't. Using a computer forced the letters out in such a neat manner that I actually started to look at the words. Before, I was afraid to look at the words. Now, instead of looking at a scribbled blurb on a page, I looked at a crisp, black-and-white image. To quote a friend of mine, it "made the words stand still." Being able to see a clear image helped me to focus on the words. I have now learned to tell when a word is wrong. I may not always be able to correct it, but the spelling check can do that for me. I have found myself trying to spell the words correctly before I put the paper through the spelling check in the word processor. Once the spelling check has checked the words, I pay attention to the change, thus reinforcing the correct spelling.

Writing in cursive is a very messy, undefined type of writing. Cursive is also an easy way out of spelling. It allows the student to compact letters together. Because of its easy flow, it does not allow the student to see how the words are actually formed. To me, it's a lazy type of writing. Before the computer, I always printed when I needed to do something right because this helped me see all the letters in the word. Even today, when I don't know a word and I don't have access to my computer, I find myself writing in cursive because it's an easy way to hide. Words I feel comfortable with, I find that I print, but words that I am not sure of, I scribble out. I believe that teachers who stress cursive writing are giving students with creative learning abilities a way out. They are allowing the student to reinforce bad habits.

Much of this chapter so far has dwelled on the subject of spelling, just as much of a person's writing education is often spent on learning to spell. If I make one point in this chapter, it is that spending so much time on trying to teach someone with a learning disability to spell might be detrimental to that person's ability to ever learn to write. I have spoken to several groups of teachers, and I am aware of how uneasy this statement makes teachers feel. However, the purpose of this book is to show what goes on in the mind of a creative learner in an attempt to explain why we have such trouble learning certain things. I cannot spell today, and it is certainly not because teachers did not try year after agonizing year to teach me. They spent so much time trying to teach me to spell that no one ever got around to teaching me how to write. To me it is an outrage that I reached college before I understood that writing is putting thoughts on paper.

For some of us spelling is impossible. Teachers and parents need to understand and accept this. It's easy for people without learning difficulties to say to the person who misspells a word to look it up in a dictionary. What they don't understand is that using a dictionary can be extremely difficult and sometimes impossible for someone who does not recognize words on paper. Distinguishing letters is extremely difficult for me. To look a word up in the dictionary takes a long time, first because I can't remember the arrangement of the letters in the word, so I have to look up different combinations until I find a word that might be close. I can often find the first two letters of a word, but the middle is always obscure. I cannot imagine what it looks like or how it sounds. When I find a word that might be close, I have no feeling about whether the word is the one I'm looking for. My feelings are more negative than anything. I'm usually more sure the word is wrong than right. An example of this is when I needed to look up the word "develop." When I first wrote this down in my notes during a psychology lecture, I spelled it "depveloup." I was so far off on the spelling that I could not begin to find it in the dictionary. This wasn't important to me because I knew what I meant the word to be and spelling has no meaning to me, but when my friends try to decipher my notes to quiz me for a test, they have no idea what language I am writing in. One thought it was French, while the other thought it surely must be Russian. My notes surely do not look as if they have been written by a good old American boy. In that same psychology class the teacher was talking about existential theory. In my notes I wrote the word "exitenal" and "extinchail" and made a note to look it up in the dictionary later. The teacher wrote the word "existential" on the board along with some others as he was speaking. I copied all the words down without realizing that this was the same word in writing that I couldn't spell. I tried looking it up in the dictionary, but I couldn't seem to recognize it there either. I might have had my finger on it, but wasn't sure it was right. I have so much doubt about the way things are written. Sometimes teachers will spell words incorrectly on the board and the class laughs. I have no idea what they are laughing about. Interestingly, I almost get angry when the teacher misspells a word. I feel like I'm missing the show even though I have a front row seat. I guess maybe that's how some people feel when they have trouble seeing between the lines in a play or opera or when reading poetry. The frustration is similar in my case but multiplied because I am missing something that is spelled out right in front of my face.

My eye is trained not to worry about spelling. I do not misspell a word the same way each time. My spelling is not at all consistent. Every time I write a word it could be different. I am really strong with words that start with "b" and "d." I don't always put them in the right place, but I know they have a place somewhere in the word. *A, i, e, c, k, ph, f, j, o, u,* and *y* are letters that seem to give me the most trouble in spelling and reading. Notice here that all the vowels are included in this list and there are no words that do not contain vowels. Basically words that I spell right consistently are words that I have been exposed to over and over again, and they are usually short. The longer the word, the more confusing it is for me. Words that I can usually spell correctly include "the, if, was, has, were, funny, time, nice, please, people, girl, friends, Georgia, and Florida." Not many people my age can list the sum total of words they can spell with confidence within a couple lines of print!

A friend of mine who is also a creative learner told me that one of the worst years of her life was when she was in the fifth grade and her teacher made a bulletin board to encourage high spelling grades. The bulletin board was designed to look like an ocean or lake. Each student made a fish which was placed on the shore. The object was to get each fish across the ocean to the other side. This was accomplished by moving the fish according to the grade scored on the weekly spelling test. The fish could be moved a certain number of inches, depending on whether the score was 100, 90, or 80. My friend's fish never left the shore. Spelling test days were terrible for her because she had to suffer the jokes from her classmates and sometimes her teacher about how she was letting her "poor fish" die being out of the water so long. Fortunately for my friend, it was this incident that convinced her teacher that someone who participated so intelligently in class discussions but could hardly read or write had some kind of problem that needed to be investigated. She was found to have unique learning abilities and, like me, writes with the aid of a computer to correct her spelling and friends to help her proof for grammatical errors.

When every effort has been made to teach someone to spell, with no positive results, it is time to admit that the time and energy would be better spent on compensation techniques rather than a "cure." Spelling needs to be taught as just one of the steps in writing; it should not be allowed to interfere with learning to express oneself. For me spelling was like a door that kept me from learning how to write; the computer was the key that unlocked that door. People who have a problem connecting sounds to their symbols need tools like the word processing software and the computer to help them unlock writing skills.

Language Deficits

After spelling, language is the next obstacle on the way to learning to write. For people who have unique learning abilities, language skills may be limited or impaired. Language is another problem I have to face when writing. The interesting thing to me is that this is an impairment I am just learning to deal with. Spelling was always the "bad guy," but now that spelling is of less concern, I have to face the fact that I cannot always find the words I want to use, and when I can, I often cannot figure out how to string the words together to make them say what I want. The computer allows me to be inventive, to go beyond the simple words I know. For some reason, I am seldom afraid to use a word on the computer, but when I am using paper and pencil, I find myself reverting back to those old feelings of wanting to hide or to avoid putting words on paper.

Now my problem is what to do with these words that I am no longer afraid to write. What do I do when writing these words? When I am writing, I see a continuous line. I don't see punctuation, I don't see commas, and, because I never see the punctuation, I don't stop when I read. I believe that when I was learning to read, I had so much trouble just figuring out the words that I never got around to seeing how the words are used or where the punctuation is. I could never get past the first step; actually, I hardly ever got to the end of a sentence. Like spelling, my teachers and parents could not "cure" this problem either. I still struggle so much with reading individual words that I don't see where sentences or paragraphs begin or end. I never see any structure when reading, therefore I don't know how to use it when I am writing.

My approach to punctuation is similar to that of a swimmer attempting to swim the English channel. The swimmer has several checkpoints along the way. Each checkpoint gives information on where the next point is, making the English channel a straight-across swim. If the swimmer does not stop at the checkpoints to find out where to go next, he or she would soon be lost. If the swimmer were to concentrate so much on the potential problems along the way, such as the cold or the possibility of sharks, he or she might swim right past all the checkpoints. A period is a checkpoint, and like the English channel swim, a paper has many checkpoints. Without them, the reader would become lost and confused. The paper would be one long sentence, a never-ending swim. Without the commas, the periods, the quotation marks, the reader gets lost, just like the swimmer.

Like the misguided swimmer, when writing, I would put my head down and pray that I could withstand the cold and that the sharks wouldn't get me, and I would just swim and swim and swim. Again, I feel like the computer helped me break this habit and forced me to see my thoughts in an orderly form. With the computer, I have learned to look up and see where I am headed. Just like a face mask would help a swimmer, the computer screen helps me with punctuation because it seems to make the thoughts clearer. When I write with pencil and paper, I can never see my complete thoughts. However, on the computer I can type rather quickly, and I do not concentrate so much on spelling, so I seem to type out a complete thought at once. I can see where the thought ends, and I know that some form of punctuation is needed in this pause or space. I am not always sure what goes in the space, but I know to stop, and I now have the confidence and knowledge to stop and figure out what goes there.

Paper and pencil were always my worst nightmare, whereas I see the computer as a friend. It is not judgmental. I don't have to be afraid of failing, even when confronted with my weaknesses, and the weaknesses are there. The mistakes stand out clearly in black and white. However, I can now view my errors as being correctable mistakes rather than failures, whereas with paper and pencil it is almost impossible to feel anything but failure and defeat. Using the computer seems to relieve my anxiety to the point that I can focus my attention on the organization of what I am writing.

When I was a freshman and was tested by the Learning Disabilities Adult Clinic, I was told that my language deficits affect my use and understanding of semantics and syntax in oral and written language. I have spent quite some time trying to figure out exactly what that means. The fact that I have deficits in understanding language interferes with my understanding the explanations of my problems. I can't understand the words and only through words can I understand!

Semantics pertains to the meaning of language or words, while syntax is the way in which the words are put together to form phrases and sentences. Once I came to realize that writing was more than spelling, I began to see how semantics and syntax, or word usage and sentence structure, were involved in the writing process. It was then that I gradually began to understand my language deficits and how these deficits interfered with my ability to express my thoughts in writing.

Semantics, or word usage, is really two different kinds of problems for me. One problem is thinking of the word that I really want to use, and the second is having to choose a different word because I cannot spell my first choice. Before I began to use a word processor to write, my written vocabulary was limited to words I could spell. Even though I knew there was a word that expressed exactly what I wanted to say, I would often go with an alternative, a simpler word. Even though the alternative would probably be misspelled, it would be closer to being recognized than the first choice. After doing this for many years, I simply stopped trying to use new words and just looked for words I could come close to spelling. After using the same words over and over, looking for the simplest choice has become a habit I am finding difficult to break.

I work on improving my vocabulary, but learning new words is difficult because I do not seem to be able to see them or hear them in my mind. I guess my worst problem with semantics is not being able to find the word I want to use. I know there is a word that would express exactly what I want to say; however, it is so difficult to find the exact word I want that I automatically replace the word I am searching for with an easier word. In composing a sentence, I place considerable concentration simply on semantics—finding the correct word.

Words and meanings are two different things to me. I can immediately attach meaning to some words simply because I have repeated them over and over. But most words, particularly larger words, simply disappear from my mind, even when I make an effort to retain them. The meaning may not be difficult to comprehend, but attaching the meaning to the word is extremely time consuming. I feel like I put as much time and effort into learning English words as most Americans would have to put into learning Russian. It would not take me any more time to learn ten simple vocabulary words in Russian than it would to learn ten difficult words in English.

I am always stopped by the letters. If individual letters have no meaning, then how can they form words that have meaning? I cannot ever remember the words because I cannot see them or hear them in any consistent form in my mind. It is not the words I cannot read or write, it is the letters. When I attempt to spell a word, I try to spell the word as a whole because I cannot break the word down into individual letters. I think I might have become a better speller if teachers had focused less on teaching the letters and more on teaching syllables. It is a natural sequence for teachers to begin with teaching the sounds and symbols that make up the words of our language. Most students would learn the sound-symbol associations and proceed to apply them to the formation of words. For students who cannot comprehend the connection, another method of teaching reading and writing must be found. With me, my education ended at this point because neither I nor my teachers ever got past the letters.

I concentrate so much on learning to connect words with meanings that I lose track of the context. The problem is compounded when I am trying to scribble out a word so that I will recognize it and know the meaning of it when I look at the paper an hour later. Sometimes I am unsure of using a new word in a paper because I might not know what the word means later. Also, I use lots of words and never have a clue as to what they mean. Somehow I pick up on the feeling of the word, and I use it because it feels right in a certain context even though I do not know what it means. For example, I really don't know what the word "propaganda" means, but sometimes I can throw it into a paper and am congratulated on how well it fits into the context of the sentence.

Once I find the words I want to use to express my thoughts, I then have to figure out the order they should go in to make sense. My poor written syntax stems from my poor oral syntax. When speaking to people my thoughts go faster than I can talk. This often happens in my writing as well. I think something and try to write it down before I forget it, and the sentence just comes out in a jumble of words that makes no sense. The lack of understanding of word definition and my poor spelling skills hold me back from writing the words as fast as I can.

Because I am not sure of the meaning of words, I often have to stop and start when trying to get out a complete thought. This results in loss of concentration. Not only do I lose what I am writing down, but I forget what I am trying to say. It's like going down a busy highway, where you're constantly having to stop at red lights or yield at yellow lights. The traffic is so stop and go that you get distracted, lose your way, and suddenly find yourself on a side street, unable to get back into the flow of traffic.

My difficulty with syntax results in sentences that are awkward. In addition to misusing words, I often leave them out. In the essay that I wrote for the Regents' Exam, I left out the main subject of the paper, the word "stool," in two sentences. I have wondered if the scorers simply overlooked the errors because it was such an unusual thing for a writer to do. Sometimes I turn words or phrases around; sometimes they come out completely backwards. Sometimes the sentences are just wordy because I am trying to get back on track with my thoughts. I cannot really explain why I write like this except that I am concentrating so much on the spelling and meaning of individual words that fluency is impossible. Using the computer has helped because it makes it easier to proof my writing. Proofing is a problem in itself because I cannot see when I have left out words or reversed their order. I read the sentences as if they were correct. But now there are computer programs that will check for grammatical errors, and I also have a few friends who I trust enough to proof my papers. I have also worked on developing a style of writing that is syntactically simple, yet adequate to express the abstract ideas that are called for in college.

I have worked for four years on developing my own style of writing. It began when I was working on trying to pass the Regents' Exam. This is an exam required by the state of Georgia to prove that students are able to read and write on a college level. The exam consists of a reading section and a writing section, and a student must pass both parts before graduating. I passed it on my second try. In order to do this, I really had to work on changing my style of writing. Because of my deficits in syntax, I often wrote extremely awkward sentences that could range anywhere from a paragraph to a page in length. These sentences were usually devoid of all punctuation. If I did use punctuation, it probably did not belong where I put it. With my learning disabilities specialist, I began to work on writing short and precise sentences. At first this was very difficult because I had difficulty expressing myself and was afraid people would not understand what I was trying to say. I had a tendency to ramble on and on trying to explain myself. I was so insecure in my writing that I was very self-conscious about what other people would think of it. I had to learn to shorten my sentences, while at the same time, get across my ideas.

There was another problem in writing short sentences. College professors seem to associate intelligent ideas with long and complex sentences. I had to learn to write short sentences that would also present my ideas in an acceptable college format. I learned to do this by practicing brevity and finding descriptive adjectives that added depth to my writing. The thesaurus became one of my best friends, and other doors opened up as I learned new words. Now my papers stood out in the classroom because they were not typical of college writing, yet they delivered the depth and understanding of a college writer.

A Change in Attitude

If I am such a terrible writer, why am I writing this book? The truth is I have learned to love writing. I find it sad that most people with unique learning abilities hate to write. I don't find it unusual because of all the problems they have to deal with in order to write a single word on paper. I have learned to put aside my fear of writing long enough for my ideas to show through. This is part of my effort to focus my anger on fighting my disability rather than being angry with the world because I have a disability.

Writing, like anything else, has many different aspects. The important aspect of writing is the substance, not the mechanics. Writing is a form of communication, and yet many people treat it as if it is a form of punishment. Writing is beautiful. It can express the depths of a person's soul. It is a way of talking without opening the mouth. Students with learning disabilities need to experience this.

I was in college before I discovered that even though the mechanics are very important, there comes a time when a person should just let go of the mechanics and write with feeling. If teachers wait to teach the communication and aesthetic aspects of writing until their students are able to perfect the mechanics, their students may never experience the true pleasure of writing. When I let go of the mechanics and began to concentrate on what I was saying, I found that my writing improved, and in turn, my mechanics improved. Before college I hated writing because it was exposing and confronting a weakness and because it simply meant that I couldn't spell or correctly punctuate a sentence. I never once realized that writing was supposed to have meaning. As it turns out, writing is a joy.

My first insight into writing as it *should* be was in my first college English class. My teacher had us keep a weekly journal. Each week I could write about anything I wanted, and I was only supposed to take ten minutes. I was not supposed to worry about punctuation or spelling.

At first this assignment scared me. I knew I would have to put more than ten minutes into it simply to get a "Pass." In fact, I typically put three hours into each journal entry.

We could bare our souls about a serious problem, describe a pretty girl walking down the street, or just describe what we had for breakfast. The point of the journals was to get us to write without being encumbered by any restraints. I found myself liking the idea of letting everything go, and even though I knew it was impossible for me to do that, I found a certain feeling of peace knowing that a grade would not be assigned to the thoughts I put on paper.

So I started to write my weekly journals. It was very hard at first. I found myself fighting to put my words on paper. I was fighting myself and the memory of years of discouragement. I did not like the fact that I had to struggle so hard and that it was so difficult to put things on paper. The freedom I longed for was not there. It was not as easy as the teacher had made it sound in class. What was supposed to be a ten-minute assignment turned out to be a week-long writing project. Then one day it happened. I was staring out the window of my dorm room and feeling sorry for myself when I saw two girls walking down the street. I had seen them around campus before. One of them was visually impaired. She had thick glasses and carried a cane. She always seemed to be smiling. She also always seemed to be alone. Walking beside her was another girl. She was a "little person" whom I had also seen around campus, also smiling. However, she, too, always seemed to be alone. I remember passing them individually on campus and trying not to feel sorry for them. I could not help thinking about how lonely each girl must have been. I never saw them with anyone. Outside my window, walking down the chilly, lamplit street, under a starry sky, they had found each other. I realized that they were no longer alone. A warm feeling came over me, and I wanted to share it with someone.

There was no one around—only my pencil and paper. For the first time I wanted to put my thoughts down on paper. And I did. Forgetting about the structure, the organization, and yes, even the spelling, for the first time I was able to concentrate on the meaning. It was such a good feeling to see two people finding each other that it overrode any fear I had of writing. After I finished I realized I had written my first real paper. The paper was lousy, but I felt fantastic. Suddenly I realized the pleasure that came with putting my thoughts down in writing. For the first time I realized that, just as the blind girl had found her friend, I had found mine—writing. I was able to free my thoughts on paper. They had always been there, in my mind, but were bound by my lack of understanding of the mechanics. For the first time the mechanics were not an obstacle.

Now the thoughts were free. I had never before done this. The fact that my journal was full of errors meant nothing. I turned it in just as it was, hoping the teacher would say how good it was. She never did. But it did not matter, because it meant something special to me, and it opened up a new world.

DIALOGUE

1. What tricks did Christopher Lee use in high school to disguise his writing problems? Discuss in your group the strategies you used in high school to outwit your teachers or to disguise shortcomings. Were they effective? Are they likely to be effective in college? Why or why not?

2. Discuss the role the computer played in helping Lee overcome his fear of writing. In what ways was the computer his friend? In what ways have computers helped you in your schoolwork?

3. Summarize Lee's specific experiences with and attitudes toward spelling. Can you relate to any of his struggles to be a good speller? Does poor spelling inhibit your ability to write or reduce your interest in doing more writing? What can you do about it?

WRITING TOPICS

1. Describe your experience with writing. Do you write for pleasure or only when it is assigned? Is writing a part of your routine or a chore? How did you come to develop your current attitude toward writing?

2. Elsewhere in the book *Faking It,* Lee shares how he felt about being called a "student with a learning disability" and how he preferred to think of himself as a "creative learner." Discuss what each of these terms implies. Which of the terms is preferable, and why?

3. Lee urges writers to let go of the mechanics of writing and "write with feeling." Explore the relationship between mechanics (spelling, syntax, punctuation) and the message or substance of the writing. Is one more important than the other? How are they interdependent in good writing?

INTERACTION

Working in small groups, discuss what aspects of learning have been especially challenging for you. Math? Taking tests? Giving a speech?

Reading or writing? What strategies have worked for you in the past? What advice can you give fellow students who face similar learning challenges?

To Err Is Human
Lewis Thomas

PREVIEW

Many students are paralyzed by the fear of failure. In this consoling essay, Lewis Thomas reminds us that everyone—including the greatest minds—makes mistakes. In fact, our capacity for error may explain the lofty status of humankind in the great chain of being. Mistakes are not only unavoidable; they are absolutely necessary to learning.

   Thomas combined an active public career in medicine (he became president of the Sloan-Kettering Cancer Center) with a more private role as a writer. In Lives of a Cell *(1974) and* The Medusa and the Snail *(1979), he wrote brilliantly about science in a style that could be easily understood by the average reader.*

Everyone must have had at least one personal experience with a computer error by this time. Bank balances are suddenly reported to have jumped from $379 into the millions, appeals for charitable contributions are mailed over and over to people with crazy-sounding names at your address, department stores send the wrong bills, utility companies write that they're turning everything off, that sort of thing. If you manage to get in touch with someone and complain, you then get instantaneously typed, guilty letters from the same computer, saying, "Our computer was in error, and an adjustment is being made in your account."

These are supposed to be the sheerest, blindest accidents. Mistakes are not believed to be part of the normal behavior of a good machine. If things go wrong, it must be a personal, human error, the result of fingering, tampering, a button getting stuck, someone hitting the wrong key. The computer, at its normal best, is infallible.

SOURCE: "To Err Is Human," copyright © 1976 by Lewis Thomas, from *The Medusa and the Snail* by Lewis Thomas. Used by permission of Viking Penguin, a division of Penguin Books, USA Inc.

I wonder whether this can be true. After all, the whole point of computers is that they represent an extension of the human brain, vastly improved upon but nonetheless human, superhuman maybe. A good computer can think clearly and quickly enough to beat you at chess, and some of them have even been programmed to write obscure verse. They can do anything we can do, and more besides.

It is not yet known whether a computer has its own consciousness, and it would be hard to find out about this. When you walk into one of those great halls now built for the huge machines, and stand listening, it is easy to imagine that the faint, distant noises are the sound of thinking, and the turning of the spools gives them the look of wild creatures rolling their eyes in the effort to concentrate, choking with information. But real thinking, and dreaming, are other matters.

On the other hand, the evidences of something like an *unconscious*, equivalent to ours, are all around, in every mail. As extensions of the human brain, they have been constructed with the same property of error, spontaneous, uncontrolled, and rich in possibilities.

Mistakes are at the very base of human thought, embedded there, feeding the structure like root nodules. If we were not provided with the knack of being wrong, we could never get anything useful done. We think our way along by choosing between right and wrong alternatives, and the wrong choices have to be made as frequently as the right ones. We get along in life this way. We are built to make mistakes, coded for error.

We learn, as we say, by "trial and error." Why do we always say that? What not "trial and rightness" or "trial and triumph"? The old phrase puts it that way because that is, in real life, the way it is done.

A good laboratory, like a good bank or a corporation or government, has to run like a computer. Almost everything is done flawlessly, by the book, and all the numbers add up to the predicted sums. The days go by. And then if it is a lucky day, and a lucky laboratory, somebody makes a mistake: the wrong buffer, something in one of the blanks, a decimal misplaced in reading counts, the warm room off by a degree and a half, a mouse out of his box, or just a misreading of the day's protocol. Whatever, when the results come in, something is obviously screwed up, and then the action can begin.

The misreading is not the important error; it opens the way. The next step is the crucial one. If the investigator can bring himself to say, "But even so, look at that!" then the new finding, whatever it is, is ready for snatching. What is needed, for progress to be made, is the move based on error.

Whenever new kinds of thinking are about to be accomplished, or new varieties of music, there has to be an argument beforehand. With two sides debating in the same mind, haranguing, there is an amiable understanding that one is right and the other wrong. Sooner or later the thing is settled, but there can be no action at all if there are not the two sides, and the argument. The hope is in the faculty of wrongness, the tendency toward error. The capacity to leap across mountains of information to land lightly on the wrong side represents the highest of human endowments.

It may be that this is a uniquely human gift, perhaps even stipulated in our genetic instructions. Other creatures do not seem to have DNA sequences for making mistakes as a routine part of daily living, certainly not for programmed error as a guide for action.

We are at our human finest, dancing with our minds, when there are more choices than two. Sometimes there are ten, even twenty different ways to go, all but one bound to be wrong, and the richness of selection in such situations can lift us onto totally new ground. This process is called exploration and is based on human fallibility. If we had only a single center in our brains, capable of responding only when a correct decision was to be made, instead of the jumble of different, credulous, easily conned clusters of neurons that provide for being flung off into blind alleys, up trees, down dead ends, out into blue sky, along wrong turnings, around bends, we could only stay the way we are today, stuck fast.

The lower animals do not have this splendid freedom. They are limited, most of them, to absolute infallibility. Cats, for all their good side, never make mistakes. I have never seen a maladroit, clumsy, or blundering cat. Dogs are sometimes fallible, occasionally able to make charming minor mistakes, but they get this way by trying to mimic their masters. Fish are flawless in everything they do. Individual cells in a tissue are mindless machines, perfect in their performance, as absolutely inhuman as bees.

We should have this in mind as we become dependent on more complex computers for the arrangement of our affairs. Give the computers their heads, I say; let them go their way. If we can learn to do this, turning our heads to one side and wincing while the work proceeds, the possibilities for the future of mankind, and computerkind, are limitless. Your average good computer can make calculations in an instant which would take a lifetime of slide rules for any of us. Think of what we could gain from the near infinity of precise, machine-made miscomputation which is now so easily within our grasp. We would begin the solving of some of our hardest problems. How, for instance, should we go about organizing ourselves for social living on a planetary scale, now that we have become, as a plain fact of life, a single community? We can assume, as a working hypothesis, that all the right ways of doing this are unworkable. What we need, then, for moving ahead, is a set of wrong alternatives much longer and more interesting than the short list of mistaken courses that any of us can think up right now. We need, in fact, an infinite list, and when it is printed out we need the computer to turn on itself and select, at random, the next way to go. If it is a big enough mistake, we could find ourselves on a new level, stunned, out in the clear, ready to move again.

DIALOGUE

1. "If we were not provided with the knack of being wrong, we could never get anything useful done." What do you think Lewis Thomas meant by this statement?
2. In what ways do computers resemble the human brain? In what ways are they different from humans?
3. Is critical thinking—the intellectual tendency to test hypotheses, verify claims, and expose fallacious reasoning—the best path to the truth? The only path? Explain your answer.

WRITING TOPICS

1. Can you think of specific examples in your own experience of an error leading to some new insight, discovery, or accomplishment?
2. List some strategies that you could use as a college student to help you profit from your mistakes.
3. "Mistakes are at the very base of human thought . . . feeding the structure like root nodules." Interview faculty in different disciplines and isolate specific examples in the history of ideas, science, politics, business, religion, and other areas that confirm the truth of this statement by Thomas.

INTERACTION

When you make a mistake or perform beneath your expectations of yourself, how do you deal with it? Working in small groups, share your individual methods for dealing with failures or mistakes in your work, relationships, and studies. Discuss steps that could be taken by members of your group to achieve more positive results.

Claiming an Education
Adrienne Rich

PREVIEW

Adrienne Rich was born in Baltimore in 1929. Since the selection of her first volume by W. H. Auden for the Yale Series of Younger Poets in 1951, her work has continually broken new ground, moving from closed forms to a feminist poetics and a radical urban imagination and politics. Her books of poetry include Collected Early Poems 1950–1970; The Dream of a Common Language; Your Native Land, Your Life; Times Power; An Atlas of the Difficult World; *and* Dark Fields of the Republic. *Prose works include* Of Woman Born: Motherhood as Experience and Institution; On Lies, Secrets, and Silence; Blood, Bread and Poetry; *and* What Is Found There: Notebooks on Poetry and Politics. *Her work has received many awards including the Ruth Lilly Prize, the Los Angeles Times Book Award, the Lambda Literary Award, the Poets' Prize, The Lenore Marshall/Nation Award, a MacArthur Fellowship, and the Dorothea Tanning Prize.*

For this convocation, I planned to separate my remarks into two parts: some thoughts about you, the women students here, and some thoughts about us who teach in a women's college. But ultimately, those two parts are indivisible. If university education means anything beyond the processing of human beings into expected roles, through credit hours, tests, and grades (and I believe that in a women's college especially it *might* mean much more), it implies an ethical and intellectual contract between teacher and student. This contract must remain intuitive, dynamic, unwritten; but we must turn to it again and again if learning is to be reclaimed from the depersonalizing and cheapening pressures of the present-day academic scene.

The first thing I want to say to you who are students, is that you cannot afford to think of yourselves as being here to *claim* one. One of the dictionary definitions of the verb "to claim" is: *to take as the rightful owner; to assert in the face of possible contradiction.* "To receive" is *to come into posses-*

SOURCE: "Claiming an Education," from *Lies, Secrets, and Silence: Selected Prose 1966–1978* by Adrienne Rich. Copyright © 1979 by W. W. Norton & Company, Inc. Reprinted by permission of the author and W. W. Norton & Company, Inc.

sion of; to act as receptacle or container for; to accept as authoritative or true. The difference is that between acting and being acted-upon, and for women it can literally mean the difference between life and death.

One of the devastating weaknesses of university learning, of the store of knowledge and opinion that has been handed down through academic training, has been its almost total erasure of women's experience and thought from the curriculum, and its exclusion of women as members of the academic community. Today, with increasing numbers of women students in nearly every branch of higher learning, we still see very few women in the upper levels of faculty and administration in most institutions. Douglass College itself is a women's college in a university administered overwhelmingly by men, who in turn are answerable to the state legislature, again composed predominantly of men. But the most significant fact for you is that what you learn here, the very texts you read, the lectures you hear, the way your studies are divided into categories and fragmented one from the other—all this reflects, to a very large degree, neither objective reality, nor an accurate picture of the past, nor a group of rigorously tested observations about human behavior. What you can learn here (and I mean not only at Douglass but any college in any university) is how *men* have perceived and organized their experience, their history, their ideas of social relationships, good and evil, sickness and health, etc. When you read or hear about "great issues," "major texts," "the mainstream of Western thought," you are hearing about what men, above all white men, in their male subjectivity, have decided is important.

Black and other minority peoples have for some time recognized that their racial and ethnic experience was not accounted for in the studies broadly labeled human; and that even the sciences can be racist. For many reasons, it has been more difficult for women to comprehend our exclusion, and to realize that even the sciences can be sexist. For one thing, it is only within the last hundred years that higher education has grudgingly been opened up to women at all, even to white, middle-class women. And many of us have found ourselves poring eagerly over books with titles like: *The Descent of Man; Man and His Symbols; Irrational Man; The Phenomenon of Man; The Future of Man; Man and the Machine; From Man to Man; May Man Prevail?; Man, Science and Society;* or *One-Dimensional Man*—books pretending to describe a "human" reality that does not include over one-half the human species.

Less than a decade ago, with the rebirth of a feminist movement in this country, women students and teachers in a number of universities began to demand and set up women's studies courses—to *claim* a woman-directed education. And, despite the inevitable accusations of "unscholarly," "group therapy," "faddism," etc., despite backlash and budget cuts, women's studies are still growing, offering to more and more women a new intellectual grasp on their lives, new understanding of our history, a fresh vision of the human experience, and also a critical basis for evaluating what they hear and read in other courses, and in the society at large.

But my talk is not really about women's studies, much as I believe in their scholarly, scientific, and human necessity. While I think that any Douglass student has everything to gain by investigating and enrolling in women's studies courses, I want to suggest that there is a more essential experience that you owe yourselves, one which courses in women's studies can greatly enrich, but which finally depends on you, in all your interactions with yourself and your world. This is the experience of *taking responsibility toward yourselves*. Our upbringing as women has so often told us that this should come second to our relationships and responsibilities to other people. We have been offered ethical models of the self-denying wife and mother; intellectual models of the brilliant but slapdash dilettante who never commits herself to anything the whole way, or the intelligent woman who denies her intelligence in order to seem more "feminine," or who sits in passive silence even when she disagrees inwardly with everything that is being said around her.

Responsibility to yourself means refusing to let others do your thinking, talking, and naming for you; it means learning to respect and use your own brains and instincts; hence, grappling with hard work. It means that you do not treat your body as a commodity with which to purchase superficial intimacy or economic security; for our bodies and minds are inseparable in this life, and when we allow our bodies to be treated as objects, our minds are in mortal danger. It means insisting that those to whom you give your friendship and love are able to respect your mind. It means being able to say, with Charlotte Brontë's Jane Eyre: "I have an inward treasure born with me, which can keep me alive if all the extraneous delights should be withheld or offered only at a price I cannot afford to give."

Responsibility to yourself means that you don't fall for shallow and easy solutions—predigested books and ideas, weekend encounters guaranteed to change your life, taking "gut" courses instead of ones you know will challenge you, bluffing at school and life instead of doing solid work, marrying early as an escape from real decisions, getting pregnant as an evasion of already existing problems. It means that you refuse to sell your talents and aspirations short, simply to avoid conflict and confrontation. And this, in turn, means resisting the forces in society which say that women should be nice, play safe, have low professional expectations, drown in love and forget about work, live through others, and stay in the places assigned to us. It means that we insist on a life of meaningful work, insist that work be as meaningful as love and friendship in our lives. It means, therefore, the courage to be "different;" not to be continuously available to others when we need time for ourselves and our work; to be able to demand of others—parents, friends, roommates, teachers, lovers, husbands, children—that they respect our sense of purpose and our integrity as persons. Women everywhere are finding the courage to do this, more and more, and we are finding that courage both in our study of women in the past who possessed it, and in each other as we look to other women for comradeship, community, and challenge. The difference between a life lived actively, and a life of passive drifting and dispersal of energies, is an immense difference. Once we begin to feel committed to our lives, responsible to ourselves, we can never again be satisfied with the old, passive way.

Now comes the second part of the contract. I believe that in a women's college you have the right to expect your faculty to take you seriously. The education of women has been a matter of debate for centuries, and old, negative attitudes about women's role, women's ability to think and take leadership, are still rife both in and outside the university. Many male professors (and I don't mean only at Douglass) still feel that teaching in a women's college is a second-rate career. Many tend to eroticize their women students—to treat them as sexual objects—instead of demanding the best of their minds. (At Yale a legal suit [*Alexander v. Yale*] has been brought against the university by a group of women students demanding a stated policy against sexual advances toward female students by male professors.) Many teachers, both men and women, trained in the male-centered tradition, are still handing the ideas and texts of that tradition on to students without teaching them to criticize its antiwoman attitudes, its omission of women as part of the species. Too often, all of us fail to teach the most important thing, which is that clear thinking, active discussion, and excellent writing are all necessary for intellectual freedom, and that these require hard work. Sometimes, perhaps in discouragement with a culture which is both anti-intellectual and antiwoman, we may resign ourselves to low expectations for our students before we have given them half a chance to become more thoughtful, expressive human beings. We need to take to heart the words of Elizabeth Barrett Browning, a poet, a thinking woman, and a feminist, who wrote in 1845 of her impatience with studies which cultivate a "passive recipiency" in the mind, and asserted that "women want to be made to *think actively:* their apprehension is quicker than that of men, but their defect lies for the most part in the logical faculty and in the higher mental activities." Note that she implies a defect which can be remedied by intellectual training; *not* an inborn lack of ability.

I have said that the contract on the student's part involves that you demand to be taken seriously so that you can also go on taking yourself seriously. This means seeking out criticism, recognizing that the most affirming thing anyone can do for you is demand that you push yourself further, show you the range of what you *can* do. It means rejecting attitudes of "take-it-easy," "why-be-so-serious," "why-worry-you'll-probably-get-married-anyway." It means assuming your share of responsibility for what happens in the classroom, because that affects the quality of your daily life here. It means that the student sees herself engaged *with* her teachers in an active, ongoing struggle for a real education. But for her to do this, her teachers must be committed to the belief that women's minds and experience are intrinsically valuable and indispensable to any civilization worthy the name; that there is no more exhilarating and intellectually fertile place in the academic world today than a woman's college—*if* both students and teachers in large enough numbers are trying to fulfill this contract. The contract is really a pledge of mutual seriousness about women, about language, ideas, methods, and values. It is our shared commitment toward a world in which the inborn potentialities of so many women's minds will no longer be wasted, raveled-away, paralyzed, or denied.

DIALOGUE

1. Adrienne Rich's remarks were addressed to an audience of female students and faculty at a women's college. To what extent are her words appropriate for all students—male as well as female?
2. Do you think that Rich is arguing for sexually segregated educational settings? Would women students be better off in women-only colleges with enlightened women professors? Why or why not?
3. Rich notes that it has been more difficult for women to comprehend their exclusion from the study of human experience and discovery than it has been for African Americans and other minority groups. Agree or disagree with this claim and explain your reasons.

WRITING TOPICS

1. Rich repeatedly uses the term *contract* in her address. Explore her use of that term in a brief essay. Who are the parties to the contract? What binding agreements or commitments are involved in it?

2. Clarify the contrast that the author sets up between *receiving* an education and *claiming* one.

3. Write an essay agreeing or disagreeing with the following statement:

   Single-sex colleges are unconstitutional.

INTERACTION

The author's criticism of higher education—that its curriculum and modes of instruction are designed by white male faculty for white male students and that they largely ignore women and minorities—contained a large measure of truth in 1977, when this address was delivered. Working in small groups, discuss whether this characterization is still accurate today. To what extent has society in general, and higher education in particular, undergone positive change over the past twenty years?

Take This Fish and Look at It
Samuel H. Scudder

PREVIEW

Occasionally, the academic routine of college is brightened by an epiphany—a moment of mental clarity when a student falls under the spell of a gifted instructor who offers encouragement and advice when it is most needed. Such an encounter is described in the following narrative by the famous entomologist Samuel Scudder. In his first year at Harvard University, Scudder walked into the laboratory of Louis Agassiz, the Swiss-born zoologist and natural history pioneer. Within a few days, Scudder learned the most valuable lesson a scientist can learn: the value of patient observation and meticulous description.

It was more than fifteen years ago that I entered the laboratory of Professor Agassiz, and told him I had enrolled my name in the Scientific School as a student of natural history. He asked me a few questions about my object in coming, my antecedents generally, the mode in which I afterwards proposed to use the knowledge I might acquire, and, finally, whether I wished to study any special branch. To the latter I replied that, while I wished to be well grounded in all departments of zoology, I proposed to devote myself specially to insects.

"When do you wish to begin?" he asked.

"Now," I replied.

This seemed to please him, and with an energetic "Very well!" he reached from a shelf a huge jar of specimens in yellow alcohol. "Take this fish," he said, "and look at it; we call it a haemulon; by and by I will ask what you have seen."

With that he left me, but in a moment returned with explicit instructions as to the care of the object entrusted to me.

"No man is fit to be a naturalist," said he, "who does not know how to take care of specimens."

I was to keep the fish before me in a tin tray, and occasionally moisten the surface with alcohol from the jar, always taking care to replace the stopper tightly. Those were not the days of ground-glass stoppers and elegantly shaped exhibition jars; all the old students will recall the huge neckless glass bottles with their leaky, wax-besmeared corks, half eaten by insects, and begrimed with cellar dust. Entomology was a cleaner science than ichthyology, but the example of the Professor, who had unhesitatingly plunged to the bottom of the jar to produce the fish, was infectious; and though this alcohol had a "very ancient and fishlike smell," I really dared not show any aversion within these sacred precincts, and treated the alcohol as though it were pure water. Still I was conscious of a passing feeling of disappointment, for gazing at a fish did not commend itself to an ardent entomologist. My friends at home, too, were annoyed when they discovered that no amount of eau-de-Cologne would drown the perfume which haunted me like a shadow.

In ten minutes I had seen all that could be seen in that fish, and started in search of the Professor—who had, however, left the Museum; and when I returned, after lingering over some of the odd animals stored in the upper apartment, my specimen was dry all over. I dashed the fluid over the fish as if to resuscitate the beast from a fainting fit, and looked with anxiety for a return of the normal sloppy appearance. This little excitement over, nothing was to be done but to return to a steadfast gaze at my mute companion. Half an hour passed—an hour—another hour; the fish began to look loathsome. I turned it over and around; looked it in the face—ghastly; from behind, beneath, above, sideways, at a three-quarters' view—just as ghastly. I was in despair; at an early hour I concluded that lunch was necessary; so, with infinite relief, the fish was carefully replaced in the jar, and for an hour I was free.

On my return, I learned that Professor Agassiz had been at the Museum, but had gone, and would not return for several hours. My fellow-students were too busy to be disturbed by continued conversation. Slowly I drew forth that hideous fish, and with a feeling of desperation again looked at it. I might not use a magnifying-glass; instruments of all kinds were interdicted. My two hands, my two eyes, and the fish: it seemed a most limited field. I pushed my finger down its throat to feel how sharp the teeth were. I began to count the scales in the different rows, until I was convinced that was nonsense. At last a happy thought struck me—I would draw the fish; and now with surprise I began to discover new features in the creature. Just then the Professor returned.

"That is right" said he; "a pencil is one of the best of eyes. I am glad to notice, too, that you keep your specimen wet, and your bottle corked."

With these encouraging words, he added:

"Well, what is it like?"

He listened attentively to my brief rehearsal of the structure of parts whose names were still unknown to me: the fringed gill-arches and movable operculum; the pores of the head, fleshy lips and lidless eyes; the lateral line, the spinous fins and forked tail; the compressed and arched body. When I finished, he waited as if expecting more, and then, with an air of disappointment:

"You have not looked very carefully; why," he continued more earnestly, "you haven't even seen one of the most conspicuous features of the animal, which is plainly before your eyes as the fish itself; look again, look again!" and he left me to my misery.

I was piqued; I was mortified. Still more of that wretched fish! But now I set myself to my task with a will, and discovered one new thing after another, until I saw how just the Professor's criticism had been. The afternoon passed quickly; and when, towards its close, the Professor inquired:

"Do you see it yet?"

"No," I replied, "I am certain I do not, but I see how little I saw before."

"That is next best," said he, earnestly, "but I won't hear you now; put away your fish and go home; perhaps you will be ready with a better answer in the morning. I will examine you before you look at the fish."

This was disconcerting. Not only must I think of my fish all night, studying, without the object before me, what this unknown but most visible feature might be; but also, without reviewing my discoveries, I must give an exact account of them the next day. I had a bad memory; so I walked home by Charles River in a distracted state, with my two perplexities.

The cordial greeting from the Professor the next morning was reassuring; here was a man who seemed to be quite as anxious as I that I should see for myself what he saw.

"Do you perhaps mean," I asked, "that the fish has symmetrical sides with paired organs?"

His thoroughly pleased "Of course! Of course!" repaid the wakeful hours of the previous night. After he had discoursed most happily and enthusiastically—as he always did—upon the importance of this point, I ventured to ask what I should do next.

"Oh, look at your fish!" he said, and left me again to my own devices. In a little more than an hour he returned, and heard my new catalogue.

"That is good, that is good!" he repeated; "but that is not all; go on"; and so for three long days he placed that fish before my eyes, forbidding me to look at anything else, or to use any artificial aid. "Look, look, look," was his repeated injunction.

This was the best entomological lesson I ever had—a lesson whose influence has extended to the details of every subsequent study; a legacy the Professor had left to me, as he has left it to so many others, of inestimable value, which we could not buy, with which we cannot part.

A year afterward, some of us were amusing ourselves with chalking outlandish beasts on the Museum blackboard. We drew prancing starfishes; frogs in mortal combat; hydra-headed worms; stately crawfishes, standing on their tails, bearing aloft umbrellas; and grotesque fishes with gaping mouths and staring eyes. The Professor came in shortly after, and was as amused as any at our experiments. He looked at the fishes.

"Haemulons, every one of them," he said; "Mr. ——— drew them."

True; and to this day, if I attempt a fish, I can draw nothing but haemulons.

The fourth day, a second fish of the same group was placed beside the first, and I was bidden to point out the resemblances and differences between the two; another and another followed, until the entire family lay before me, and a whole legion of jars covered the table and surrounding shelves; the odor had become a pleasant perfume; and even now, the sight of an old, six-inch, worm-eaten cork brings fragrant memories.

The whole group of haemulons was thus brought in review; and, whether engaged upon the dissection of the internal organs, the preparation and examination of the bony framework, or the description of the various parts, Agassiz's training in the method of observing facts and their orderly arrangement was ever accompanied by the urgent exhortation not to be content with them.

"Facts are stupid things," he would say, "until brought into connection with some general law."

At the end of eight months, it was almost with reluctance that I left these friends and turned to insects; but what I had gained by this outside experience has been of greater value than years of later investigation in my favorite groups. (Scudder 1874)

DIALOGUE

1. Describe Professor Agassiz's teaching methods. Were they effective? Explain.
2. "Facts are stupid things," Agassiz said to his students. What did he mean? For true scientific learning to take place, what is required beyond mere observation?
3. What is the most important lesson Samuel Scudder learned from his observations of the fish? Why is it important?

WRITING TOPICS

1. List three common characteristics that good scientists and good writers share. Explain how both groups make use of these characteristics in their work.
2. Reconstruct the process by which Scudder came to his complete vision of the fish. Describe each distinct step, from his initial effort to his final revelatory insight.
3. Scudder suggests that the lesson learned by observing the fish could be "extended to the details of every subsequent study." In what ways can the lesson he learned be applied to the study of art? Literature? A foreign language? Choose the academic area you are most interested in and transfer Scudder's lesson to the observations and learning associated with that field.

INTERACTION

In small groups, describe to each other a favorite teacher you have had or an experience in school from which you learned a valuable lesson. What did you learn? Is it still valuable today?

I Thought I Was a Terrific Teacher
Until One Day . . .
Marcia Yudkin

PREVIEW

The average age of American undergraduates has been creeping steadily upward as more and more adult students enroll in college for career advancement, to certify themselves for a career change, to keep up in a rapidly changing world, or simply for the joy of learning. Returning adults, a large percentage of whom are women, have forced faculty and administrators to rethink and recast an educational system designed for students of traditional age. In this article, Marcia Yudkin, a Boston-based novelist, freelance writer, and occasional college instructor, describes her own encounter with adult learners and how she responded to their special needs.

When I surveyed the faces in my "Philosophy and Women" class at Smith College last September, I felt a thrill of anticipation. Of 33 students, about one third were Ada Comstock Scholars—women who had been out of school for some time, now finishing up their undergraduate degrees. Like most Smith instructors, I relished the diversity of experience and perspective that "Adas" contributed. I envisioned more productive discussions than usual and thus a better learning environment for the entire class.

Near the end of the semester, it seemed that something had gone wrong. From a cluster of Adas in the back of the room came hostile demands to negotiate their grades and harsh criticisms of the supposed nonhierarchical structure of the course. Later I learned that a few days before, several Adas had visited my department chairman with similar complaints: my grading system was too vague and the course lacked substance.

The sudden jelling of dissatisfaction, unprecedented in my teaching, stunned me. When I pondered the "revolt," I couldn't get around the apparent connection with age. Some Adas during the semester had enlightened me about Smith's inhospitableness to their children and about

SOURCE: Marcia Yudkin, "I Thought I Was a Terrific Teacher Until One Day . . ." Ms. Magazine, October 1987. Reprinted by permission of Ellen Levine Literary Agency. Copyright © 1987 by Marcia Yudkin.

professors and administrators belittling the Adas' previous careers. Did my course somehow fit into a pattern of insensitivity to adult students? Even though we were contemporaries, what did I know about their needs? Partly for myself and partly because older college students represent a trend, I launched an investigation.

Nationwide, according to the U.S. Bureau of the Census, between 1975 and 1985 women students over 25 jumped from 11.8 percent to 17.4 percent of all undergraduates. Because of the well-known dearth of 18-year-olds, the greater abundance of 30- and 40-year-olds, and the much larger number of women than men who have delayed finishing their education, older women look more and more attractive to many college administrators. But as I learned from talking with Smith Adas, as well as students at other schools and their advocates, older women do have some distinctive needs. And the way they exploded some of my own assumptions about education may indicate challenges ahead for even the best-intentioned efforts to broaden the age spread at colleges.

Right off, one of my former older students warned me against convenient generalizations. "Our going back to school isn't a *trend,*" explains Lucinda Butler, an ex-secretary and divorced mother who graduated from Smith in May at age 40 and hopes to go on for a doctorate in sociology. "It's a survival mechanism, a way of rerooting our lives. And you have to keep in mind, we're so different from one another—we're women with grown-up children, women with young children, women with no children. Some of us live on campus, some off. We have tremendous class differences." Nevertheless, I found consensus on the following:

- Unlike most traditional-age students, who enroll in college as the normal next step in their development, older women must defend and explain their decision to children, husbands, and bosses. Often they face a heavy burden of guilt. Ruth Wynkoop, who started classes at Greenfield Community College in Massachusetts as the first female manager of the local Burger Chef and mother of two young children, says she had to leave her job because of the owners' disapproval. For Jill St. Coeur, who entered the University of Massachusetts when her 14-year marriage was falling apart, her going back to school became an issue in a bitter custody trial.

- Having been out of school for some time, older women return unsure of their academic abilities. According to Barry Sheckley, professor of education at the University of Connecticut, their self-esteem, whether low or high, generally drops during their first semester back. Robin Greiner, head resident last year in a Smith house with four times as many Ada Comstocks as traditional students, observes: "The new Adas were

45

really nervous because they'd pulled themselves out of a whole other lifestyle. One woman had been a professional in broadcasting, another a ballerina. Others had dropped out of college before and saw this as their last chance. Suddenly they had no income and were in debt. They went to class five minutes early with three pencils, overstudied, and were tired all the time."

- Grades become the concrete sign for older women that they do belong in school. "Adas are less willing to get B's than are traditional-age students," says Greiner.
- One particular strength of older women, their greater wealth of experience and practical knowledge, doesn't always translate into an advantage in college, where narrowly academic skills matter most.
- Emergencies, ranging from children's chickenpox or parents' cancer to running out of money or suddenly losing one's apartment, more often disrupt the semester of older students. "Burnout stuff," says St. Coeur, whose saga of how she earned her degree includes innumerable 20-mile drives to see her kids, doing free-lance work at home because she couldn't afford child care, and tracking down special counseling to help her cope with having lost all her psychological and material security. Adds Wynkoop, who recently graduated from Smith and is now completing a book of interviews with working-class women who attended college, most as older students, "College is more traumatic for older students because we want to do our best but sometimes can't."

Talking with authorities on adult learning heightened my awareness of tensions inherent in treating adult women as proxy 18-to-22-year-olds. "There's no consensus about adult learning versus younger learning, just as there's no consensus about women's versus men's learning," cautions Elinor Miller Greenberg, a regional executive officer for the Council for Adult and Experiential Learning. "Adults come back to school to get something they think they're missing. They have a heavy experience base and want to be able to make sense of it. They're seeking 'why,' whereas younger students seek 'how.'"

According to Frances Mahoney and Maurice Olivier of the School for Lifelong Learning in New Hampshire, the college curriculum itself embodies assumptions that clash with adult needs. "For example," offers Olivier, a founder of SLL, "we assume there needs to be a sequence of courses, from beginning to more advanced, that you need prerequisites to take more advanced courses. But the adult may have learned about a subject area from life, or have taken various courses. For adults, it's not appropriate to run a college like a winery—the longer it takes the better it will taste—and to ignore what the adult learner already knows."

Where I had failed my students, I finally saw, was in thinking of a course as an entity apart from the students it should be educating. Only in retrospect did it sink in that I had designed my course, reasonably well received before, to remedy certain deficiencies characteristic of younger students. I emphasized group projects to give students an experience of cooperative discovery, which many Adas had already gained from work or community involvement. By de-emphasizing grades and my professorial authority so that students would learn to trust themselves as inquirers, I deprived the older students of the guidance, feedback, and expertise they preferred. Most didn't need another dose of experiential learning, either—and hence, their frustration. I suspect that similar problems exist in more traditional courses as well.

I also came to understand the relevance of Adas in my class to the "revolt" that took place. One of the women involved later told me that until I fell sick and canceled a class, she and the others had felt vaguely dissatisfied with the course, but they hadn't compared their feelings with each other. After they did, they marched off to my chairman as a gesture of Ada solidarity. As with other minorities, constituting a real presence rather than the isolated case undoubtedly helped them articulate and assert the legitimacy of their needs. I believe what happened in my class may foreshadow other challenges to entrenched assumptions on college campuses as older women students gather individual and collective strength.

My experience reminded me that implementing true equality of opportunity for any long-excluded group requires imagination and a willing ear in addition to good intentions. Because the extent to which policies on everything from financial aid to housing inappropriately generalize younger students' needs to older women may be apparent only to those affected, colleges should invite dialogue on ways to make school less stressful for those with equal ability but more complicated lives. Wellesley College Dean Bonnie Leonard likes to brag that older women students often walk off with a disproportionate share of honors at graduation, despite the obstacles. I trust the maxim "You're never too old to learn" can hold true for 100-year-old (and more and less venerable) institutions too.

DIALOGUE

1. A large percentage of adult learners are women. What reasons can you think of for this gender imbalance?

2. What life roles do adult learners play in addition to their role as students? How do these roles both help and hinder their ability to learn and complete a college degree?
3. What unique contributions can adult learners make to a college classroom?

WRITING TOPICS

1. Define the term *adult learner* by comparing and contrasting adult learners with traditional-age college students.
2. According to two sources at the School for Lifelong Learning, "the college curriculum itself embodies assumptions that clash with adult needs." List at least three features of the curriculum at your college that support this idea.
3. Argue for or against the following statement in an essay:

   The solution to the problem of adult women learners is to segregate them from other students and then provide a separate academic track that accommodates their uniqueness.

INTERACTION

Working in groups, take turns describing your own preferred learning styles and special needs. Under what circumstances do you learn best? What would you tell your instructor about yourself that would help him or her be more effective in helping you learn? Keep a list of the group's suggestions and share them with the other groups.

Part I Reflections

Review the ideas you expressed at the beginning of this part in "Write Before You Read." How have your ideas changed as a result of reading the articles in this part? Explain in the space below.

1. What motivates you to learn _____

_____

_____

_____

_____

_____

2. Your greatest fears about college _____

_____

_____

_____

_____

_____

3. What you hope to get from your college experience _____

_____

_____

_____

_____

_____

Part I Writing Assignment

People pursue formal education beyond high school for many different reasons—hunger for learning, personal ambition, financial gain, to earn good grades, to please others. At the same time, we have all encountered individuals who have no apparent motivation to acquire new knowledge or to advance themselves intellectually.

Interview at least five fellow students about the nature of their motivation to attend college. What drives them to achieve and succeed in their studies? What prevents them from realizing their full academic potential? The responses will reflect the different personal circumstances of each student.

Summarize and characterize the response you receive. Classify them according to the probable outcome of each student's motivation or lack of it. Draw a general conclusion about the motivation to attend college as it has been expressed by your peers.

Part II

Learning to Learn

INTRODUCTION

Success in college requires a battery of skills—time management and prioritizing tasks, rapid and critical reading of a text, listening carefully and taking notes from a lecture, active participation in class discussion, studying for and taking tests, using the library, writing essay exams, and conducting research. These skills are only superficially taught, if at all, at most high schools and colleges.

Over the past twenty-five years, the number of first-year college students who had ever checked out a book from a library declined 40 percent. The number who had done any nonrequired reading declined 24 percent. The number who had argued with a teacher declined 20 percent. The number who expected that they would need special tutoring in college doubled, and 77 percent admitted that they had cheated on tests.

To be successful in college, you will need to acquire basic skills in the mechanics of learning: you will need to learn how to learn. The basic skills of learning—reading, writing, oral communication, critical thinking and problem solving, analysis and synthesis, and the conduct of original research—must be mastered before you begin work in more specialized areas of study. These skills are emphasized in the courses required of all college students. Grouped together, they are called general, basic, or liberal studies, or simply "the core." Because these required courses are intended to free students from the chains of ignorance and prejudice, they are often referred to as the liberal arts, from the Latin word *liber,* meaning "free."

These foundation courses are the subject of the first essay in this part by A. Bartlett Giamatti, the late commissioner of Major League Baseball and former president of Yale University, who answers the question so often asked by college students eager to get on with their major courses and a career: What is the earthly use of a liberal education?

The next essay by David Daniels examines not *what* is taught in college but *how* it is taught. Daniels is frankly critical of the lecture approach that still predominates in many college classrooms. "Most students learn best," he says, "by engaging in frequent and even heated debate." He explains why both college instructors and administrators often prefer the lecture method and acknowledges that they have a place in upper-division courses, while making a strong case for more active learning at the lower level. "After all," he concludes, "students must learn to listen before they can listen to learn."

The authors of the next essay, "Writing Under Pressure," remind us that most of the writing tasks that will be expected of us after college must be done under deadline pressure. College instructors prefer essay exams because they are both a tool for learning and evidence of learning. Since there is no "correct answer" to an essay question, the challenge for the students is to construct a response that demonstrates expertise in the subject and to present it in a coherent, organized, and interesting manner. This useful article breaks the process down into six basic steps.

Many first-year students are overcome by the fear of not measuring up academically, a fear that is intensified by the grading system. Students are pressured to achieve high grades by parents, a shrinking job market, and their own expectations of themselves. In this pressure-cooker atmosphere of graded papers, quizzes, and exams, real learning is often sacrificed in favor of joyless hack work and rote memorization.

Grade pressure can drive students to desperate acts, such as cheating and plagiarism. Since intellectual integrity is a prized virtue in the academy, penalties for cheating may be severe. In "When Students Resort to Cheating," William and Pamela Kibler examine the many possible reasons and motivations for academic dishonesty and suggest some ways that colleges can help such students beyond simply catching and punishing offenders.

The complex job of being a college student requires careful time management. The final essay in this part, "Managing Your Time" by Edwin Bliss, offers practical tips on one of the most important skills a college student can possess: managing and prioritizing tasks. He offers ten proven techniques for using time effectively. The effective time manager, he reminds us, doesn't waste time regretting the past or worrying about the future. "Today," he quotes an anonymous philosopher as saying, "is ready cash. Use it!"

Write Before You Read

A. After you've read the introduction, take a few minutes to survey the contents of this part. Then write three questions you expect will be answered in the course of your reading.

1. _____

   _____

2. _____

   _____

3. _____

_____

B. Briefly reflect on each of the following topics. Then write freely and rapidly about what you already know about the topic, relevant experiences you have had, and any opinions you have formed about it.

1. Tests and the grading system _____

_____

_____

_____

_____

_____

2. Cheating and plagiarism _____

_____

_____

_____

_____

_____

3. How you manage your time _____

_____

_____

_____

_____

_____

The Earthly Use of a Liberal Education
A. Bartlett Giamatti

PREVIEW

As the child of Italian immigrants, A. Bartlett Giamatti dreamed of two conflicting careers—literature and professional baseball. He ended by achieving both, becoming a professor of comparative literature and eventually president of Yale University and, a few years before his death from cancer in 1989, being named commissioner of Major League Baseball.

As president of Yale, it was Giamatti's annual custom to address the incoming freshman class. In the speech reprinted here, given in September 1983, he compares the intrinsic values of a liberal arts curriculum (general studies or core courses) with the more practical values of vocational courses. (The "Yale College" referred to throughout the text is the undergraduate liberal arts component of Yale University.)

The summer before college is the time when in a thousand different circumstances mythology dresses up as epistemology. Parents, older siblings and friends, former teachers, coaches, and employers, dimly but vividly remembering how it was, propound with certainty how they know the way it might, or should, or could, or will be.

By and large, the versions of your life to come are well meant. All summer long, however, you have simply wanted to get on with it. There, of course, is the rub. Despite all you have heard and read, no one can tell you what it is you are now so desirous of getting on with. Nor can anyone tell you what it, whatever it is, will be like. You wonder, Will everyone else know? Will he or she be more sure, less insecure, less new? Will I ever get to know anyone? Will I be able to do it? Whatever *it* is.

I will tell you, in a moment, what I think *it* is. I cannot tell you with certainty what it will be like; no one can. Each of us experiences college differently. I can assure you that soon your normal anxieties will recede

SOURCE: From *A Free and Ordered Space: The Real World of the University* by A. Bartlett Giamatti. Copyright © 1988, 1987, 1986, 1985, 1984, 1983, 1982, 1981, 1980, 1979, 1976 by A. Bartlett Giamatti. Reprinted by permission of W. W. Norton & Company, Inc.

and a genuine excitement will begin, a rousing motion of the spirit unlike anything you have experienced before. And that will mark the beginning of it, the grand adventure that you now undertake, never alone but on your own, the voyage of exploration in the freedom that is the development of your own mind. Generations have preceded you in this splendid opening out of the self as you use the mind to explore the mind, and, if the human race is rational, generations will come after you. But each of you will experience your education uniquely—charting and ordering and dwelling in the land of your own intellect and sensibility, discovering powers you had only dreamed of and mysteries you had not imagined and reaches you had not thought that thought could reach. There will be pain and some considerable loneliness at times, and not all the terrain will be green and refreshing. There will be awesome wastes and depths as well as heights. The adventure of discovery is, however, thrilling because you will sharpen and focus your powers of analysis, of creativity, of rationality, of feeling—of thinking with your whole being. If at Yale you can experience the joy that the acquisition and creation of knowledge for its own sake brings, the adventure will last your whole life and you will have discovered the distinction between living as a full human being and merely existing.

If there is a single term to describe the education that can spark a life-long love of learning, it is the term *liberal education.* A liberal education has nothing to do with those political designer labels *liberal* and *conservative* that some so lovingly stitch on to every idea they pull off, or put on, the rack. A liberal education is not one that seeks to implant the precepts of a specific religious or political orthodoxy. Nor is it an education intending to prepare for immediate immersion in a profession. That kind of professional education is pursued at Yale at the graduate level in eleven graduate and professional schools. Such training ought to have in it a liberal temper; that is, technical or professional study ought to be animated by a love of learning, but such training is necessarily and properly pointed to the demands and proficiency requirements of a career or profession. Such is not the tendency of an education, or of the educational process, in Yale College.

In Yale College, education is "liberal" in Cardinal Newman's sense of the word. As he says in the fifth discourse of *The Idea of the University,*

> . . . that alone is liberal knowledge which stands on its own pretensions, which is independent of sequel, expects no complement, refuses to be *informed* (as it is called) by any end, or absorbed in any art, in order duly to present itself to our contemplation. The most ordinary pursuits have this specific character, if they are self-sufficient

and complete; the highest lose it, when they minister to something beyond them.

As Newman emphasizes, a liberal education is not defined by the content or by the subject matter of a course of study. It is a common error, for instance, to equate a liberal education with the so-called liberal arts or *studia humanitatis.* To study the liberal arts or the humanities is not necessarily to acquire a liberal education unless one studies these and allied subjects in a spirit that, as Newman has it, seeks no immediate sequel, that is independent of a profession's advantage. If you pursue the study of anything not for the intrinsic rewards of exercising and developing the power of the mind but because you press toward a professional goal, then you are pursuing not a liberal education but rather something else.

A liberal education is defined by the attitude of the mind toward the knowledge the mind explores and creates. Such education occurs when you pursue knowledge because you are motivated to experience and absorb what comes of thinking—thinking in order to create new knowledge that others will then explore. A liberal education at Yale College embraces physics as well as French, lasers as well as literature, social science and physical and biological sciences as well as the arts and humanities. A liberal education rests on the supposition that our humanity is enriched by the pursuit of learning for its own sake; it is dedicated to the proposition that growth in thought, in the power to think, increases the pleasure, breadth, and value of life.

"That is very touching," I will be told, "that is all very well, but how does someone make a living with this joy of learning and pleasure in the pursuit of learning? What is the earthly use of all this kind of education later on, in the practical, real world?" These are not trivial questions, though the presuppositions behind them puzzle me somewhat. I am puzzled, for instance, by the unexamined assumption that the "real world" is always thought to lie outside or beyond the realm of education. I am puzzled by the confident assumption that only in certain parts of daily life do people make "real" decisions and do "real" acts lead to "real" consequences. I am puzzled by those who think that ideas do not have reality or that knowledge is irrelevant to the workings of daily life.

To invert Plato and to believe that ideas are unreal and that their pursuit has no power for practical or useful good is to shrink reality and define ignorance. To speak directly to the questions posed by the skeptic of the idea of a liberal education, I can say only this: ideas and their pursuit define our humanity and make us human. Ideas, embodied in data and values, beliefs, principles, and original insights, must be pursued because they are the stuff of life. There is nothing more necessary to the full, free, and decent life of a person or of a people or of the human race than to free the mind by passionately and rationally exercising the mind's power to inquire freely. There can be no more practical education, in my opinion, than one that launches you on the course of fulfilling your human capacities to reason and to imagine freely and that hones your abilities to express the results of your thinking in speech and in writing with logic, clarity, and grace.

While such an education may be deemed impractical by those wedded to the notion that nothing in life is more important than one's career, nevertheless I welcome you to a liberal education's rigorous and demanding pleasures. Fear not, you will not be impeded from making a living because you have learned to think for yourself and because you take pleasure in the operation of the mind and in the pursuit of new ideas. And you will need to make a living. The world will not provide you with sustenance or employment. You will have to work for it. I am instead speaking of another dimension of your lives, the dimension of your spirit that will last longer than a job, that will outlast a profession, that will represent by the end of your time on earth the sum of your human significance. That is the dimension represented by the mind unfettered, "freely ranging onley within the Zodiack of his owne wit," as the old poet said. There is no greater power a human being can develop for the individual's or for the public's good.

And I believe that the good, for individuals and for communities, is the end to which education must tend. I affirm Newman's vision that a liberal education is one seeking no sequel or complement. I take him to be writing of the motive or tendency of the mind operating initially within the educational process. But I believe there is also a larger tendency or motive, which is animated by the pursuit of ideas for their own sake. I believe that the pleasure in the pursuit of knowledge joins and is finally at one with our general human desire for a life elevated by dignity, decency, and moral process. That larger hope does not come later; it exists inextricably intertwined with a liberal education. The joy of intellectual pursuit and the pursuit of the good and decent life are no more separable than on a fair spring day the sweet breeze is separable from the sunlight.

In the common pursuit of ideas from themselves and of the larger or common good, the freedom that the individual mind wishes for itself, it also seeks for others. How could it be otherwise? In the pursuit of knowledge leading to the good, you cannot wish for others less than you wish for yourself. Thus, in the pursuit of freedom, the individual finds it necessary to order or to limit the surge to freedom so that others in the community are not denied the very condition each of us seeks. A liberal education desires to foster a freedom of the mind that will also contribute, in its measure, to the freedom of others.

We learn, therefore, that there is no true freedom without order; we learn that there are limits to our freedom, limits we learn to choose freely in order not to undermine what we seek. After all, if there were, on the one hand, no restraints at all, only anarchy of intellect and chaos of community would result. On the other hand, if all were restraint, and release of inquiry and thought were stifled, only a death of the spirit and a denial of any freedom could result. There must be an interplay of restraint and release, of order and freedom, in our individual lives and in our life together. Without such interplay within each of us, there can be no good life for any of us. If there is no striving for the good life for all of us, however, there cannot be a good life for any one of us. We must learn how freedom depends for its existence upon freely chosen (because rationally understood) forms of order.

At Yale College, you will find both the spur for freedom or inquiry and civility's curbing rein. One could, I suppose, locate these conditions in the classroom and in the residential colleges; one could posit that in the classroom the release of the mind is encouraged and in the residential colleges the limits to civil behavior are learned. That view is oversimplified, for in both contexts, as well as on playing fields, in community service, in extracurricular activities, in services of worship, in social events, the interplay of freedom and order obtains. In all these contexts, as in each one of us, the surge of freedom and the restraint that compounds freedom's joy and significance occur all the time.

The ideal of this community is therefore composed of intellectual and ethical portions, the freedom of the mind and the freedom to express the results of the mind's inquiry disciplined by the imperative to respect the rights and responsibilities of others. It is a community open to new ideas, to disagreement, to debate, to criticism, to the clash of opinions and convictions, to solitary investigation, to originality, but it is not tolerant of, and will not tolerate, the denial of the dignity and freedoms of others. It will not tolerate theft of another's intellectual product. It will not tolerate denials of another's freedom of expression. It will not tolerate sexist or racist or other acts or expressions of bigotry based on prejudices about ethnic or religious backgrounds or about personal sexual preference or private philosophic or political beliefs. It will not tolerate these denials, because the freedom we possess to foster free inquiry and the greater good is too precious. What I have stated are matters of moral conviction. They are also matters of University policy. The policies that reflect those convictions are designed to protect an environment where individual rights are respected because responsibilities are shared. They are designed to create a community where freedom exists because order is sustained by the moral courage to affirm the good by all members of the community.

I have told you what I think it is, the "it" I guessed you might be concerned with upon your arrival. It is a quest to become the best in all that is meant by being human. This quest has been going on in this college for a long time, in this old New England city by the water. In 1701 Yale made a promise to itself and a pact with America, to contribute to the increase of scholarship, service, and spiritual enlightenment. You now assume part of the obligation of that promise. And you will be essential to maintaining the faith of that pact. As you become deepened in the commitment to ideals and in the excellence I know you possess, this community will continue to shape itself in intellectual and ethical ways that are faithful to our ancient roots and in ways that are ever new.

DIALOGUE

1. How does A. Bartlett Giamatti define a liberal education, and what arguments does he use to justify its value?
2. The author maintains that "our humanity is enriched by the pursuit of learning for its own sake." How does he support this claim? Do you agree or disagree with it? Explain.
3. What are the characteristics of an academic community, and what can students do to help create such a community?

WRITING TOPICS

1. Define what Giamatti means by the term *civility*.
2. Giamatti is speaking to students who are about to embark on the great adventure of a college education. Describe some of your feelings, anxieties, expectations, fears, and excitement as you begin what he calls the "voyage of exploration in freedom."
3. Support or refute the following statement:

   The central mission of a college or university is to provide students with specific skills that prepare them for employment and professional careers.

INTERACTION

Working in groups, read and discuss the mission statement and rationale for general studies requirements in your college catalog. What values do these statements express? Do you agree with them? Why or why not? Do you feel that a person who enrolls in your college has an obligation to endorse and uphold these values? Compare your reactions with those of the other groups.

College Lectures: Is Anybody Listening?
David Daniels

PREVIEW

American higher education was modeled after the European system, in which a professor, garbed in academic regalia, entered from a private door near the podium, delivered a lecture, and exited by the same door. At most American colleges, the lecture system is still in force, despite a growing body of research showing that passive learning (listening, taking notes, and repeating the lecture on a test) is the least effective kind.

In the following essay, David Daniels explains why the lecture system is popular with college instructors and administrators and why, in certain classes, lectures may be necessary. But he makes a plea for active learning, which requires "energy, imagination, and commitment" from both instructors and students.

A former teacher of mine, Robert A. Fowkes of New York University, likes to tell the story of a class he took in Old Welsh while studying in Germany during the 1930s. On the first day the professor strode up to the podium, shuffled his notes, coughed, and began, *"Guten Tag, Meine Damen und Herren"* ("Good day, ladies and gentlemen"). Fowkes glanced around uneasily. He was the only student in the course.

Toward the middle of the semester, Fowkes fell ill and missed a class. When he returned, the professor nodded vaguely and to Fowkes's aston-

---

SOURCE: David Daniels, "College Lectures: Is Anybody Listening?" is reprinted by permission of the author.

ishment, began to deliver not the next lecture in the sequence but the one after. Had he, in fact, lectured to an empty hall in the absence of his solitary student? Fowkes thought it perfectly possible.

Today, American colleges and universities (originally modeled on German ones) are under strong attack from many quarters. Teachers, it is charged, are not doing a good job of teaching, and students are not doing a good job of learning. American businesses and industries suffer from unenterprising, uncreative executives educated not to think for themselves but to mouth outdated truisms the rest of the world has long discarded. College graduates lack both basic skills and general culture. Studies are conducted and reports are issued on the status of higher education, but any changes that result either are largely cosmetic or make a bad situation worse.

One aspect of American education too seldom challenged is the lecture system. Professors continue to lecture and students to take notes much as they did in the thirteenth century, when books were so scarce and expensive that few students could own them. The time is long overdue for us to abandon the lecture system and turn to methods that really work.

To understand the inadequacy of the present system, it is enough to follow a single imaginary first-year student—let's call her Mary—through a term of lectures on, say, introductory psychology (although any other subject would do as well). She arrives on the first day and looks around the huge lecture hall, taken a little aback to see how large the class is. Once the hundred or more students enrolled in the course discover that the professor never takes attendance (how can he?—calling the role would take far too much time), the class shrinks to a less imposing size.

Some days Mary sits in the front row, from where she can watch the professor read from a stack of yellowed notes that seem nearly as old as he is. She is bored by the lectures, and so are most of the other students, to judge by the way they are nodding off or doodling in their notebooks. Gradually she realizes the professor is as bored as his audience. At the end of each lecture he asks, "Are there any questions?" in a tone of voice that makes it plain he would much rather there weren't. He needn't worry—the students are as relieved as he is that the class is over.

Mary knows very well she should read an assignment before every lecture. However, as the professor gives no quizzes and asks no questions, she soon realizes she needn't prepare. At the end of the term she catches up by skimming her notes and memorizing a list of facts and dates. After the final exam, she promptly forgets much of what she has memorized. Some of her fellow students, disappointed at the impersonality of it all, drop out of college altogether. Others, like Mary, stick it out, grow resigned to the system and await better days when, as juniors and seniors, they will attend smaller classes and at last get the kind of personal attention real learning requires.

I admit this picture is overdrawn—most universities supplement lecture courses with discussion groups, usually led by graduate students, and some classes, such as first-year English, are always relatively small. Nevertheless, far too many courses rely principally or entirely on lectures, an arrangement much loved by faculty and administrators but scarcely designed to benefit the students.

One problem with lectures is that listening intelligently is hard work. Reading the same material in a textbook is a more efficient way to learn because students can proceed as slowly as they need to until the subject matter becomes clear to them. Even simply paying attention is very difficult; people can listen at a rate of four hundred to six hundred words a minute, while the most impassioned professor talks at scarcely a third of that speed. This time lag between speech and comprehension leads to daydreaming. Many students believe years of watching television have sabotaged their attention span, but their real problem is that listening attentively is much harder than they think.

Worse still, attending lectures is passive learning, at least for inexperienced listeners. Active learning, in which students write essays or perform experiments and then have their work evaluated by an instructor, is far more beneficial for those who have not yet fully learned how to learn. While it's true that techniques of active listening, such as trying to anticipate the speaker's next point or taking notes selectively, can enhance the value of a lecture, few students possess such skills at the beginning of their college careers. More commonly, students try to write everything down and even bring tape recorders to class in a clumsy effort to capture every word.

Students need to question their professors and to have their ideas taken seriously. Only then will they develop the analytical skills required to think intelligently and creatively. Most students learn best by engaging in frequent and even heated debate, not by scribbling down a professor's often unsatisfactory summary of complicated issues. They need small discussion classes that demand the common labors of teacher and students rather than classes in which one person, however learned, propounds his or her own ideas.

The lecture system ultimately harms professors as well. It reduces feedback to a minimum, so that the lecturer can neither judge how well students understand the material nor benefit from their questions or comments. Questions that require the speaker to clarify obscure points and comments that challenge sloppily constructed arguments are indispensable to scholarship. Without them, the liveliest mind can atrophy. Undergraduates may not be able to make telling contributions very often, but lecturing insulates a professor even from the beginner's naive question that could have triggered a fruitful line of thought.

If lectures make so little sense, why have they been allowed to continue? Administrators love them, of course. They can cram far more students into a lecture hall than into a discussion class, and for many administrators that is almost the end of the story. But the truth is that faculty members, and even students, conspire with them to keep the lecture system alive and well. Lectures are easier on everyone than debates. Professors can pretend to teach by lecturing just as students can pretend to learn by attending lectures, with no one the wiser, including the participants. Moreover, if lectures afford some students an opportunity to sit back and let the professor run the show, they offer some professors an irresistible forum for showing off. In a classroom where everyone contributes, students are less able to hide and professors less tempted to engage in intellectual exhibitionism.

Smaller classes in which students are required to involve themselves in discussion put an end to students' passivity. Students become actively involved when forced to question their own ideas as well as their instructor's. Their listening skills improve dramatically in the excitement of intellectual give and take with their instructors and fellow students. Such interchanges help professors do their job better because they allow them to discover who knows what—before final exams, not after. When exams are given in this type of course, they can require analysis and synthesis from the students, not empty memorization. Classes like this require energy, imagination, and commitment from professors, all of which can be exhausting. But they compel students to share responsibility for their own intellectual growth.

Lecturers will never entirely disappear from the university scene both because they seem to be economically necessary and because they spring from a long tradition in a setting that rightly values tradition for its own sake. But the lectures too frequently come at the wrong end of the students' educational careers—during the first two years, when they most need close, even individual, instruction. If lecture classes were restricted to junior and senior undergraduates and to graduate students, who are less in need of scholarly nurturing and more able to prepare work on their own, they would be far less destructive of students' interests and enthusiasms than the present system. After all, students must learn to listen before they can listen to learn.

DIALOGUE

1. Why has the college lecture system persisted for so long? What roles do faculty and administrators play in preserving the lecture system in its present form? Do students play a role as well? How?

2. Do you agree with David Daniels that "listening intelligently is hard work"? Do you think listening attentively or concentrating over an extended period is especially difficult for the current generation of traditional-age college students? Explain.

3. Considering the high enrollments and limited resources of many colleges, are there any practical alternatives to the lecture format? If no alternative teaching system can be developed, what reforms of the lecture approach do you recommend?

WRITING TOPICS

1. Describe your classroom experience with lectures. How do you react as a student to the lecture format? Is it a positive, negative, or neutral involvement?

2. Define the terms *passive learning* and *active learning*. Which of the two ideas best characterizes your learning experience in school? With which style of learning are you most comfortable? Do you plan to pursue one style or another in college?

3. Daniels claims that "the time is long overdue for us to abandon the lecture system and turn to methods that really work." In an essay, develop arguments that support or refute this statement. If you agree with the statement, consider what "methods that really work" should be used as substitutes for lectures.

INTERACTION

Working in groups, critique Daniels's hypothetical portrayal of the student Mary in a lecture situation. Discuss which aspects of Mary's experience are fairly represented and which may be exaggerated or overgeneralized. How does Daniels's characterization conform to or contradict the lecture experiences of the group's members?

Writing Under Pressure

Stuart C. Brown, Robert Mittan, and Duane Roen

PREVIEW

Most first-year college students prefer objective exams to essay exams. With objective tests, an answer is either right or wrong, so it's possible to guess at the right answer. Essay exams are more subjective and there is no right answer: depending on your writing skills, knowledge of the subject, and the time available to you to write, your answer can be continually improved. Even if an answer is technically correct, it may be incomplete or contain writing flaws or gaps in logic.

College instructors tend to prefer essay to objective exams (especially in the humanities, social sciences, and business) not because they enjoy grading them, but because essay exams test higher-order thinking skills rather than rote memorization. A good essay exam (like a good essay) tests a student's ability to think critically and to organize information under pressure—resources you are more likely to need and use in your career than stored knowledge of facts and figures.

The following essay offers some practical tips on how to prepare for and take an essay exam.

Since we too are under pressure (our publisher wants this book done NOW!), this discussion will be brief and practical. That's not to say that this topic is unimportant to us. Nor is writing under pressure unimportant to you, either in school or on the job. In fact, both our own experiences and that of our students tell us that there is never enough time to write something as well as we could, or want to write it. Events happen too quickly. People need things done immediately.

Next time you take a plane trip, observe what goes on in the first-class section. Get beyond your envy of the bigger seats, the nicer meals, the free drinks. Most likely, the majority of those passengers are using the larger seats so that they can work more easily. Dictation equipment, laptop computers, fax machines, cellular phones are technologies developed to speed the communication process and to get the most out of employ-

SOURCE: From *The Writer's Toolbox* by Stuart C. Brown, Robert Mittan and Duane Roen. Copyright © 1997 by Allyn and Bacon. Reprinted by permission.

ees wherever they are. Nowadays, many documents are drafted on the airplane ride to the meeting where they're presented.

The writing and thinking processes that we present throughout this book, and that most of us would *prefer* to use, go out the window because some audience or some purpose is snatching at our documents as fast as we can get them off the printer. Federal Express and other next-day mail services, not to mention fax machine and modem manufacturers, make a lot of money as a result of the constant time pressures most of us face as professionals. But the kinds of tests you're subjected to as a student, especially those that involve writing under time pressure, will help you prepare for some of the professional demands made on your writing.

In schools, one popular forum for you to demonstrate your learning, thinking, and writing capabilities is the essay test. You're no doubt familiar with them. Most likely you'll become more and more familiar with them before you finish your degree. Increasingly, colleges and universities across the United States are implementing exit examinations that you must pass before graduating, examinations that involve an assessment of your writing. Other approaches include sophomore- or junior-level essay exams to diagnose your capabilities for the writing expected of you in your upper-level course work.

Writing-intensive or writing-emphasis courses are also increasingly common to our educational system. These courses often require essay or in-class writing situations, whether the traditional "here is a question and write your brains out until time is called" or more creative approaches involving case studies and elaborate scenarios in which you present solutions or analyses within a very tight time frame.

If you are planning to continue on to professional or graduate school, you face even more writing under pressure once you get there. And getting there usually involves a writing trial-by-fire. Almost all of the professional school exams such as the Law School Admissions Test (LSAT) and the Medical College Admissions Test (MCAT) now have essay components that weigh heavily.

Thus, writing under pressure—writing without the benefit of extensive time for adequate reflection and revision—is inevitably encountered by professionals and students alike. The following suggestions will help you produce better documents under limited time constraints. We focus on how to prepare for and take essay exams because they are a relatively universal experience—and frequently frustrate students. But professionals and experts in all disciplines apply these same strategies almost daily as they draft, revise, polish, and print out documents just in time to rush them to their readers.

Anticipation: Strategies for Preparing

Central to adequately preparing for an essay exam is recognizing that your response, your answer to the test situation, must be *constructed.* Many situations, a statistics test, for instance, require you to recognize a problem and its immediate answer: you apply a particular formula to the situation and then solve that formula to derive the expected answer. Usually, there is only one correct response. But in situations involving writing, the *nature* of your response, or how you present your answer, is as important as what the answer is. And in writing situations, there is usually a range of possible responses. Or there is no "correct" answer at all, but rather one that you present as feasible or probable. The central concern of a reader (the evaluator) in this case is to determine if you demonstrate proficiency, knowledge, expertise. Your job, then, is to construct, control, and present your expertise knowledgeably and proficiently.

Although the individual nature of the exam situations depend, like every other communication situation, on your audience and purpose, it's useful to conceive them, like a play, in terms of three acts:

1. Construct your response.
2. Organize your response.
3. Write your response.

Of course, the reader also expects all of the features of well-crafted prose—clarity, conciseness, freedom from error—features you do not have much time for in these situations. So, we add a short epilogue:

4. Revise and edit your response.

Preparation is the key to making the most of your time in an exam situation. You usually have forewarning. You may not know specifically what you will be expected to respond to but you should have a general idea of the topics to be covered. Many instructors announce in advance the number of questions, the time available to you, and even the specific topics that will be covered on the exam. In some cases, you can review exams given at other times to get a clearer sense of the exam. A sample test, when available, provides an idea of the structure of the exam and often identifies main issues or focuses on a topic.

Another way to prepare is to review your class notes and texts to determine the main points covered in the course. Using the strategies we discuss in Unit 2 for generating reading notes really pays off when tests come up. Once you've identified potential topics, focus on particular areas.

Creating your own essay-type questions is useful. Look at previous exams, from any course, and model your questions on those written by instructors. This forces you both to analyze the way questions are constructed—a key to constructing your own responses, which we discuss a little later—and to synthesize the material. One instructor we know often asks his students to each submit three possible questions from which he builds the final exam in his course. Having written exams ourselves, we can assure you it's one of the most challenging writing assignments that an instructor could give.

Keep in mind, however, that anticipating potential questions is not necessarily predicting the future. "Your question" may not actually appear on the exam, although there's always the chance, especially if you really have been paying attention. But writing possible questions helps you discover what you know well and also what you're weak on. You can then use your time filling in the gaps of your understanding with more study, further research, or questions to the instructor during class or office hours. Forming a study group to create and share possible questions is also effective.

Once you or your group has created a set of questions, respond to them. Set up the time constraints you expect and take your own exam, imitating the conditions you expect in the actual exam as nearly as possible. Then, exchange your responses, or put yourself in your instructor's position, and judge your efforts. This is an effective way of analyzing your audience, another important aspect of preparing. If your efforts fall short of what you think your audience expects, you still have time to do more reading, writing, and thinking. If, on the other hand, you have difficulty deciding what is expected, you need to investigate your audience further.

Most instructors are quite clear about what they are looking for in responses on their tests. If you are unsure, *ask*. Find out the instructor's goals or purposes for the test. Exams, especially essay exams, are not usually intended to discover how little you know, but rather to demonstrate how much you know and how well. Asking an instructor the specific goals for a test increases your chances of meeting them.

Also find out whether notes, the textbook, or other resources will be allowed. If so, much of your preparation time can be spent organizing these materials for easy use during the exam. For instance, you might annotate your notes and textbook and create an index, as we describe in Unit 2. If you sort, arrange, and paper clip or mark with Post-It notes your materials according to specific topics, you will save valuable time otherwise used shuffling through for just the right page of notes during the exam. On the job, this is called filing, and it's a highly valued skill that you need to develop. Finally, consider whether you need to take a dictionary. Used too much, it may slow you down unnecessarily. On the other hand, if you can wait to use it until you've finished writing and are revising and editing, it may be invaluable. A misspelled word crossed out once and corrected neatly indicates your preparation and attention to detail, not your ignorance.

Execution: Strategies for Writing

Here we'll start with the obvious: Be on time (or a little early) and bring with you exactly—and only—what you need.

Not quite so obvious, perhaps, is what to do once you have the exam in your hands. We offer the following strategy, which we have seen work successfully for dozens of students. You will need to modify it to your individual situation; but if you keep these steps in mind, you will be far ahead of those who don't. Here are the six steps:

1. Scan the exam
2. Budget your time
3. Reread, analyze, and choose
4. Plan your response
5. Write your response
6. Revise, edit, and proofread

Your first instinct on being handed an exam is probably to hunch over it, begin at the top, and work your way to the end—all the while disregarding the clock ticking off the minutes. A better strategy is to scan the whole thing quickly first to get an idea of what you're facing. And we mean *very* quickly. Look over the directions for key phrases such as "Choose one of the following" or "Answer each in a short essay." Note key topic words in the question(s) as well, words that trigger memories of discussions, notes you've written, or stacks of material you have ready to use. This brief overview lets you know where you need to concentrate your efforts. It also alerts you to possible black holes in your preparation or your memory that you either want to avoid, if possible, or devote extra time to filling in.

Once you have a sense of the number, the type, and the topics of the questions, pause to make a time budget. When we suggest this to students in our classes, they usually look aghast and say, "But I don't have enough time to worry about the time!" And we say, "You don't have enough time *not* to worry about it." The seconds it takes to establish a time budget result in a better piece of writing. Write down your time budget—inside the front cover of your exam book, perhaps—and indicate the actual clock times to be finished with each phase. For instance, given one question to respond to in a two-hour exam, your budget might look like this:

Planning 1/2 hour	10:30
Writing 1 hour	11:30
Revising 1/2 hour	12:00

If you must answer several questions, or if your exam is divided into several parts, consider how much each piece of writing is worth. Instructors often list the point value of each item so you can do this. Some even suggest the amount of time you should spend on each item. Use this information to budget your time. Then, stick to it faithfully. Like money, time gets spent faster without a budget.

Now you're ready to return to the exam for a much closer reading. Take each question apart by asking yourself

- What *task* does this question ask me to perform?
- What is the specific *topic* it focuses on?
- What *hints* does it give me about my response?

The following prompt, for example, can be quickly analyzed this way:

"Define the term xeriscape *in relation to southwestern urban planning."*

- What *task* does this question ask me to perform? define
- What is the specific *topic* it focuses on? *xeriscape*
- What *hints* does it give me about my response? relate to southwestern urban planning

Granted, not every exam question works that well. We know; we've written a few clunkers. But these three elements—task, topic, hints—are used by many question writers. Besides *define,* some other common task words to watch for include *explain, compare, describe*—essentially all of those words that describe language activities.

This is also the time to make choices, if you have the opportunity. If you spot a topic word that you are less prepared to write about, immediately eliminate that question and never look at it again. If you must face it, schedule it in the middle of your time budget, after you've handled an easier question or two but before you feel the crush of the clock.

Rereading, analyzing, and making choices should take no more than a few minutes. Planning your response, the next step, will take longer, depending, of course, on the number of responses you must write. Again, most students balk at the notion of spending valuable writing time planning. But once again, we assure you, it's time well spent.

To plan your response, use any of the usual writing strategies that help you get started writing. Outlining is effective, and fast, for many writers. But you may also find that quickly reviewing your notes or a specific passage in your textbook, if they are available to you, will suggest the approach you want to take. And we've seen some interesting pictures sketched inside the covers of exam books that helped writers "see" what they wanted to say.

One caution: Don't spend too much time fussing over introductions. We've seen some beautifully crafted beginnings, like half-built bridges, that went nowhere. In fact, we suggest that, when you begin writing, you leave the first page blank for an introduction yet to be written. After all, that *is* the way most texts are produced anyway: middle, end, beginning. And it's much more effective to dazzle your reader with the "meat" of your response. Finally, if you run out of time or can't come up with something more delightful, your introduction can be a rephrasing of the question or of your conclusion. Given the speed with which most exams must be read, bland introductions are quickly forgotten.

Here are a few more suggestions to keep in mind while writing your response:

- Write in the clearest, most direct language possible.
- Choose simplicity and repetition over elegance and diversity.
- Use technical language if it is efficient and appropriate to your audience.
- Let purpose and audience guide you.
- Repair weak sentences during revision and editing, not during writing.
- End conclusively, not abruptly.

Effective writing, whether composed over ten years or in ten minutes, requires revision, editing, and proofreading. Taking the time to read through your writing to spot and fix those weak sentences and fill in punctuation marks thought but not written will definitely add to the quality of your writing. Readers notice these touches, sometimes unconsciously, as their eyes glide over the page.

But sometimes there just isn't enough time to do as much of this as you'd like. There are some shortcuts. As you write, mark in the margin a sentence or word that needs fixing, or leave a blank space if you can't think of the word you want. Then, if you don't have much revising time, you can scan through and at least fix these few items you know about. In some instances, you may discover when revising a whole paragraph that you need to reorganize: you have all the pieces, but they're jumbled. Don't waste your time recopying; simply number the elements in the correct order and add a note to your reader: "Read as numbered." This works equally well for parts within a sentence and even large chunks of your text. And it's usually much easier to follow than arrows.

Finally—and it's embarrassing to have to bring this up—write legibly. Most readers' response to illegible writing is to assume it's concealing ignorance, not wisdom. Regardless of what you've heard about doctors, illegible writing is not professional.

Desperation: Strategies of Last Resort

Sometimes—rarely, we hope—you need strategies of last resort. You haven't the faintest idea how to respond to a question, or you're sure you've never even heard of the topic before. Write something, anything. Writing, as we point out throughout this book, is the best way to think. You may find out that you did pick up a little bit, perhaps accidentally, from sitting in class. Or, you may find another angle on the topic, one that you can write from.

If nothing else, you can use the time to write out your excuse, and your apology, and your personal guarantee that such a mishap will never occur again. Even if you don't show it to your instructor, spending the exam time writing it will certainly improve your oral delivery of it. And improve your character. Our best advice for such instances is, quite obviously, don't get yourself into them. Using the strategies we've outlined here and those discussed throughout this book, you should be fully prepared to meet any writing situation, no matter how short the time. If you are to become an expert,

[*Publisher's note: Due to time constraints, this sentence was not finished.*]

DIALOGUE

1. The authors provide several suggestions for writing an essay exam. Which did you find most helpful, and why?
2. In what ways does time management figure into the writing of an essay exam?
3. Share with your group a personal horror story about taking an exam. How did you feel at the time? How do you feel about it today? What things do you do differently today as a result of the experience?

WRITING TOPICS

1. Describe your previous experience with essay exams. Has it been positive or negative? Why?
2. Discuss your reactions to situations that call for writing under pressure. Are you able to demonstrate your best writing and thinking skills in such situations? If not, why not?
3. How is the essay exam different from an essay? In what ways does the writing of essay exams prepare you to write effective essays?

INTERACTION

Divide into two teams and debate the following issue:

Resolved: *Essay exams do not allow sufficient time for reflection or revision and therefore should be abolished as a testing format.*

Each team selects a captain, then each team member is given one minute to make a statement. The teams alternate turns until each student has had a chance to speak. The debate concludes with each team captain summarizing the views expressed by his or her team (maximum five minutes).

When Students Resort to Cheating
William L. Kibler and Pamela Vannoy Kibler

PREVIEW

One reason for the high incidence of cheating in college (according to one recent study, two out of three college students cheat) is the intense pressure generated by competition for admission, grades, and jobs. Most college students understand why cheating is wrong and the possible consequences of their behavior, but their motivation to cheat overrides their values and their fear of punishment.

According to William L. Kibler, associate director of student affairs at Texas A&M University, and Pamela Vannoy Kibler, a counselor at Blinn College, students who cheat need to understand why they do it

SOURCE: William L. Kibler and Pamela Vannoy Kibler, "When Students Resort to Cheating," *The Chronicle of Higher Education* (July 14, 1993), B1–2. Reprinted by permission of the authors.

and how it hurts them. They also need to be equipped with strategies and skills that increase their chances for academic success while building their self-esteem. Citing research on the relationship between cheating and self-esteem, they propose a comprehensive program that combines evaluation and counseling, disciplinary action, and education for students who cheat.

College students face an intense and competitive environment on many campuses as the pressures for academic excellence grow. Higher education has created a "survival of the fittest" subculture where the need to get good grades often is the focal point of students' educational experience. The need for students to develop survival strategies expands as the competition for admission to the "right" college or graduate school and for landing the "right" job increases.

There are, of course, many positive strategies that students can use to be successful academically. They include development of study skills such as good methods for note taking, memorization, and reading; time-management techniques; and the utilization of academic-advising and career-planning offices. But despite these avenues, research indicates that academic dishonesty is becoming the survival technique of choice for a growing number of students. Donald McCabe of Rutgers University, for example, conducted a study in 1991 in which 67 percent of the students responding—who attended 31 highly selective colleges and universities—admitted to cheating in college.

The challenge for colleges and universities is to understand why students choose cheating rather than more appropriate strategies for academic survival. Understanding students' motivation to cheat is necessary if we are to intervene effectively and change their behavior. Many studies of cheating have concentrated on "situational" factors that may influence students to cheat, including tests or assignments that make cheating easy, excessive difficulty of course work, and students' perception that "everyone" is cheating.

Several other researchers have examined issues of ethics and moral development to try to discover what motivates students to cheat. This approach assumes that the tendency to cheat is directly related to a lack of moral development or a lack of understanding of the ethics of cheating. But based on recent research that we have conducted, we contend that most college students understand that cheating is wrong and unacceptable, and most understand the potentially negative consequences of this behavior. But they choose to cheat anyway. Their motivation to cheat is greater than their moral and ethical principles and more powerful than their fear of the consequences.

Many of the studies of cheating have recommended what institutions and instructors should do to address and redirect dishonest behavior. Such recommendations include improving teaching techniques, designing assignments and tests that make it harder to cheat, and addressing the moral and ethical development of students through educational seminars and classes. Although there is value in such approaches, none has proved to be a significant deterrent for academic dishonesty.

If we are to truly have an impact on dishonest behavior, we must pay attention to the internal factors that move a student to cheat. Studies done over the last 25 years reinforce the idea that dishonest behavior is consistent with low self-esteem. Students with low self-esteem have a greater tendency to cheat for three basic reasons—they lack self-confidence, their behavior is dictated more by circumstances or people around them than it is by a feeling that they can control what happens to them, and they fear failure.

For various reasons, students who cheat do not believe in their own worth. David Ward of Washington State University, in a study reported in *The Journal of Social Psychology* in 1986, discussed the relationship between self-esteem and dishonest behavior. He found that subjects low in self-esteem seemed to be more prone to dishonest behavior, because dishonesty was consistent with their negative feelings about themselves. Thus, if an individual is tempted to cheat, it is easier to yield to this temptation if self-esteem is low rather than high. Cheating seems to be inconsistent with generally high self-esteem.

Students who cheat perceive themselves as being incapable of effectively meeting challenges and of solving problems on their own. They believe that they are failures who cannot independently succeed. Lacking feelings of self-worth and inner strength, they have become dependent on their external world to survive.

In the classroom, these students look outside themselves for ways to meet their academic challenges. Cheating, whether it is copying from a fellow student, using crib sheets, or more sophisticated means of dishonesty such as theft of exams or the use of "term-paper mills," becomes a way for students with low self-esteem to achieve their academic goals and avoid failure. Students who lack self-esteem fear failure because it reinforces their feelings of incompetence and inadequacy. Although cheating involves risk, the feeling of inadequacy and the fear of failure are greater than the fear of being punished.

However, achieving good grades through dishonesty may exacerbate students' lack of self-esteem. Knowing that their choice to cheat is wrong morally and ethically can produce feelings of guilt and shame that compound the students' negative feelings about themselves and increase their fear of failure. This heightened fear of failure, in turn, contributes to their continuing dependency on external means such as cheating to survive. Thus, the environment for an addictive cycle of cheating may be established.

Interventions designed to address dishonest behavior from a purely disciplinary perspective, such as giving students a failing grade or suspending them from college, are often ineffective because they focus only on the undesirable behavior. Educational interventions such as ethics seminars and training in academic skills may also be ineffective if they do not include information about the relationship between self-esteem and cheating.

To promote academic integrity, institutions must take a comprehensive approach to preventing and detecting academic dishonesty. They should design programs that address the emotional, as well as the disciplinary and educational, needs of student cheaters. We propose the following intervention strategy:

- *Evaluation and counseling.*   Beginning with an initial assessment, students should be helped to identify the internal and external factors motivating them to cheat. Information derived from social and family histories, stress evaluations, and self-esteem inventories can assist the counselor and student in determining appropriate psychological interventions. Such interventions can range from a limited number of individual counseling sessions to group counseling or referral for specialized treatment, depending upon the psychological and emotional needs that are identified.
- *Discipline.*   Actions such as being assigned failing grades, academic probation, and required participation in counseling and other activities are necessary, because they contribute to the development of the student's understanding of community standards. Although punitive sanctions alone may contribute to lower self-esteem, when such sanctions are combined with appropriate counseling and educational interventions, the damaging results can be mitigated. Appropriate disciplinary actions can help clarify the importance that the institution places on integrity.
- *Education.*   Seminars that enhance students' academic skills and help them respond better to future ethical dilemmas must be offered. In the

academic-skills portion, students should learn about test anxiety and develop time-management and study and writing skills. This will equip them with strategies that should increase their chances for academic success without cheating and help build self-esteem. Then discussions, case studies, and role playing can be used to help students recognize and respond more appropriately to future ethical dilemmas.

Such a comprehensive approach—combining counseling, discipline, and education—can help students understand why they are tempted to cheat, build self-esteem, and equip them to succeed without cheating.

DIALOGUE

1. Some studies refer to academic cheating in colleges as an epidemic. What is your perception of the incidence of cheating in high school and college? Is it prevalent or less common than researchers claim?
2. Students are often uncertain about what constitutes academic dishonesty, especially what qualifies as plagiarism. On what issues of academic dishonesty (definitions, policies, sanctions) do you think there is confusion or ambiguity?
3. Should colleges be in the business of building students' self-esteem? Has the self-esteem-building approach of some elementary and secondary schools (gold stars, happy faces, word-processed certificates) created in students an illusory sense of self-worth? Explain your answer.

WRITING TOPICS

1. Review your college's policy on academic integrity (or cheating). Is there anything about the policy that surprised or distressed you? Comment on whether the policy needs to be rethought or rewritten. What specific changes do you recommend?
2. Describe your thoughts about cheating and plagiarism. Have you confronted the temptation to be dishonest in your schoolwork? How have you handled the situation? What do you think about students who cheat?
3. About fifty colleges have an honor system, which requires students to sign a pledge not to cheat and to report those they observe cheating. Write an essay in which you advocate or oppose the establishment of an honor system at your college.

INTERACTION

In groups, analyze the following list of factors that are often cited as causes of student cheating. Add others to the list if you wish. Discuss each factor, then rank the factors from least likely to most likely to influence a student to cheat.

- Competition for grades/graduate school placement
- Large, impersonal classes
- Indifferent professors
- Tests/assignments that make cheating easy
- Excessive difficulty of work
- "Everyone" is cheating
- Arrested moral/ethical development
- Lack of self-esteem
- Ignorance of the rules/policies
- Policies against cheating not enforced

Managing Your Time
Edwin Bliss

PREVIEW

One of the joys—and greatest perils—of college life is the relative freedom students enjoy in the management of their lives. For those accustomed to being told what to do and when to do it, the management of discretionary time can be a major challenge. In this essay, Edwin Bliss, an internationally known time management consultant, offers some practical advice on how to use time effectively.

I first became interested in the effective use of time when I was an assistant to a U.S. Senator. Members of Congress are faced with urgent and conflicting demands on their time—for committee work, floor votes, speeches, interviews, briefings, correspondence, investigations, constituents' problems, and the need to be informed on a wide range of sub-

SOURCE: Edwin Bliss, "Managing Your Time." Reprinted with the permission of Scribner, a Division of Simon & Schuster, from *Getting Things Done: The ABC's of Time Management*, Revised, and Updated Edition by Edwin C. Bliss. Revised and Updated Edition Copyright © 1991 by Edwin C. Bliss. Copyright © 1976 by Edwin C. Bliss.

jects. The more successful Congressmen develop techniques for getting maximum benefit from minimum investments of time. If they don't, they don't return.

Realizing that I was not one of those who used time effectively, I began to apply in my own life some of the techniques I had observed. Here are ten I have found most helpful.

1. Plan.   You need a game plan for your day. Otherwise, you'll allocate your time according to whatever happens to land on your desk. And you will find yourself making the final mistake of dealing primarily with problems rather than opportunities. Start each day by making a general schedule, with particular emphasis on the two or three major things you would like to accomplish—including things that will achieve long-term goals. Remember, studies prove what common sense tells us: the more time we spend planning a project, the less total time is required for it. Don't let today's busywork crowd planning-time out of your schedule.

2. Concentrate.   Of all the principles of time management, none is more basic than concentration. People who have serious time-management problems invariably are trying to do too many things at once. The amount of time spent on a project is not what counts: it's the amount of *uninterrupted* time. Few problems can resist an all-out attack; few can be solved piecemeal.

3. Take Breaks.   To work for long periods without taking a break is not an effective use of time. Energy decreases, boredom sets in, and physical stress and tension accumulate. Switching for a few minutes from a mental task to something physical—isometric exercises, walking around the office, even changing from a sitting position to a standing position for a while—can provide relief.

Merely resting, however, is often the best course, and you should not think of a "rest" break as poor use of time. Not only will being refreshed increase your efficiency, but relieving tension will benefit your health. Anything that contributes to health is good time management.

4. Avoid Clutter.   Some people have a constant swirl of papers on their desks and assume that somehow the most important matters will float to the top. In most cases, however, clutter hinders concentration and can create tension and frustration—a feeling of being "snowed under."

Whenever you find your desk becoming chaotic, take time out to reorganize. Go through all your papers (making generous use of the wastebasket) and divide them into categories: (1) Immediate action, (2) Low priority, (3) Pending, (4) Reading material. Put the highest priority item from your first pile in the center of your desk, then put everything else out of sight. Remember, you can think of only one thing at a time, and you can work on only one task at a time, so focus all your attention on the most important one. A final point: clearing the desk completely, or at least organizing it, each evening should be standard practice. It gets the next day off to a good start.

5. Don't Be a Perfectionist.   There is a difference between striving for excellence and striving for perfection. The first is attainable, gratifying, and healthy. The second is often unattainable, frustrating, and neurotic. It's also a terrible waste of time. The stenographer who retypes a lengthy letter because of a trivial error, or the boss who demands such retyping, might profit from examining the Declaration of Independence. When the inscriber of that document made two errors of omission, he inserted the missing letters between the lines. If this is acceptable in the document that gave birth to American freedom, surely it would be acceptable in a letter that will be briefly glanced at en route to someone's file cabinet or wastebasket!

6. Don't Be Afraid to Say No.   Of all the time-saving techniques ever developed, perhaps the most effective is frequent use of the word *no*. Learn to decline, tactfully but firmly, every request that does not contribute to your goals. If you point out that your motivation is not to get out of work, but to save your time to do a better job on the really important things, you'll have a good chance of avoiding unproductive tasks. Remember, many people who worry about offending others wind up living according to other people's priorities.

7. Don't Procrastinate.   Procrastination is usually a deeply rooted habit. But we can change our habits provided we use the right system. William James, the father of American psychology, discussed such a system in his famous *Principles of Psychology*, published in 1890. It works as follows:

1. Decide to start changing as soon as you finish reading this article, while you are motivated. Taking the first step promptly is important.
2. Don't try to do too much too quickly. Just force yourself right now to do one thing you have been putting off. Then, beginning tomorrow morning, start each day by doing the most unpleasant thing on your schedule. Often it will be a small matter: an overdue apology; a confrontation with a fellow worker; an annoying chore you know you

should tackle. Whatever it is, do it before you begin your usual morning routine. This simple procedure can well set the tone for your day. You will get a feeling of exhilaration from knowing that although the day is only 15 minutes old, you have already accomplished the most unpleasant thing you have to do all day.

There is one caution, however. Do not permit any exceptions. William James compared it to rolling up a ball of string; a single slip can undo more than many turns can wind up. Be tough with yourself, for the first few minutes of each day, for the next two weeks, and I promise you a new habit of priceless value.

8. Apply Radical Surgery. Time-wasting activities are like cancers. They drain off vitality and have a tendency to grow. The only cure is radical surgery. If you are wasting your time in activities that bore you, divert you from your real goals and sap your energy, cut them out, once and for all.

The principle applies to personal habits, routines, and activities as much as to ones associated with your work. Check your appointment calendar, your extracurricular activities, your reading list, your television viewing habits, and ax everything that doesn't give you a feeling of accomplishment or satisfaction.

9. Delegate. An early example of failure to delegate is found in the Bible. Moses, having led his people out of Egypt, was so impressed with his own knowledge and authority that he insisted on ruling personally on every controversy that arose in Israel. His wise father-in-law, Jethro, recognizing that this was poor use of a leader's time, recommended a two-phase approach: first, educate the people concerning the laws; second, select capable leaders and give them full authority over routine matters, freeing Moses to concentrate on major decisions. The advice is still sound.

You don't have to be a national leader or a corporate executive to delegate, either. Parents who don't delegate household chores are doing a disservice to themselves and their children. Running a Boy Scout troop can be as time-consuming as running General Motors if you try to do everything yourself. One caution: giving subordinates jobs that neither you nor anyone else wants to do isn't delegating, it's assigning. Learn to delegate the challenging and rewarding tasks, along with sufficient authority to make necessary decisions. It can help to free your time.

10. Don't Be a "Workaholic."   Most successful executives I know work long hours, but they don't let work interfere with the really important things in life, such as friends, family, and fly fishing. This differentiates them from the workaholic who becomes addicted to work just as people become addicted to alcohol. Symptoms of work addiction include refusal to take a vacation, inability to put the office out of your mind on weekends, a bulging briefcase, and a spouse, son, or daughter who is practically a stranger.

Counseling can help people cope with such problems. But for starters, do a bit of self-counseling. Ask yourself whether the midnight oil you are burning is adversely affecting your health. Ask where your family comes in your list of priorities, whether you are giving enough of yourself to your children and spouse, and whether you are deceiving yourself by pretending that the sacrifices you are making are really for them.

Above all else, good time management involves an awareness that today is all we ever have to work with. The past is irretrievably gone, the future is only a concept. British art critic John Ruskin had the word "TO-DAY" carved into a small marble block that he kept on his desk as a constant reminder to "Do It Now." But my favorite quotation is by an anonymous philosopher:

> *Yesterday is a canceled check.*
> *Tomorrow is a promissory note.*
> *Today is ready cash. Use it!*

DIALOGUE

1. Are you typically late for classes, appointments, and meetings? Are you often unprepared? Do you tend to put off doing unpleasant chores? If you answered yes to any of these questions, what techniques mentioned in the essay could you use to change these behaviors?
2. Are you satisfied with the balance between work and fun in your life? If not, what techniques does the author suggest to help you achieve a better balance?
3. What is your reaction to people who are workaholics? Do you admire their dedication or see their work addiction as a serious problem? Explain.

WRITING TOPICS

1. If you feel you have an effective system for managing your time, describe it. If time management is an area that needs improvement, what are some things you could do differently to make the best use of your time?
2. Think of a person in your experience whose time management you admire. Comment on that person's habits and organization. Specify which attributes you find commendable.
3. Clarify the difference between striving for excellence and striving for perfection. Use examples from your experience as a student to illustrate the difference between the two concepts.

INTERACTION

Which of the ten strategies outlined by Edwin Bliss do you consider most important in managing your time effectively? Which ones are you least likely to practice? Discuss these questions in small groups and compare responses with the other groups.

Part II Reflections

Review the ideas you expressed at the beginning of this part in "Write Before You Read." How have your ideas changed as a result of reading the articles in this part? Explain in the space below.

1. Tests and the grading system _____

_____

_____

_____

_____

_____

2. Cheating and plagiarism _____

  _____

  _____

  _____

  _____

  _____

3. How you manage your time _____

  _____

  _____

  _____

  _____

  _____

Part II Writing Assignment

Over the course of five working days, keep a log in which you record how you spend your time. When the five days are over, analyze your log and write an evaluative summary of your time management performance in relation to the ten techniques in Bliss's essay. Which techniques did you practice? Which techniques did you ignore or neglect?

Part III

Campus Culture

INTRODUCTION

College students lead a double life. The first is lived in the classrooms, labs, libraries, and study centers. The other consists of everything students do besides studying and going to class: the cocurriculum. The cocurriculum is pursued in the gym, at the mall, at a part-time job, in community service, at a frat party, or over coffee at the student union.

This second life expresses and shapes the campus culture. It is, according to Michael Moffatt, "what college is *really* like." The first text in this section is from Moffatt's best-selling 1989 book *Coming of Age in New Jersey*, in which he describes his infiltration of the residence halls of Rutgers University. As a young-looking assistant professor at Rutgers, Moffatt was able to pass himself off as an undergraduate. Living incognito among the natives, he studied the campus culture firsthand from the perspective of a trained anthropologist.

In "The Legal Drug," *New York Times* columnist Anna Quindlen explores the phenomenon of binge drinking on American college campuses. A generation that has shunned cancer-causing cigarettes and harmful drugs continues to spend far more on beer than on books. Although alcohol has been a concern of parents and college administrators since the colonial period, binge drinking is a comparatively recent and widespread practice. Whereas illicit drug use has declined 60 percent over the past ten years, Quindlen says, "beer is the dope of the quad" and "an accident waiting to happen."

The headquarters of the college party scene has always been the fraternity. As a living option, fraternities and sororities offer distinct advantages: the opportunity to form a support network of lifelong friends and business associates, social activities, and opportunities to develop leadership and communication skills. For some college students, joining a fraternity or sorority makes perfect sense. Others may be happier in a residence hall, a shared apartment, a single room, or commuting from home. In "I Swallowed the Greek Bait," Andrew Cohen, a Bucknell senior, explains his original motivation for joining a fraternity, as well as his ultimate decision to withdraw from it.

Since the founding of Harvard, the first American college, in 1636, college students have found an outlet for their energies in athletic competition. From footraces and tugs of war in the eighteenth century and intramural and club sports in the nineteenth century have evolved today's high-tech, billion-dollar industry of intercollegiate athletics. In "Our Schools for Scandal," columnist George Will surveys the scene of big television contracts, sports scandals, and shockingly low graduation rates of college athletes and asks the disturbing question, What can this possibly have to do with education?

Increasing numbers of college students are devoting a portion of their cocurricular time to volunteer activities on campus or in their communities. Volunteer work has come to be called "academic service learning" because it teaches valuable skills that employers desire: leadership, teamwork, resourcefulness, sensitivity to people with special needs, and a practical understanding of real-world problems. In "Student Greens Get Practical," Steve Lerner describes how thousands of college students are treating their own campuses as sustainable ecosystems and conducting environmental audits of their own college communities.

It may be that college students live not two lives but one life with two sides: a life designed both for learning and growing and for deriving the maximum enjoyment possible.

Write Before You Read

A. After you've read the introduction, take a few minutes to survey the contents of this part. Then write three questions you expect will be answered in the course of your reading.

1. _____

_____

2. _____

_____

3. _____

_____

B. Briefly reflect on each of the following topics. Then write freely and rapidly about what you already know about the topic, relevant experiences you have had, and any opinions you have formed about it.

1. Your initial impressions of your campus and fellow students _____

_____

_____

_____

_____

_____

2. Activities you'd like to pursue outside of class _____

_____

_____

_____

_____

3. Your attitude toward volunteerism and academic service learning

_____

_____

_____

_____

_____

_____

What College Is *Really* Like
Michael Moffatt

PREVIEW

In 1977, Michael Moffatt enrolled as a freshman at Rutgers College and moved into the residence hall—an ordinary event in itself, except for the fact that Moffatt was only posing as a college student. In actuality, he was a thirty-four-year-old professor of cultural anthropology at Rutgers. He continued to study Rutgers students off and on for the next ten years by "going native"—living among the students on a daily basis. He recorded his observations in the bestseller Coming of Age in New Jersey *(1989). Taking its title from anthropologist Margaret Mead's seminal work,* Coming of Age in Samoa, *Moffatt's book is an unvarnished tale of student life on a mainstream American college campus.*

My first, most vivid impression from the dorms was how different college looked from the point of view of the undergraduates. . . . [T]he students had no idea of most of what the professors spent their time doing and thinking about: research, publication, and department politics. Student friends in the dorms who knew I was a faculty member were surprised to discover I had written a book, or even that I had my Ph.D. Two sophomore friends once admitted to me that they had always privately thought that "tenure" meant a faculty member had been around for "ten years." Most students were not sure of the relation between the two most immediate authorities in their lives, the dean of students and the dean of Rutgers College. And very few of them could name any of the higher-level university officials between these two deans at the bottom of the administration and the president of Rutgers at the top.

Most Rutgers professors, on the other hand, would not have known how to do what the students had to accomplish successfully every semester—how to balance college and major requirements against the time and space demands of Rutgers classrooms, how to get to their classes on time on the overcrowded campus bus system, and how to push their academic needs through a half-efficient, sometimes impolite university bureaucracy. Most faculty members no longer possessed the ability to sit

SOURCE: Michael Moffatt, *Coming of Age in New Jersey: College and American Culture,* copyright © 1989 by Rutgers, The State University. Reprinted by permission of Rutgers University Press.

passively through long lectures without ever once getting a chance to open their own mouths. Few faculty members could have named the dean of students at Rutgers College. Most of them had never heard of some of the commoner terms in undergraduate slang in the 1980s. Almost all of them would have been confused and uncomfortable in the average dorm talk session, and none of them would have had any inkling of how to go about locating a good party on the College Avenue Campus on a Thursday night.

The different perspectives of the students and of campus adults were also rooted in generation, of course. Professors and other campus authorities were not in the same position in the typical American middle-class life cycle as college adolescents. College was a profession for most campus adults. It was the way station to a hoped-for profession—not to an academic one, in most cases—for most students. Presumably you had already come of age if you were a campus adult. Usually you were still coming of age if you were a student.

And generational differences, finally, were historical differences. In an effort to empathize with the students, campus authorities sometimes tried to think back to when they were college youths. They almost always got it wrong. Memory was selective, of course. But aside from this, student culture and youth culture have changed every ten or twenty years in two centuries of the history of higher education in the United States. And the relation of every undergraduate generation to historical and social events in the wider world has always been different. One's own past student experience never serves as an adequate map for the present.

I came of age in college in the early 1960s, for example. I was on the peak of the postwar baby boom wave. Everything was always cresting for my generation. The economy was always growing; our schools were always expanding; our SATs were always going up. I knew I could study whatever I was interested in; I would always get a good job after college. In college my first year at Dartmouth, we still observed some of the old traditions established in the late nineteenth century—hats, hazing, college patriotism, and so on. I was in graduate school during the late sixties. That was the first time I had ever allowed myself to pay attention to noncollegiate youth culture, to rock-and-roll. I was also grateful for the onset of the second American sexual revolution in the twentieth century during those years, my early twenties. And, though I was not particularly active politically, I found the late sixties exciting times to be young and on campus. It seemed like something new was always going on. It was difficult to be bored.

My student friends at Rutgers in the late seventies and early eighties, on the other hand, had been on the downside of the same demographic wave from which my own generation had benefited. They had grown up in much more uncertain, cynical-making times than I had, during the Vietnam collapse, Watergate, and the pallid years of Jimmy Carter's America. The economy was tighter. If your college education did not get you into the job market, what would? In high school, almost none of them would have dared to neglect the sort of universal youth culture centering on music that had thoroughly established itself in the sixties. They had also lived in a more extensively sexualized culture than I had. In college, the late sixties were ancient history to them. The occasional campus demonstrations were exciting events, part of college life as they expected to find it in the late seventies and early eighties. But students in the 1980s also expected the ambience of the typical college demonstration to be slightly archaic—to be a culture capsule from the sixties, as it were. And most of them had never heard of the quaint old customs of college life whose last vestiges I had experienced at Dartmouth in the early sixties. . . .

For most faculty members, *the* purpose of higher education is what goes on in the classroom: learning critical thinking, how to read a text, mathematical and scientific skills, expert appreciation and technique in the arts, and so on. Some educational theorists propose broader, more humanistic goals for a college education, especially for the liberal arts: to produce "more competent, more concerned, more complete human being[s]" (Boyer 1987:1); to give students a "hope of a higher life . . . civilization" (Bloom 1987:336). And, almost all college authorities assume, whatever is valuable about college for the undergraduates is or ought to be the result of the deliberate impact, direct or indirect, of college adults such as themselves on the students.

Professors and other campus authorities do know, of course, that the students get up to other things in college. Many of them remember that they themselves got up to other things in college. But, in their present mature opinions, the "other things" that contemporary students are getting up to at the moment are either to be ignored or to be discouraged. Or they are, at best, the trimmings of higher education. The main course—the essence of college—is its serious, high-minded goals as articulated and understood by its adult leaders.

The Rutgers students I knew in my research agreed that classroom learning was an important part of their college educations. College would not be college, after all, without "academics"—professors, grades, requirements, and a bachelor's degree after four years. Most students also agreed that college should be a broadening experience, that it should make you a better, more open, more liberal, more knowledgeable person.

But, in the students' view of things, not all this broadening happened through the formal curriculum. At least half of college was what went on outside the classroom, among the students, with no adults around.

Beyond formal education, college as the students saw it was also about coming of age. It was where you went to break away from home, to learn responsibility and maturity, and to do some growing up. College was about being on your own, about autonomy, about freedom from the authority of adults, however benign their intentions. And last but hardly least, college was about fun, about unique forms of peer-group fun—before, in student conceptions, the grayer actualities of adult life in the real world began to close in on you.

About the middle of the nineteenth century, American undergraduates started calling this side of college—the side that belonged to them, the side that corresponded to late-adolescent development in college the way *they* wanted to experience it—"college life" (Horowitz 1987:23–55, Kett 1977:174–182, Moffatt 1985a). And so they still referred to it in the late twentieth century. American college life was originally a new adolescent culture entirely of the students' own creation, arguably the first of the modern age-graded youth cultures that were to proliferate down to preteens by the late twentieth century. It was a boisterous, pleasure-filled, group-oriented way of life: hazing and rushing, fraternities and football, class loyalty, college loyalty, and all the other "old traditions" celebrated in later alumni reminiscences.

College life had changed almost out of recognition a century later, however. By the 1980s, it was much closer to the private lives of the students. It no longer centered on the older organized extracurriculum. Nor was it an elite culture of youth any longer. Now it was populistically available to almost all students on campus, and it was for "coed" rather than for strictly masculine pleasures. But college life was still very much at the heart of college as the undergraduates thought of it in the late twentieth century. Together with the career credential conferred on them by their bachelor's degree, it was their most important reason for coming to college in the first place, their central pleasure while in it, and what they often remembered most fondly about college after they graduated. Let us look at its contours in more detail, as the students thought of it and experienced it at Rutgers in the late 1970s and mid-1980s.

Work and Play

College life, first of all, involved an understanding among the students about the proper relationship between work and play in college, about the relative value of inside-the-classroom education versus extracurricular fun. A century ago, the evaluation was a simple one. Extracurricular fun and games and the lessons learned in the vigorous student-to-student competitions that "made men"—athletics, class warfare, fraternity rushing—were obviously much more important than anything that happened to you in the classroom, as far as the students were concerned.

College students could not make the same aggressive anti-intellectual judgments in the late twentieth century, however. Most modern Rutgers students, like undergraduates elsewhere in the United States, instinctively knew what historian Helen Lefkowitz Horowitz has pointed out in an important new book on American undergraduate culture. Despite periodic crises of confidence in higher education in the United States (one is occurring as I write, in 1987), American parents have sent higher proportions of their children to college every single decade since 1890, and the trend continues in the 1980s. Why? Because, in the increasingly bureaucratic, impersonal, modern American economy, a college baccalaureate—and a good one with good grades—has become the indispensable initial qualification leading to the choicest occupations and professions via law school, business school, medical school, graduate school, and other types of professional postgraduate education. Once there were several routes to comfortable upper-middle-class status in the United States. And once, college could be a lazy affair. You could drift elegantly through Harvard as a "gentleman C" and still wind up in a prime law firm thanks to your family connections. No longer for other than a tiny portion of the American elite (Horowitz 1987:4–10).

What was the relation between work and play in contemporary student culture, then, and what were the preferred forms of play? . . . One way to figure out actual undergraduate priorities was to examine a crucial set of student actions: how they budgeted their time in college. Both years in the dorms, I asked hundreds of students to fill out simple time reports: "Please tell me, as precisely as possible, what things you have done, and how long each has taken, since this time twenty-four hours ago." Most of the reports were made on weekdays in the middle of the semester. On these reports, 60 to 70 percent of the students suggested that they studied about two hours a day. Another 10 to 15 percent indicated harder academic work, up to six or seven hours a day—usually, but not always, students in the more difficult majors. And the rest, about a quarter of those who filled out the time reports, hardly studied at all on a day-to-day basis, but relied on frenetic cramming before exams.

How did the students spend the rest of their time in college? They did a surprising amount of sleeping, an average of just over eight hours a day. They spent about four hours a day in classes, on buses, or dealing with Rutgers bureaucracy. A quarter of them devoted small amounts of their remaining free time, one or two hours a day, to organized extracurricular activities, mostly to fraternities or sororities, less often to other student groups. One-eighth worked at jobs between one and four hours a day. One-tenth engaged in intramural or personal athletics. And two-fifths mentioned small amounts of TV watching, less than the average for American children or adults.

The students' remaining free time was given over to friendly fun with peers, to the endless verbal banter by which maturing American youths polish their personalities all through adolescence, trying on new roles, discarding old ones, learning the amiable, flexible social skills that constitute American middle-class manners in the late twentieth century. Friendly fun was thus the bread and butter of college life as the undergraduates enjoyed it at Rutgers in the 1980s. It consisted almost entirely of spur-of-the-moment pleasures; with the exception of one type of campus organization (fraternities and sororities) . . . very little of it had to do with the older extracurriculum. Friendly fun included such easy pleasures as hanging out in a dorm lounge or a fraternity or a sorority, gossiping, wrestling and fooling around, going to dinner with friends, having a late-night pizza or a late-night chat, visiting other dorms, going out to a bar, and flirting and more serious erotic activities, usually with members of the opposite sex. And the students managed to find an impressive amount of time for such diversions in college. Across my entire sample, the average time spent on friendly fun on weekdays in the middle of the semester was a little over four hours a day.

On the face of it, then, the students were fooling around about twice as much as they were studying in college. But this is a deceptive conclusion. For from their point of view, college work also included going to classes, and the total of their classroom time plus their study time was about six hours a day. They also almost all worked more and played less around exams or when big papers or other projects were due. It was fairer to say instead that the students acted as if they assumed that academic work and friendly fun were, or ought to be, about equally important activities during one's undergraduate years.

In many ways, they also said that this was the case. Incoming freshman usually had two goals for their first year in college: to do well in classes and to have fun (or to make friends, or to have a good social life). Older students looked back on college as either an even or a shifting mixture of work and fun. . . . The two halves of college ought to be *complementary* ones in the opinion of modern college students. You came to college for the challenge, for the work, and to do your best in order to qualify for a good career later in life, most students assumed. College life was the play that made the work possible and that made college personally memorable.

Autonomy

Modern college life, like college life in the mid-nineteenth century, was also about autonomy, about experiencing college one's own way, independent of the influence and the intentions of adults. At first in the dorms, however, it was more difficult to figure out where the students were not autonomous than where they were. On initial impressions, they did not really seem to be oppressed or controlled by adults in any part of their lives.

Most of them had led peer-centered existences for years before arriving at college. In their public high schools and in their homes and families, they had become masters at avoiding the close scrutiny of adults, or at manipulating adult authority when they could not avoid it. Incoming freshmen women and men also typically said that their parents had voluntarily given them more freedom—later nighttime curfews, fewer questions about their private behavior—in their last few years at home, in anticipation of their leaving daily parental authority when they did go away to college. Once they arrived at Rutgers, most of them really felt that they were on their own on a daily basis. . . .

Looked at more carefully, however, the students actually lived in two different zones of relative autonomy and control in college in the 1980s. They were freest in their private lives. Rutgers, like other American colleges, had officially renounced *in loco parentis* authority over the personal conduct and moral behavior of its students in the late 1960s. Many of the other reforms that the protesting students of the sixties had tried to make in higher education had long since been rolled back by the late seventies and early eighties. But this fundamental change in college authority had endured for a generation.

It had not been an uncontested change, however. Since the sixties, adult critics had regularly deplored the new arrangements, often imagining that good old American college life had now degenerated into a noisy, dirty, hedonistic world of sex and drugs. And in the mid-1980s, with renewed public concern about teen alcoholism and, more recently, about a possible heterosexual AIDS epidemic, deans of students all over the country were thinking about new ways of intervening more directly in the personal lives of the students once again. At Rutgers in the late 1980s, however, the basic redefinition of undergraduate autonomy arrived at in the late sixties was still holding. In the dormitories, the authority of the deans stopped at the doors to the students' rooms.

The students were least free, on the other hand, when it came to their formal education at Rutgers. Here, they had to submit in certain ways to adult authority—to professors, who gave them grades, their fundamental institutional pay. They had to sit passively in scheduled classes. They had to learn the material the professors thought was important. They often felt that they had to think like their professors to get a good grade, whether they agreed with them or not. They had to meet "requirements."

However, the students also had a degree of autonomy and of choice even in this least free side of college. College was not mandatory like high school. The undergraduates had chosen to come to college in the first place, knowing that it would be full of academic work. In college, they did not have to get to know their professors on a personal basis; they usually would not get to know them at Rutgers even if they had wanted to. So faculty authorities were not breathing down their necks. General academic requirements at Rutgers in the mid-1980s were exceptionally loose and open-ended ones. Once the students chose majors, they often had a tighter, more demanding set of academic things they had to do. But at least they had chosen those requirements. . . .

Private Pleasures and the Extracurriculum

Late-nineteenth-century college life had been a group-oriented way of life. The students had claimed that college life did teach individualism, the "rugged individualism" of the era, the ability to impose one's character and one's will on other people. But it had done so through collective activities, through an extracurriculum of organized groups created and run entirely by the students: college classes, fraternities, glee clubs, campus newspapers, yearbooks, intramural and intercollegiate sports teams, and other student organizations. Not one college authority had had anything to do with these extracurricular student groups for forty or fifty years. Despite the claims of college officials that the professors and good bourgeois families in college towns kept an eye on the private lives of the undergraduates, the students in most American colleges were actually almost entirely on their own outside the classroom before about 1900. . . .

Rutgers students in the 1980s gave considerably less energy to organized extracurricular groups than they did to their private pleasures. The Rutgers Student Activities Office was proud that there were 155 duly constituted student groups on the campus in 1987, not counting the fraternities and the sororities. Most undergraduates probably had a formal affiliation with one or two of them. But, according to the student time reports and the estimates of knowledgeable undergraduates, no more than one in ten of the students were really active in any of them. Freshmen often said that they intended to concentrate on their studies and their social life during their first year in college, and then possibly to "go out for something" in later years. In their accounts, an extracurricular involvement sounded like a duty that they felt might be good for them, somewhere between the fun of their private pleasures and the work of academics. Most students managed to avoid this duty entirely.

The students did make distinctions among the organized extracurricular activities in the 1980s, however. The radio station was so focal to the interests of American youth culture that it was a prestigious involvement, even if the deans ultimately oversaw its operations. So, too, was the Concerts Committee of the Program Council, the student committee that selected musical performers on campus. Another respected student organization, however, the campus newspaper, had made itself independent of college oversight. Student government, on the other hand, was a joke in the opinion of most students. The undergraduates voted for its representatives in the tiniest of turnouts. Student leaders must be lackeys of the administration, the students imagined. Even if they were not, they had no chance of accomplishing anything against the weight of deanly bureaucratic power. The only reason to become a student leader was to get to know some dean for reasons of your own, many students assumed.

The undergraduates had also invented intercollegiate athletics in the late nineteenth century. In the Original Football Game, in fact, played between Rutgers and Princeton in 1869, Rutgers undergraduates had legendarily been in on the very creation both of intercollegiate athletics and of American football. In the twentieth century, however, following nationwide trends, the alumni and a growing professional coaching staff had taken sports out of the hands of the students. Rutgers had more recently gone big time in intercollegiate sports. By the 1980s, most students in the dorms did not know any Rutgers varsity athletes personally. (Football players were carefully housed separately from other undergraduates.) Some students enjoyed intramural athletics. Others jogged or worked out. Most of them were as likely to be fans of nearby professional teams as of any of the college teams.

There was one exception to the students' generally casual interest in the organized extracurriculum in the late twentieth century, however, an exception that proved the rule. Rutgers students in the 1980s were strongly split in their opinions of the fraternities and the sororities. But for those of them who liked them, a quarter to a third of the students, the fraternities and sororities were going strong in the mid-1980s and getting stronger by the year. Why? Because, though the deans had attempted to "work with" the fraternities and sororities as much as with the rest of the extracurriculum, they had not really succeeded in penetrating and controlling them despite seventy years of trying. In their ritual constitutions, the fraternities were intrinsically secret, and the intense peer solidarity created by their initiations could be extended into other aspects of their operations. The members also held their houses in private ownership; the deans did not have the same right to place preceptorlike supervisors inside them as they did in the dorms. And the fraternities often produced loyal alumni who could, as influential adults in the college, counteract deans or other authorities possibly unfriendly to the Greek community.

Thus, in the late twentieth century, the fraternities still gave undergraduates an opportunity for real autonomy in a group setting rather than only in their informal private lives. Such a zone of collective autonomy had not been available elsewhere in student culture at Rutgers or at other American colleges since about 1900. What fraternity and sorority members chose to do with this autonomy, however—unfortunately—was not likely to warm the hearts of many adults who believed in freedom and autonomy for college youths. . . .

Boys and Girls Together

Until recently in American culture, friendships usually formed between men and men or between women and women; they did not ordinarily occur between the sexes, especially for youths over ten or eleven years old. As late as 1970 a sociologist could generalize about American gender relations: "Except during courtship, [American] men and women are not expected to pursue interaction voluntarily with one another. And they are not expected to form friendships with one another, but to try to find a marriage partner, thus the assertion that 'men and women can be lovers but never friends'" (Kurth 1970:145). By the late 1970s and mid-1980s, however, over a third of hundreds of reciprocated close friendships reported to me by students in the Rutgers coed dorms were cross-sex relationships. Most students carefully distinguished these friendships from erotic or "romantic" ties, though stable girlfriend-boyfriend unions were also usually considered close friendships as well. And most students made it clear that they valued their cross-sex friends for their personalities, for the perceived closeness of their true selves, rather than for their sexual attractiveness:

> *Sophomore male:* My best friend is a girl named Debby. She is really *special.* I first met Debby two days after I got here [my freshman

year]. . . . I like her 'cause she's different from a lot of other girls. We seem to be on the same level. She understands what I'm saying and I understand what she's saying. Towards the end of the first semester we became good friends. Even over the summer we kept in touch. Even after I graduate and we go our separate ways, I think we still will keep in touch.

Anthropologist: We're not talking about a romantic relationship here, are we?

Sophomore: No. She's just someone I always know will be there to talk to.

It was true that students of both sexes sometimes made friends with persons of the opposite sex in hopes that something closer would develop between them. Cross-sex friendships could include an erotic interest, usually unilaterally. But eroticism was not an invariant part of such connections, most students insisted; and if lust was all that was going on, then the relationship was not really a friendship. The students not only distinguished between friendships and sexual relationships at a formal, definitional level; they also observed cross-sex codes of conduct toward "girls-who-were-friends" and "guys-who-were-friends" different from the behavioral codes that signaled predominantly erotic or romantic attraction. The details of these codes varied from friendship group to friendship group, but they tended to be based on older male-friendship conventions. One of them was busting. Male friends usually initiated busting, but many female undergraduates in the 1980s were adept at busting back. Busting typically marked friendship rather than romance.

American friends of either sex were also supposed to be physically as well as emotionally close. Heterosexual males dealt with mainstream homophobia by putting their physical contacts in certain acceptable frames. One of these was "athletic": wrestling or horsing around together. Another was "alcoholic": falling down drunk together. A third might be called "homosexual ironic," in which male friends implied that they were so manly that they could act "gay," for fun, because no one would ever believe that *they* were really homosexual.

Cross-sex friends did not have to worry that their physical contacts would brand them as homosexuals, but they did have to handle closeness in such a way as to rule out the possibility that they were heterosexually interested in one another. "Brother-sister" and "little kids at play" were handy frames for friendship between women and men among the students—tickle fights, pillow fights, and the like. And, unlike American male friends past the age of puberty, cross-sex friends could sit with companionable arms around each other, but not for too long. Or one of them could lie with her or his head in the other's lap. But they generally could not hold hands; holding hands meant "romance." More provocatively, males might pretend-assault female friends, usually in the presence of a protective audience of peers, being careful about where they placed their hands. Females, conversely, might pretend-seduce male friends in the same stagy manner.

Cross-sex friendships in the Rutgers dorms were thus relatively mutual, egalitarian relationships. Their high incidence suggests how far what historian Mary Hartman calls "gender crackup" had proceeded in contemporary middle-class American culture by the 1980s (Hartman n.d.). In ways for which there are no real parallels in the American past or in other cultures and societies, these young American women and men were trying to deal with one another as persons rather than as sexually defined human beings, at least some of the time. But there were also limits to contemporary American sexual egalitarianism as it was practiced in Rutgers dorms in the 1980s.

One of them had to do with which sex's patterns were being used to be egalitarian in. Gender convergence had taken place in some instances. According to common undergraduate stereotypes about different sorts of dorm floors, for example, all-men's floors were often said to be dirty, noisy, and "rowdy." All-women's floors, conversely, were considered "uptight" and "catty"; women supposedly had a harder time dealing with their hostilities than men did. But on coed floors, the students said, the more commendable traits of each sex were typically brought into a new combination. Coed floors were quieter and cleaner "because of the girls," and they were more amiable and relaxed "because of the guys."

But more often, the price that the women had had to pay for being treated as near equals in the coed dorms was to act like the men, to move more in the direction of older male gender patterns than males had moved toward older female patterns. The standard convention for daily banter on coed dorm floors in the 1980s, for example—competitive busting—was an old male norm rather than a female one. And males still took the lead in busting on the coed dorm floors, and thus, with some exceptions, unmistakably dominated informal social processes among the students.

Likewise, the unisex style of dress common on the average coed dorm floor, one that served to minimize erotic awareness between the sexes, was a relatively masculine style. Girls wore pants and jeans and T-shirts and sweats. Guys did not, on the average dorm floor in the late 1970s or mid-1980s, ordinarily wear jewelry or other detectably feminized fashions. Finally, many of the fundamental pleasures in contemporary student life were also older male pleasures. "Partying," drinking to excess, and sexual "scoring," now done somewhat mutually by women and men, were stereotypically masculine pleasures or desires a college generation or two ago.

Another limitation to modern gender egalitarianism among the undergraduates was that in private, among themselves, many of the men simply did not go along with it at all. Perhaps a third of them were obviously happier among their all-male peers, still viewing women as physical objects, still thinking of them in traditional locker-room sensibilities. They were happier with the older, more traditional American double standard. They were threatened by "women who acted like men." And they often found the combination of asexual friendship and sexual tension on coed dorm floors particularly difficult to deal with. They wanted the women to be sex objects again, and they resented them for not automatically "giving" them sexual satisfaction. Yet they would not have "respected" them if they had.

Their generally more liberal peers usually kept these males in line on the coed dorm floors. But many of them moved as quickly as possible into their more natural habitats in late-twentieth-century undergraduate society—the fraternities. At the worst, their attitudes became actions; incidents of sexual abuse and "acquaintance rape" continued to blight the female undergraduate's college experience at Rutgers and at other American colleges in the 1980s.

Aside from these male traditionalists, however, Rutgers students had not somehow lost erotic interest in persons of the opposite sex just because they were able to define some of them as coequal persons and friends. Quite the contrary. If relaxed, friendly fun was the private pleasure to which students devoted most of their free time in the late twentieth century, sexual and erotic fun were the even-more-private pleasures that they found most intensely interesting and enjoyable. Older college authorities had been sure they knew exactly what late-adolescent college females and males would get up to if they were given the chance, if they were not carefully sequestered from one another. In the 1980s, the students were living the unsupervised private lives that the older authorities had feared. And the authorities had been right in their premises if not in their judgments that adolescent sex was immoral and corrupting. Rutgers students in the 1980s did have a great deal of sexual fun with each other. Sexual fun, in fact, could be said to be at the very core of college life as the students defined it in the late twentieth century.

Females had access to about as much sexual pleasure as males. Perhaps because of this and perhaps because they had not yet encountered modern American gender asymmetry in the real world—occupational inequities, the special women's problems of combining career and family, the changing sexual balance between women and men as they grew older—most women undergraduates were not especially impressed by feminist or other political critiques of gender inequality.

Undergraduate women sometimes implied that such arguments sounded dated to them. Most of them apparently assumed that there were a few "natural" differences between the sexes: "naturally" girls had to be more careful about sexual danger than guys, "naturally" girls had a more direct investment in birth control than guys, and so on. But, judging by their replies when asked about their political attitudes toward sex and gender in the 1980s, most of them seemed to feel that these natural differences were no big deal compared to the real sexual autonomy they now enjoyed and to their near equality with undergraduate males in most other aspects of their daily lives in college. In my two years in the dorms, I never heard an undergraduate woman spontaneously complain that she had been subjected to sexism by her professors or by other college authorities—and most women, when I asked them about this directly, said such things had never happened to them. In the opinion of most female undergraduates in the dorms, apparently, the political battles for the equality of the sexes had largely been won.

If Rutgers students enjoyed a considerable amount of sexual fun and sexual freedom in modern college life, there were also many limits to their sexual behavior. Considering the potential, the late-adolescent women and men who lived together on most coed dorm floors maintained remarkably discreet, self-monitored sexual codes among themselves without adult supervision. In the dorms and in the student body more widely, a significant minority of both sexes were probably sexually inactive at any given time, either out of choice, out of lack of opportunity, or out of ineptitude. And most of the students who were sexually active were guided by the same sexual moralities that most middle-class Americans under the age of forty-five followed or preached in the 1980s.

The principal peer-group activity associated with student sexuality at Rutgers in the 1980s was "partying." Through parties, students tried to meet new erotic partners or got in the mood for sexual pleasures with partners they already knew. A party could be a scheduled event with a time and a place. Or it could be any time that a few students gathered together with the necessary ingredients: liquor, music, and members of the opposite sex—or of the same sex, for homosexuals—who were not "just friends," who were erotically interested in one another. And the students evidently did quite a bit of partying. One sample of twenty-eight students from Hasbrouck Fourth, for instance, quizzed about their use of time over the past week in the middle of the fall semester in 1984, reported an average of 2.5 parties a person, 11.5 hours of partying time. The champion was a young woman—not a bad student—who claimed to have partied for a total of 40 hours, 8 hours every evening, Wednesday through Sunday inclusive.

Liquor lubricated undergraduate partying, and restoring the minimum drinking age to twenty-one at Rutgers in the fall of 1984, mandated by the state of New Jersey, did nothing to alter this fact. To ask the students to stop drinking was about as popular as it would have been to ask the professors to stop reading books—or to stop drinking. Soft and hard drugs were used in smaller amounts and by fewer Rutgers students, in frequencies on which I have no good information. . . .

Coming of Age

The age grading that characterized most of American childhood and adolescence in the 1980s first developed for small numbers of middle-class college students a century and a quarter ago. And with age grading, college students also formulated stereotypical notions of their own physical and mental maturation in college. Drawing on older images of the Ages of Man, late-nineteenth-century undergraduates pretended that they progressed from infancy to maturity during their four short years in higher education. One typical image from Rutgers in the 1880s showed the freshman as a precocious baby, the sophomore as a drunken youth, the junior as a suave ladies' man and the senior as a care-worn, middle-aged bourgeois. And for two-thirds of a century, college class histories repeated the same conceits. Freshmen and sophomores were carefree, childish pranksters; juniors and seniors were more manly in body and in mind.

Rutgers students no longer drew such drawings or wrote such histories in the 1980s. But they still had similar concepts of the typical stages of their personal development in college, which they still enacted with some faithfulness. Freshman were foolish and inexperienced. Sophomores were wild men (and women), the leading troublemakers in the dorms. Then, with a predictability that resembled that of some form of pupating insect, juniors almost always discovered that they had matured beyond the juvenilities of dorm culture. Dorm fun was now dorm foolishness. And the inescapable intimacies of collective living—everyone else knowing almost everything about you—had grown tiresome with time.

Juniors usually decided that they were ready for something closer to an independent adult existence in the real world, usually an off-campus apartment. Seniors often wanted a maturer life style still. Or they might typically consider themselves to be "burned out," victims of mild or severe cases of "senioritis," weary of college, apprehensive about what came next. Sexual maturity was no longer peculiar to college upperclassmen in the 1980s. Now it could characterize students in any of the four college classes. But the older you were, the more likely you were to be sexually active.

In student opinion, you were pushed through these stages of development in college in the 1980s by the various formal and informal learning experiences that characterized modern undergraduate college life. Students sometimes felt that college adults did have some impact on them in college. Four out of five students in a large class in 1987 said they thought that looking back twenty years after college they would remember a professor or two as people who had inspired them in college, who had made a real difference in what they were today as adults in the real world. But most of the time the students believed that they came of age in college thanks to what they learned among themselves on their own, student to student, or, paradoxically, thanks to what they learned from dealing with precisely the least personal, most uncaring sides of official Rutgers.

College from the students' point of view was a combination of academic and outside-the-classroom education. Academic learning gave you the credentials you needed to progress toward a good career, and perhaps it made you a broader, more knowledgeable person. Outside-the-classroom education, on the other hand, was often the greater influence on your personal development, many of the students believed. About half the same large class in 1987 said that academic and extracurricular education had been "different, but equally important" aspects of college learning for them so far. About one in five of the remaining students considered academic learning more important than extracurricular learning, and about four in five made the opposite judgment. So, for about 40 percent of these students, the do-it-yourself side of college was the most significant educational experience. And for all but 10 percent, extracurricular learning had been at least half of what had contributed to their maturation so far in college.

One form of outside-the-classroom education in college, according to the students, resembled academic learning in content but not in context: the extracurricular intellectual learning that they did among themselves. Like the rest of college life as the students enjoyed it in the 1980s, most of this intellectual fun took place in private, in long talks about philosophy, morality, politics, and other serious interests, usually with friends. Some of it also took place due to the extracurricular programming available on campus, the students said, thanks to speakers, concerts, and other performances, thanks to an intellectual environment richer than anything they had typically known in their hometowns and high schools before college. . . .

*   *   *

The academic work was more difficult than it had been in high school. Your teachers no longer knew you personally or cared about you. Guidance counselors were not tracking your every move any longer. Your parents were not sure what you were doing on a daily basis. You had a more flexible schedule and more free time than you had ever had in high school—and more distractions all around you. It was not easy under these circumstances to remember the serious purposes for which you had probably come to college in the first place. Learning to balance college work against college play was one of the tougher challenges of your college years, the students maintained. . . .

Rutgers mirrored the real world in the diversity of its undergraduate student body, the students often asserted. As a public institution, it brought students together from suburban hometowns and high schools that were often more homogeneous by class, by race, and by ethnic group. And here again, Rutgers resembled the real world much more than fancier colleges did:

> I have an old girlfriend from high school who now goes to Mt. Holyoke. It's all like "high-up Suzie Sorority" there. Like they're all just the *same*. My girlfriend is sheltered from life. I have to deal with more. Because this is a state university, they have to let in all kinds of people. You just can't imagine the *friends* you have at a place like this!—Sophomore male, 1985

The actual ability of Rutgers students to deal with real cultural diversity as I observed it in the dorms was often very limited. Many students could not tolerate it at all, but sealed themselves into little friendship groups of people as much like themselves as they could find. Virtually all the undergraduates believed in the value of diversity, however. For "diversity"—like "friendship" and "community" as they were ideologically defined—was simply one more entailment of late-twentieth-century American individualism. What was the point of being an individualist if everyone and everything was the same? Real choice required a diverse universe within which to choose.

Diversity, moreover, was an easily shared value because it was almost empty of content. Real cultural diversity to an anthropologist might mean the difference between an American middle-class youth from a white ethnic background raised in northern New Jersey and a student who had recently arrived in the United States from a small city in south

Asia. To an undergraduate, on the other hand, it might mean a roommate who liked mellow music while you yourself liked punk, a nerdy roommate while you yourself were a jock, or (somewhat more culturally) a friend whose third-generation white ethnic identity was different from yours—Italian versus Irish, for instance.

Nevertheless, undergraduate Rutgers was almost inevitably more diverse than anything most students had known to date, and was probably more diverse than the world in which most of the professors and other college adults lived. At the very least, the students at Rutgers had to learn to get along with people they did not like for reasons of cultural differences. At best, the students sometimes did learn valuable things at Rutgers about themselves and the world from other students who were really different from themselves.

> All in all I am very glad I came to Rutgers. Many people say it's too big. However, I really believe that is an advantage. There are so many different opportunities here. . . . [Also,] being somewhat of a conservative, it was great being exposed to those "damn liberals."—Senior male

> In high school, everyone in my classes was either Irish, Italian or Polish. Here, I go to classes with Asians, Indians, Blacks, Puerto Ricans and many others, from whom I get different viewpoints.—Senior male

> Above all else, college is a breeding ground for interrelationships between students. If nothing else, a college student learns how to interact with his or her peers. The ability to form lasting relationships is of great value to the graduating adult. College is a step in the mental and psychological development of an individual.—Senior female

> One attribute of mine . . . that was well developed through the years I spent at Rutgers . . . is that of being a true partier. . . .—Senior female

> My social development [in college] seemed to help me as much, if not more, than my academic development into shaping me into what I am today. . . .—Senior male

In the end, the students claimed, even the fun of college life was a learning experience. And with this claim, the dichotomy between formal education (work, learning) and college life (fun, relaxation) collapsed entirely for the students. In the end, you learned from everything that happened to you in college, the students asserted. And, anthropologically speaking, they were not far from wrong. For they did spend those four hours a day in informal friendly fun, working on their real identities through such activities and practicing the "bullshit" necessary to the well-tuned American social self in the real world in the late twentieth century. And they did devote about the same amount of imaginative and real energy to "learning to pick up girls or guys" as they did to seeking out "meaningful relationships" during their college years. All these personal skills would undoubtedly continue to be useful to them long after they graduated from college. In their refinement, in their opinion—as much as in the intellectual learning that they acquired in college—they came of age, they progressed toward something like adult maturity during their four years at Rutgers.

DIALOGUE

1. Michael Moffatt's observations about college students are based on a particular sample: students at a large, selective, residential campus during the 1980s. What similarities and differences does the author observe between these students and their attitudes and those of his own generation (Dartmouth in the 1960s)?
2. According to Moffatt, students and faculty have very different expectations and attitudes about college. How are they different? Can you think of ways that students and staff on your campus could achieve a better understanding of each other?
3. What nonacademic experiences have you had that proved to be valuable learning opportunities? What cocurricular activities do you plan to pursue in college? How do these activities relate to your academic or career plans?

WRITING TOPICS

1. List several similarities and differences between the Rutgers campus culture of the 1980s as described by Moffatt and your own campus culture. Draw general conclusions about the relationship between the two campuses.
2. Prepare a time report of your activities for a twenty-four-hour period during the semester. Record all the activities performed as precisely as possible and indicate how long each activity took. Prepare an analysis of the time report in which you note time spent on academic work, sleeping, and organized and unorganized cocurricular activities. What does the time report suggest about your time management and priorities? What is the balance between formal education (classroom work, study) and college life (fun, relaxation)?

CAMPUS SKETCH

In the space below, draw a picture of your college campus. It doesn't have to be realistic. Draw it in a way that is meaningful to you. For example, if you spend a lot of time looking for a parking space, draw a bunch of parking lots with a few buildings sprinkled about. If you're familiar with only a few areas of your campus, draw those and leave blank the parts you're unfamiliar with. Use labels if you like—STUDENT UNION, ADMISSIONS OFFICE, BASEBALL DIAMOND, etc.

3. Moffatt states that many students believed that "outside-the-class-room education . . . was often the greater influence . . . on personal development." Write an essay in which you support or challenge this statement based on your college experience to date.

INTERACTION

While a "student" at Rutgers, Moffatt asked actual students to create topographical maps of the campus as they saw it from their personal perspectives. A football player, for example, might have drawn a large football field at the center of the campus, even if it was actually on the edge. On the preceding page, draw a sketch of your campus from your current perspective. Share your drawing with your small group and explain its significance to you. Later in the text, in the "Reflections" section at the close of Part 4, you will be invited to draw a second sketch to see how much your perceptions have changed over the course of the quarter or semester.

The Legal Drug
Anna Quindlen

PREVIEW

The consumption of alcohol has long been a part of the American college scene, but in recent years this traditional rite of passage has taken some disturbing turns. According to a 1994 study by the Columbia University Center on Addiction and Substance Abuse, more and more students are binge drinking (consuming five or more drinks at a time), and more and more binge drinkers are women. Excessive drinking is a factor in 95 percent of all violent crimes on campus, including 90 percent of campus rapes. Of the women diagnosed as having contracted a sexually transmitted disease such as herpes or AIDS, 60 percent were drunk at the time of infection.

In this 1994 editorial, New York Times *columnist Anna Quindlen describes the ambivalent and often hypocritical attitude Americans have taken toward alcohol and suggests that, as a matter of public policy, alcohol should be treated as what it really is: a legal drug.*

SOURCE: Anna Quindlen, "The Legal Drug," *New York Times* (June 11, 1994), p. 15. Copyright © 1994 by The New York Times Co. Reprinted by permission.

For some it is a beverage, for some a habit, for some an addiction.

And those differences, perhaps more than anything else, explain why we have yet to come to terms with the vast damage that alcohol can do, with those it kills, those it harms, those who can't get loose from its sharp fishhook.

While even young children know that cocaine and heroin are nothing but trouble, while even young children know that cigarettes cause cancer, what they know about booze and beer and wine is different because it is the drug their parents keep in the refrigerator and use themselves. And that can be confusing.

The Center on Addiction and Substance Abuse at Columbia University quantified some of the results of that confusion this week. A commission report shows that "binge drinking is the number one substance abuse problem in American college life," far outweighing the use of drugs. The widespread use of alcohol at nearly every American school affects everything from the prevalence of venereal disease to the failure rate.

Ninety percent of all reported campus rapes occur when either the victim or the assailant has been drinking. At least one in five college students abandons safe sex practices when drunk that they'd use when sober. Two-thirds of college suicide victims were legally intoxicated at the time of death. Estimates of alcoholism range from 10 to 15 percent of the college's population.

What's wrong with this picture? These statistics would normally be the stuff of vocal lobbies, calls for action and regulation. Instead alcohol manufacturers openly court the college market, advertising in campus newspapers despite the fact that many of the readers are too young to drink legally. In a 1991 report on alcohol promotion on campus, one marketing executive was quoted on the importance of developing brand loyalty in a student. "If he turns out to be a big drinker, the beer company has bought itself an annuity," the executive said.

"When parents visit, their concern is drugs," says one college administrator. "They're surprised if we want to talk about drinking. A few are even annoyed."

The demonization of drugs allows delusion about alcohol to flourish. There are 18.5 million people with alcohol problems and only 5 million drug addicts. More people who commit crimes are drunk than high. Illicit drug use on campus has decreased 60 percent in the last decade. Beer is the dope of the quad.

Colleges and universities are cautious in confronting alcohol use on campus; if they accept responsibility for policing it, administrators are concerned they will be held legally responsible for its effects. And for many parents, the legality of alcohol is a convenient excuse not to delve too deeply into the issues it raises for their kids, issues not only about drinking but about self-image. Research being done at Mississippi State University showed that many students drank to escape from anger and loneliness, to feel accepted and at ease.

College authorities and parents both have to find some way to communicate that using alcohol to anesthetize doubt and insecurity can become a lifelong habit as fast as you can say A.A. And that way lies disaster, disappointment, even death. The other day Betty Ford came with her daughter, Susan, to a symposium at the Center on Addiction and Substance Abuse so both could talk about how her family had to force her into treatment. "I suddenly found myself making excuses so that I wouldn't have to spend too much time over at the house," Susan said of the time when the former First Lady was addicted to booze and pills.

Cynthia Gorney, in an exquisite essay in *The Washington Post* last year, wrote of her mother: ". . . she was a woman of curiosity and learning and great intelligence. She died in March, of cirrhosis of the liver, which is also what kills the men under blankets by the sewer grates."

But kids won't even begin to understand that until everyone starts to treat alcohol like what it is: a legal drug. That can be confusing too, since there are many who can drink with no ill effect and never come close to addiction. But just because many of us are safe drivers doesn't mean we don't acknowledge the existence of car accidents. And in the lives of many young adults, alcohol is an accident waiting to happen.

DIALOGUE

1. Some people argue that drinking has always been a prominent feature of American college life and that this is not likely to change. Do you agree? Why or why not?
2. A fairly recent change in college student drinking patterns is a sharp increase in binge drinking: 42 percent of college students drink to get drunk, compared to 33 percent of their nonstudent counterparts age eighteen to twenty-one. The percentage of women students who drink to get drunk has increased from 10 percent to 35 percent over the past fifteen years. What explanations can you give for this trend? What have you observed about the drinking patterns of your fellow students?
3. Has alcohol played a prominent role in the social life of the schools you have attended? Do you feel alcohol or drugs will be a problem for

you? Are you concerned with the drinking habits of a roommate or friend?

WRITING TOPICS

1. Reconstruct a memorable event in your experience in which alcohol played a prominent role.
2. Quindlen writes that, "For some it is a beverage, for some a habit, for some an addiction." Under what circumstances is alcohol just a beverage? A habit? An addiction? Make clear distinctions between these three conditions and provide examples or illustrations of circumstances to which each term applies.
3. In an essay, develop three arguments supporting or opposing the following statement:

   Considering the damage caused by alcohol abuse on college campuses, the advertisement and promotion of alcohol products in the campus newspaper or on campus bulletin boards should be prohibited.

INTERACTION

Working in small groups, rank the effectiveness of the following measures to reduce alcohol abuse on campus (1 = most effective; 5 = least effective):

1 2 3 4 5   1. Ban alcohol in the residence halls.

1 2 3 4 5   2. Ban alcohol at all campus events, including those attended by faculty and administrators.

1 2 3 4 5   3. Pass a federal law requiring colleges to report whether drug or alcohol abuse was the cause for rapes, assaults, vandalism, and other campus crimes.

1 2 3 4 5   4. Ban the advertising and promotion of alcohol in all campus publications and at all campus events.

1 2 3 4 5   5. Launch a campaign to educate college students, faculty, and staff about the dangers of alcohol abuse and provide a full range of counseling and support services for alcohol abusers and their victims.

Following group discussion of the above measures, suggest other ideas and initiatives that would educate the college community about alcohol abuse.

I Swallowed the Greek Bait

Andrew Cohen

PREVIEW

The popularity of fraternity and sorority life on American college campuses rises or falls with each new generation. Considered "uncool" in the seventies, fraternities and sororities enjoyed a boom in the eighties. In the nineties, membership is once again on the decline. The following article was written when the author, Andrew Cohen, was a senior majoring in economics and philosophy at Bucknell University. It was first published in the school paper, the Bucknellian, *and later republished in the* Chronicle of Higher Education. *He describes how his initial enthusiasm gradually turned to disenchantment as he lived out every collegian's inner struggle to reconcile his social identity with his sense of self.*

Two and a half long years ago I witnessed what I thought to be my first "casualty of rush." A woman who lived downstairs had decided to drop out of rush before the first round of cuts were returned. To my sophomoric first-year intellect, the reason for her decision was clear: she knew that she was not good enough to get into the sororities that she wanted so she cut her losses. The woman was invited back to all eight sororities, and, in truth, she was too good for them. However, this realization has been a long time coming for me.

I swallowed the Greek bait, hook, line, and sinker. People said, "Going Greek is a good experience. You get to meet people, you have a body of brother/sisters so close they'll do anything for you, you have leadership opportunities, and besides, the social scene here is so Greek-based you've got to do it."

Nothing could be further from the truth.

I joined a fraternity and served as its vice-president and public-relations chair. I was elected by the presidents of the fraternities to the Interfraternity Council Executive Board, where I served until my deactivation in the spring of 1992. I do not speak from a disenfranchised perspective, but rather as someone who experienced the "essence" of the system.

SOURCE: Andrew Cohen, "I Swallowed the Greek Bait," *The Chronicle of Higher Education* (March 3, 1993), B5. Reprinted by permission of the author.

It is also important that I am honest about my reasons for leaving. I left not because of any moral awakening, but because I could barely stay sober long enough to write my name. This was my problem, not the system's. Yet my time away from Greek life has led me to realize that while in the system, there is a tendency to forget the "kind of person" you think you are, in favor of the inclinations of the herd.

As a first-year student, I came to Bucknell University berating my parents for their interference in my life. I was my own person, not their juvenile, dependent son. I came to school eager to experience my individuality for the first time. Yet, within a few months, the burden was too great, and I sought refuge in the acceptance of a group.

I said that I was only going to rush. But it was so enticing. People seemed to like me. With no more than a beer in hand and an hour or so of small talk in common, I decided that they were going to be my best friends.

From the very first, the things that were me, that were pointedly Andrew Cohen, that comprised my very soul, began to die. The physical pain of being paddled bare-assed was, at that point in my life, indescribable. Some "pops" (older fraternity members picked as big brothers for pledges) and their "sons" never talked after that night. But I learned that *silence* was precious. I did not let out a peep, and the brothers "respected that," many shook my hand. They made it all *worth* it. I was proud of my welts, they were a badge of *courage*.

However, it was the psychological torture during pledging that really broke me. I was expected to sit in silence when I saw things that made me sick to my stomach. When brothers senselessly decried my very being, made me feel inhuman, I had to suck it up, to let go of my thoughts, to ignore them, to become numb. This was a hard lesson for me to swallow, and I voiced objections. I even mentioned the word "hazing," as I was told to do at an anti-hazing program we had been required to attend. I found out from an officer of the house that I was not being hazed because I could disassociate myself at any time.

It was too late. My identity was bound into the group. So I learned to ignore myself. One of the brothers told me that it was a simple psychological process whereby the individual is broken down only to be built up as a member of the group. It worked.

By the end of "Hell Week," I had discarded any remnants of myself as an individual and rather began to enjoy my debasement. I was so excited that I would soon become a member and there would be others for me to terrorize. By the next year, I had become what I had held in contempt.

I miss my friends from my first year at Bucknell. After pledging, it was never the same. Paradoxically, my social opportunities were enlarged and shrunken all at once. I had an instant group of friends called brothers. But everyone outside of the group was somehow not as good as those in it. Social options immediately became limited by a set of letters.

As a brother, little changed. I ceased to be a thinker, if I ever was one. I was always busy jumping on the bandwagon or trying to lead one. But as for doing anything for myself, that was impossible; my self had long since left. The silence I had learned as a pledge took a turn for the worse; I put on my mask and joined the masses.

It was really no one's fault. An opening for a sexist remark or act would occur, someone would take it, everyone would take it. Never in my year and a half as an active member did I hear anyone really stand up against sexism during the hundreds of times that it occurred. I did not pride myself as a sexist, but it was just so damn funny, everyone roared with *approving* laughter.

I always thought I was the "kind of person" who deplored racism. Yet, when a small group got together and began making racist remarks, my courage had disappeared like the welts. Dumb silence pervaded my psyche. I did not know what to say, how to say it. Everyone was having such a good time, how could I spoil it?

Frequently, Jews were the target of disparaging remarks. While the anger rose within me, I shut up and smiled. Now it was my so-called "people." How could there be "my people" when there was no *me?*

So it was that I forgot myself. My insecurity had been filled by the ethos of the herd. I was now a leader of the system. I wrote scathing newspaper stories against those who opposed it. And I made the thing look so beautiful on paper that no one would dare write the libel you are reading. I wrote letters praising "our diverse brotherhood which maintains a close-knit sense of unity." All the while, my *experience* told a very different story.

I do not believe that Greeks are bad people. The majority of my close friends are Greek. But I do think that the system encourages people to value their membership in the group above their individuality and sense of self, which makes it easy for people to become foreign to themselves.

Students need not be slaves to the system. *Students can change the way things are.* If they do not *validate* the system, it will cease to rule a university's social climate. People will be able to transcend the herd mentality to embark upon genuine relationships that are supportive of their individuality. Such a decision takes a lot of courage, though, a lot more than I had during my time in a fraternity.

DIALOGUE

1. What are some of the arguments for and against joining a fraternity or sorority?
2. Do you agree with the author that membership in a fraternal organization is an expression of a herd mentality? What similarities and differences can you think of between Greek organizations and religious cults?
3. What living situation would you consider ideal while you are attending college? If you currently live on campus, what improvements would you make in housing and food services? Would you be willing to pay higher room and board rates if it meant having more amenities, better food, and improved service?

WRITING TOPICS

1. Develop a proposal to be presented to the Panhellenic Council on your campus in which you argue for the abolition of all "hell week" activities. What would be gained or lost by banning all traditional hell week rituals?
2. Imagine that the president of your college has announced that the Greek system is under review at your campus and student input is requested. Prepare a letter to the president in which you argue to retain or dismantle the current Greek system at your college.
3. Write a critique of Andrew Cohen's essay in which you defend the Greek system. To what extent are Cohen's objections to Greek life rooted in his own perceptions and judgments? Do his criticisms overlook the positive aspects of Greek life?

INTERACTION

Working in groups, describe a personal experience in which you were forced to choose between conflicting loyalties—to your personal integrity and to a group to which you belonged. Discuss with the group how you felt about the conflict and how you resolved it. How do you feel about your decision now?

Our Schools for Scandal
George Will

PREVIEW

After a brilliant career as a student at Oxford and Princeton and brief stints as a professor of political science at Michigan State and the University of Toronto, George Will entered politics as a congressional aide and speechwriter for Jesse Helms and Ronald Reagan. Now a widely syndicated newspaper columnist, Will can be relied on for writing that is consistently conservative, iconoclastic, and clever. In this 1986 Newsweek *article, he identifies the major scandals of college sports and proposes some modest reforms.*

During a royal visit in 1957 Queen Elizabeth, at a Maryland–North Carolina football game, asked Maryland's governor, "Where do you get all those enormous players?" He replied: "Your Majesty, that's a very embarrassing question." Big-time college football is grinding into gear yet again, and permanent embarrassment may account for the tradition of nervous joking. A wit once defined college coaches as "a class of selfless sufferers who go on building character year after year, no matter how many states they have to import it from." A Cincinnati University coach once said that 90 percent of all colleges abide by the rules and the other 10 percent go to bowl games. When hired at Nebraska a coach joked, "I don't expect to win enough games to be put on NCAA probation. I just want to win enough to warrant an investigation." An Oklahoma University president joked, "We're trying to build a university our football team can be proud of." Ho, ho.

Not funny. Big-time college sports are a continuing scandal, corrupting and exploiting. A proximate cause of this is coaches' insecurity, but that insecurity is produced by the stakes: bushels of money and rabid legions of alumni. Insecurity? Lou Holtz, Notre Dame's new coach, once joked, "I have a lifetime contract. That means I can't be fired during the third quarter if we're ahead and moving the ball." A Michigan State coach once got this telegram from alumni: "Coach, we're all behind you—win or tie."

SOURCE: George Will, "Our Schools for Scandal." Copyright George F. Will. First published in *Newsweek,* September 15, 1986. Reprinted by permission.

The worst scandal does not involve cash or convertibles. It involves slipping academically unqualified young men in the back doors of academic institutions, insulating them from academic expectations, wringing them dry of their athletic-commercial usefulness, then slinging them out the back door even less suited to society than they were when they entered. They are less suited because they have spent four years acquiring the idea that they are exempt from normal standards. A Texas A&M basketball coach once joked to an athlete who received four F's and a D, "Son, looks to me like you're spending too much time on one subject." The sports system that generates such jokes has an ugly racial dimension.

Many football and basketball programs prosper by exploiting the heartbreaking belief of ghetto boys that sports are a broad paved road to riches. This year the NCAA is implementing requirements for freshmen athletes—a minimum grade-point average in a core high-school curriculum and a very minimal score on a standard aptitude test. At least 8 of the 47 football players on *Parade* magazine's 1985 high-school All-America team are ineligible to play this year. The Dallas *Times Herald* reports that in the 105 Division I football programs, 206 (9 percent) of 2,227 entering freshmen are ineligible. All but 31 of the 206 are black. High schools deserve a large dollop of blame for not having "no pass, no play" rules. But colleges are especially guilty of exploitation because they are the end of the road for most "student athletes."

A survey of 1,359 black athletes who entered colleges in 1977 revealed that only 14 percent graduated in four years and only 31 percent in six years. Among 4,067 white athletes the figure was deplorable but better: 53 percent graduated in six years. But many "graduates" glided through on cushy courses. Remember Kevin Ross, who played basketball for Creighton University in Omaha and then enrolled in a seventh-grade class to learn to read and write.

Many athletes live in an atmosphere of permanent exemption—exemption from all the rules and rigors of academic life. Not surprisingly, some young people come to think they are exempt also from physiological limits. "Cocaine? Can't hurt me." An attorney for some University of Georgia officials said: "We may not make a university student out of [an athlete], but if we can teach him to read and write maybe he can work at the post office rather than as a garbage man when he gets through with his athletic career." However, even if the athletic departments had such kindness in mind, it is a preposterous enterprise for an institution of higher—higher than what?—education. Anyway, what is really involved is higher math. This season the 105 Division I football programs will raise and spend nearly $1 billion while entertaining 25 million spectators and zillions of TV viewers. Ticket and concession sales often top $500,000 for a single game. Winning teams go to bowl games and swim in gravy. Penn State's share from last year's Orange Bowl was $2.2 million.

In addition to money, a sprawling multiversity can get from a successful team a unifying focus. As Alabama's Bear Bryant once noted, "It's kind of hard to rally round a math class." And sports can give useful glamour to an institution. A Boston College official gives much credit to the 1984 football team of quarterback Doug Flutie for the increase from 12,500 to 16,000 in freshman applications from 1984 to 1985. Also, it is not fair to say, as a wit did, that football bears the same relation to education that bullfighting does to agriculture. Sport is a realm of discipline, skill and excellence, and hence has a legitimate role on campuses. Furthermore, many institutions such as Penn State, Notre Dame, Georgetown and Duke are proving that athletic excellence is compatible with academic responsibility.

Many small reforms could make a big difference in big-time sports. Freshmen should not be allowed to compete on varsity teams. Joe Paterno, Penn State's football coach, says something is out of whack when a kid plays football games before attending his first class. There should be none of those special dormitories where athletes eat and sleep and do not study together in splendid isolation from real students. Schools should not be allowed to give the full quota of athletic scholarships unless the graduation rate among athletes is as high as the rate for the entire student body. Eligibility and graduation should not be faked using ludicrous "courses" such as the one some University of Nevada at Las Vegas basketball players "took" during a 16-day playing tour of the South Pacific. *Sports Illustrated* reports that they were required to spend several hours a day on "field trips," read two books and write a term paper. Some players received six credits. The average full-term credit load at UNLV is 15. The course was called Contemporary Issues in Social Welfare, and should itself be an issue. *Sports Illustrated* suggested the title Palm Trees 101.

DIALOGUE

1. What is the "ugly racial dimension" in college sports? Is it evident at your school?
2. Are the terms *student athlete* and *athletic scholarship* contradictory, misleading, or hypocritical? Are unfair demands placed on students in performance-based areas such as athletics, music, art, dance, and the-

ater? If there are any such students in your class, ask them to share their strategies for balancing academic commitments with obligations to their performance areas.

3. To what extent do you think school spirit is related to or dependent on a successful and visible intercollegiate athletic program?

WRITING TOPICS

1. George Will suggests that there are several institutions where "athletic excellence is compatible with academic responsibility." How do some schools achieve this balance? Are they special institutions, or could their formula be implemented by other colleges?

2. Prepare a proposal in which you argue that college athletics should be fully commercialized. Players should be paid for services, programs should be required to generate enough income to be self-sustaining, and the policy that ties athletic eligibility to academic performance should be abolished. Market conditions should dictate the success or failure of intercollegiate sports, and National Collegiate Athletic Association (NCAA) oversight should be discontinued.

3. Will says that "sport is a realm of discipline, skill, and excellence, and hence has a legitimate role on campuses." In a brief essay, elaborate on the proper role of athletics on a college campus.

INTERACTION

In small groups, evaluate the following proposals suggested by Will for reforming college sports. Try to reach a consensus on the possible negative and positive consequences of each:

a. Eliminate all athletic scholarships.
b. Pay athletes in revenue-producing sports a salary.
c. Outlaw the televising of athletic contests.
d. Tie the number of permitted athletic scholarships to the number of athletes who graduate.

Student Greens Get Practical

Steve Lerner

PREVIEW

Environmental activism is on the rise on campuses throughout the United States. The first annual national student environmental conference in 1989 at the University of North Carolina attracted two thousand students. At the 1990 conference on the campus of the University of Illinois, the number of participants more than tripled. Chapters of the Student Environmental Action Coalition (SEAC) have been formed on more than seven hundred campuses; their marching papers are the campus environmental audit described in Campus Ecology: A Guide to Assessing Environmental Quality and Creating Strategies for Change *by April Smith.*

"Student Greens Get Practical" describes how some students and staff at the University of Wisconsin came to view their own campus as a fragile ecosystem. While the contemplation of global environmental problems—oil spills, rain forest destruction, and ozone depletion—can lead to despair, these students discovered that they could make a meaningful contribution to the quality of the environment on their campus.

Steve Lerner is research director for Commonweal *magazine. "Student Greens Get Practical" originally appeared as an article in the* Amicus Journal *and now forms a chapter in Lerner's book* In Search of Sustainable America: Success Stories of 16 Environmental Pioneers *(MIT Press, 1995).*

Daniel Einstein can trace his family tree to his famous cousin twice removed, Albert. But the relative he admires most is a cousin who invented a rotating lawn sprinkler. This preference for the practical over the theoretical is typical of the thirty-six-year-old Einstein, who occupies a key position in one of the nation's most innovative campus environmental programs at the University of Wisconsin at Madison. A lanky graduate student working on his master's degree in land resources, Einstein channels the energies of undergraduates into finding more pragmatic ways to make the campus more ecologically sustainable.

SOURCE: Steve Lerner, "Life Studies: Student Greens Get Practical at the University of Wisconsin." Copyright Summer 1994, The Amicus Journal, a quarterly publication of the Natural Resources Defense Council, 40 West 20th Street, New York, NY 10011. Reprinted by permission. NRDC membership dues or non-member subscription: $10.00 annually.

Convincing students to be practical isn't always easy. "Students want to prevent pollution, stop global climate change, and save the rain forest," Einstein says with a smile. This description fits Suzanne Tegen, a senior majoring in German literature, who says she was "struck by save-the-worldness" during a recent trip to East Germany, where she was appalled by the degraded condition of the environment. "I wanted to rush back here and solve all the environmental problems," she says now, laughing at her own idealism.

But when she arrived back at college, Einstein was there to bring her down to earth to work on projects she could complete in one semester. "I want students to get their hands on something doable and feel at the end of the term that their work has made a difference," says Einstein, who created a job for himself as the university's Environmental Management Coordinator, brokering projects that bring students, faculty, and staff together to work on solving campus-based environmental problems.

Scaling down her ambitions, Tegen joined a team of students Einstein supervises who are looking for ways to reduce the campus waste stream. She zeroed in on one small piece of the problem—the large number of student newspapers going to waste. After two months monitoring thirty sites around campus, she estimated that every day a total of approximately 11,500 copies of *The Badger Herald* and *The Daily Cardinal* were never even taken out of the newspaper racks. To help other students understand the monumental waste of resources involved, during Earth Week Tegen built a tower of student newspapers twenty-one feet high that accounted for only half the newspapers wasted on campus every day. Her research, she is confident, will force the student publishers to cut their press runs or collect their own unread papers for recycling.

Einstein makes no bones about the fact that he is training environmental activists. In order to give students a positive experience and increase the chance that their work will be acted on, Einstein pairs each student with a member of the university staff who has an interest in improving some aspect of the campus environment.

This kind of match-up between student researcher and administration "client" worked well recently when Einstein introduced Lori Kay, Director of Transportation Services, to senior honors student Tabitha Graves. Graves subsequently helped devise a number of incentives for students to use mass transit instead of driving their cars when commuting to campus.

As a first step, Graves addressed the single most difficult hurdle for mass transit advocates everywhere: flexibility. She helped design and won administrative approval for a "guaranteed ride home" program, which assures students that if they take mass transit to school and have to return home for an emergency, they can take a taxi, save a receipt, and be reimbursed for 90 percent of their expenses. Second, Graves was involved in negotiating a "flex parking" program, which provides a discount on campus parking fees for students who reduce by at least one day a week the number of days they travel to campus in a single-occupancy vehicle. Third, she had a hand in expanding the university's telecommuting program, which permits some university staff to work at home on certain days.

Looking back, Graves says that the work was frustrating at times because progress came so slowly, but ultimately satisfying. "This work is more rewarding than the advocacy work I did in the past because I know these programs are going to be implemented," she observes.

This sense of accomplishment and excitement that students feel when they are instrumental in solving real-world problems also appeals to David J. Eagan, a doctoral candidate in educational administration, who is writing his thesis, not coincidentally, on whether or not college is providing students with the skills they will need in the workplace. A red-bearded teaching assistant, Eagan has become a second connecting point for students interested in making the university more environmentally friendly.

"It is curious that in a place where inquiry is highly prized, the environmental impact of the campus has gone virtually unquestioned," Eagan writes in the book he co-authored with David W. Orr, *The Campus and Environmental Responsibility.* The reason for this oversight, he contends, is that college campuses are often depicted as ivory towers walled off from the real world. Eagan takes exception to this view. "At the University of Wisconsin," he writes, "the impact of 60,000 individuals and a billion-dollar budget is about as real world as you can get." With 42,000 students and 17,000 faculty and staff on a campus of 900 acres, 220 buildings, twelve miles of roads, and four miles of lake shore, the University of Wisconsin at Madison constitutes Wisconsin's eighth largest city. As such, the university has a huge environmental impact, and students should use it as a laboratory for finding solutions to environmental dilemmas, he argues. Eagan is well placed to help, as the teaching assistant leading the UW's Institute for Environmental Studies capstone certificate seminar, which gives academic credit to students who do research on the campus environment.

Eagan's students have spent the last semester chipping away at some of the more wasteful practices on campus. One student convinced the librarian at the Education Library to use recycled paper in the copy machines by stocking one machine with virgin paper and the other with recycled—disproving the myth that recycled paper causes more jams. Another student, Matt Mitby, studied the fate of the 200,000 university bulletins and 70,000 timetables the university prints and distributes to students. Mitby found that 60 percent of the students ended up throwing these publications in the trash, and argued successfully that the administration should indicate on the covers of the publications that they are recyclable.

Jason Frost, a soft-spoken third-year sociology student, spent the semester working with a team of other students streamlining the way the university collects and redistributes laboratory chemicals on campus. In the past, the university collected unused chemicals from its labs and then advertised the chemicals available for redistribution through a newsletter published only a couple times a year. Frost adapted a state-run computer program so that the information could be posted immediately on a computer network and chemists constantly updated what is available. He anticipates that the new system will reduce the volume of chemicals disposed of at hazardous waste facilities and diminish the amount that must be purchased.

These individual changes are limited in scope. But the incremental approach to social change has its advocates. In an article entitled "Small Wins: Redefining the Scale of Social Issues" in *American Psychologist*, Karl Weick writes that "Once a small win has been accomplished, forces are set in motion that favor another small win. When a solution is put in place, the next solvable problem often becomes more visible. This occurs because new allies bring new solutions with them and old opponents change their behavior. Additional resources also flow toward winners, which means slightly larger wins can be attempted."

Of course, it helps if the "small win" brings some resources along with it. For instance, Einstein struck gold recently supervising Dan Jaffe, a graduate student who examined the university's contract with a waste-paper hauler. The university was paying $37,000 a year for the privilege of trucking its waste paper to a company that then resold the material to a recycling outfit. By rewriting the contract, cutting out the middlemen, and selling the waste paper directly to the recycling company for some $13,000, Einstein and his student researcher saved the university about $50,000 yearly.

But the decisive resource for Einstein and Eagan is the support of critical allies—their ability to broker projects that bring together students, faculty, and administrators. Indeed, one of the most important reasons that practical steps are being taken at the University of Wisconsin is that Einstein has ensconced himself within the bureaucracy that makes decisions about the university's physical plant. Specifically, he has developed a good working relationship with his boss, Duane Hickling, Assistant Vice Chancellor for Facilities Planning and Management.

Hickling, a transplant from the University of Southern California, is part of a new breed of facility manager on campus who sees environmental responsibility as an important part of his mission. When Donna Shalala, now Secretary of Health and Human Services, was Chancellor of the University of Wisconsin in 1988–1993, she made it clear that the university was going to become a responsible member of the community, running its facilities in an environmentally efficient and accountable fashion.

There is ample evidence that Hickling takes this mission seriously. When he noticed that excavation at a construction site on campus was coming dangerously close to a cluster of 125-year-old American Elms, he questioned his staff about plans to save the trees—and was told they were scheduled to be cut down so a storm water sewer could be installed where they stood. "There was a full minute of silence while I collected myself after hearing that," Hickling recalls. Then, without mincing words, he told his staff that they were not going to deface the university by carrying out such a project. Einstein notes that, since then, other construction plans have been altered to protect nature.

Through Hickling, Einstein has access to members of the grounds crew and custodial staff, and he diligently cultivates their trust. For example, when he applied for and won the governor's award for recycling, one of the people he chose to bring with him to the award ceremony was John Harrod, Director of Physical Plant. In the parking lot of the governor's mansion, just before the presentation, Harrod asked Einstein to find a student who could research methods for reducing the amount of salt used in the sand spread on roads and sidewalks during the winter to keep ice from forming. He was concerned that salt-water runoff was killing vegetation and polluting the fresh water of Lake Mendota.

"Here is what appears to be a simple problem," says Einstein from his modest office overlooking the campus. "You have a pile of sand and a pile of salt. The sand is going to freeze unless you mix some salt in it. So a member of the grounds crew operates a piece of heavy equipment and dumps a bucket of salt on the sand. He then runs the front-end loader back and forth across the pile to mix it. Now you have salt and sand." But the simple problem turns complex when you try to measure the amount of salt in a pile of sand, a task complicated by the fact that the two materials are unevenly mixed.

Convinced that the answer to the problem lay in mixing the salt and sand more evenly, the student researched equipment available for the purpose. Whether the university will ever purchase this equipment is still unclear. But, building on this research, an ad hoc committee formed to deal with the road-salt issue is looking into the possibility of closing off some roads and sidewalks that are little traveled in the winter.

These practical puzzles seem to delight Einstein, who has a peripatetic background: directing summer Youth Conservation Corps programs in California and Oregon, leading outdoor adventure/education programs in New York State, working as an energy auditor in Massachusetts, installing energy-efficient boilers in Maine, building housing in Nicaragua, and supervising a construction crew building a chimpanzee research station in Uganda. It was in Uganda, driving a jeep through the outback one hot afternoon, that Einstein decided he could have a greater impact as an environmental organizer if he worked among his own people instead of in Africa.

When he returned to the United States and enrolled in graduate school at the University of Wisconsin, Einstein was part of a growing number of students who felt it was important to help protect the environment. A 1993 survey shows that 29 percent of the U.S. college freshmen wanted to become involved in programs to clean up the environment, and 84 percent wanted the government to do more on pollution, reports Paul Rogat Loeb in his soon-to-be-published *Generation at the Crossroads: Apathy and Action on the American Campus.*

But despite this evidence of environmental interest among undergraduates, Einstein cautions us to keep the scale of student environmental activism in perspective. At the University of Wisconsin, Einstein estimates that there are only about fifteen dedicated activists in the UW Greens, forty in the Wisconsin Public Interest Research Group, and another fifteen in the local chapter of the Student Environmental Action Coalition. Thus, while he recognizes that there are many environmentalists on campus who are not affiliated with organized groups, by his calculation there are no more than seventy hard-core activists out of a total of 42,000 students.

Einstein attributes the relatively small number of committed activists to a profound sense of despair and powerlessness prevalent among students. As a teaching assistant, he received many course evaluations from students who wrote that they were depressed to learn that environmental problems were so bad, and that they did not think they could do anything to solve them. Perversely, then, classes designed to provide students with useful information about the environment were leaving them paralyzed by the scope of the problem. To fight this sense of hopelessness and despair, Einstein provides one student at a time with the opportunity, the contacts, and the supervision necessary to bring about positive environmental change on campus.

For his part, Einstein wants students not only to find ways to make the university more environmentally friendly, but also to see the campus as a living ecosystem—not just the place where they go to classes. When they walk on the grounds of this university, founded in the wilderness 140 years ago, Eagan wants them to remember that this land was once prairie with scattered clusters of oaks. He wants them to know that student activists brought about the restoration of an important marsh on campus. He wants them to know that the great conservationist John Muir was a student at the university, and that Aldo Leopold taught here and initiated projects in prairie and woodland restoration. Eagan hopes that, in the process of learning about the natural history of the campus, students will become stakeholders involved in protecting it.

Another way to bind students to the place where they live is to get them involved in physical restoration work. "When you sweat and grunt and get your hands dirty, you become connected with a place," notes Eagan, who himself volunteers for work-bees at a folk organization outside Madison. Students who plant a tree on campus come back year after year to see how it is doing, he observes. To encourage this kind of physical connection with the land, he led volunteers on a work project recently to cut out exotic plants that are crowding out native species in the woods on campus. He has also received permission to organize some members of the staff, who work in the science building, to plant and care for native species nearby. And some of his students have gone out into the woods on campus and driven stakes into the ground to take surveys of all plants, shrubs, and trees within a twenty-foot radius. Their intention is to turn this into a long-term survey so that future generations will understand how the local flora are changing.

This hands-on learning approach spills over into Eagan's seminar, where he sometimes asks his students to sort through the trash and recycling bins at the student union. Trash-sorting teaches them at first hand what materials are going into the trash that could be recycled, and what trash is contaminating the recycling bins. This information can then be used to devise strategies for reducing the waste stream.

While the campus environment may seem an obvious focus for study, in fact it is often ignored, says Eagan, who peers out from behind steel-rim glasses. "Professors are famous for knowing everything there is to know about the tropical rain forest but almost nothing about what is growing from the soil right outside their windows," he continues. In an effort to reverse this trend, he started a collection of insects and lichen that inhabit the campus. And he invited Douglas Thiessen, the university pest control specialist, to talk to his class. Thiessen, who describes himself as the un-official campus wildlife manager, told students that his philosophy is, "if insects or animals aren't bugging anyone, then leave them alone."

Eagan is also keen to have students acknowledge their own contribution to environmental degradation and the wasting of precious resources. Dorms across America have had to be rewired and energy consumption has soared, he notes, as students have brought to school personal computers, printers, TVs, mini-fridges, microwaves, hair-dryers, and sound systems. It is always less painful to look at problems that other people create than those we are responsible for ourselves, he observes. In an effort at self-examination, one team of students in Eagan's seminar looked into areas on campus where the grass had been trampled by students cutting across the green. After conferring with members of the grounds crew, the students planted native plants in these areas to try to alter student herd behavior.

To ensure that the information students collect in their projects is compiled for future use, Eagan has compiled a library of research papers on various aspects of the campus environment. The papers have been indexed so that one can now see the breadth of subjects already investigated. There are papers on pesticide use, biohazardous waste disposal at the veterinary building, disposal of wood pallets, the use of individual paper packets of sugar in the student union, the pros and cons of paper towels vs. hot-air hand dryers, the handling of toxic materials in the Art Department, student light-switching behavior in bathrooms, and a host of other issues.

While many student groups around the country have done environmental audits of their campus, Eagan prefers to see this compilation of student research as an environmental profile of the university. "The word audit is very confrontational. If you audit someone, you are looking for something that is wrong. The IRS does audits. We do assessments or profiles," he says. "I don't want to sneak up on anybody and embarrass them," he adds. "We are not taking an adversarial approach and trying to find dirty linen on campus. My position is that we are all in this together; it is not just us against them." So, rather than march into the Chancellor's office with a master plan to reform the university overnight, Eagan and Einstein have mapped out a long-term campaign, in which gains can be made one step at a time.

"Although it requires a stretch of the imagination," Eagan writes, "campus environmental stewardship offers students the opportunity to contribute to the construction of a new sort of monument—a sustainable campus."

DIALOGUE

1. What do you know about the natural history of your college campus? What distinctive environmental features and issues would need to be addressed to shape a sustainable campus at your college?
2. To what extent are problems of energy waste and environmental degradation caused by students? To what extent are they caused by administrative neglect? Whose responsibility is it to solve them?
3. Consider the environmental features and issues you noted in question 1. Select one problem with your campus environment that you think would be fairly easy and inexpensive to solve and whose solution would contribute significantly to the quality of life on campus. Then answer the following questions:
    a. What preliminary data need to be collected to understand the exact nature of the problem?
    b. What are the most serious obstacles to a solution of the problem?
    c. What resources are needed to solve the problem?
    d. What are the benefits of solving the problem?

WRITING TOPICS

1. To what extent are you an activist? Do you get involved in causes and projects? Have you joined organizations and volunteered your time? Does the idea of improving the quality of your campus environment inspire the activist in you? Based on how you spend your free time, what things do you care most about?
2. Try to locate campus environmentalists on the World Wide Web. If no listserv or web site exists, start one. Survey the environmental activism at several campuses and compare the results in a report.
3. Survey students at your college to determine their interest in becoming involved in programs to clean up the campus environment. Prepare several questions to ask each person. Draw conclusions about the level of interest and willingness to get involved in these issues on your campus.

INTERACTION

What examples of energy waste, pollution, and environmental neglect have you observed on your campus? Working in small groups, brainstorm a list of such abuses and then create a campus environmental assessment by combining all groups' lists.

Part III Reflections

Review the ideas you expressed at the beginning of this part in "Write Before You Read." How have your ideas changed as a result of reading the articles in this part? Explain in the space below.

1. Your initial impressions of your campus and fellow students _____

_____

_____

_____

_____

_____

2. Activities you'd like to pursue outside of class _____

_____

_____

_____

_____

3. Your attitude toward volunteerism and academic service learning ___

_____

_____

_____

_____

_____

Part III Writing Assignment

Develop a student bill of rights—a list of five to ten essential liberties for college students. Provide a rationale for each right you list. Operate on the assumption that your list will require approval by the Faculty Senate and Student Senate. Show your rough draft to at least five students and one faculty member, ask for feedback, and revise your draft accordingly.

Part IV

Sex and Relationships

INTRODUCTION

As if the academic challenge of the first year of college were not enough, the lives of college students also are complicated by their personal relationships. The process of maintaining, developing, and defining meaningful relationships can be deeply satisfying, but it can be draining, too. Success in a relationship, like success in the classroom, takes hard work.

Male-female relationships have been complicated in recent years by the feminist movement and the close scrutiny of gender roles it has inspired. The feminist demand for equality in American society is at least as old as the biological idea that there are fundamental genetic differences between men and women and that these differences limit opportunities: a man lacks the opportunity, for example, to bear a child; women, on average, are smaller and physically weaker than men. But the challenge of achieving gender equity is not to deny or eliminate the intrinsic differences between the sexes, but to transform a world that has been designed by men according to male needs.

Julia T. Wood, professor of communication studies at the University of North Carolina, discusses the differences between men and women in "Gendered Close Relationships," the first essay in this part. Men are taught to be strong, independent, aggressive, and emotionally reserved. Women are trained for nurturing, emotional connectedness and openness, responsiveness, and support. Because men and women are socialized differently, their perspectives on issues are often diametrically opposed and may lead to conflict. Understanding the difference between the sexes is an important first step in establishing a strong relationship.

Biological differences between men and women—the out-of-control hormones of nineteen-year-old males and female teasing and coquetry—are often used as explanations and justifications for incidents of violent sexual assault, often called date rape or acquaintance rape, on college campuses. Although the extent of the problem is difficult to determine—partly because many college women who have been raped are too frightened to report it, partly because there is no commonly accepted definition of rape, and partly because the statistical base is unreliable and easily manipulated for political ends—there is no question that date rape is a major problem on American campuses. In "College Women Should Take Precautions Against Date Rape," Pamela Cantor, a columnist for the *Los Angeles Times*, offers some sensible advice to young women: remain in control and don't accompany your "no" with sugarcoated kisses.

Myra and David Sadker's "Higher Education: Colder by Degrees" describes the barriers college women face in an institution created by men and still dominated by them today. The essay is taken from their

1994 book *Failing at Fairness: How America's Schools Cheat Girls*, a power-ful indictment of our educational system. The Sadkers describe how girls are marginalized and discriminated against from infancy through gradu-ate school, often by well-meaning parents, teachers, and administrators whose values are themselves the products of a system designed by men for men.

The goal of affirmative action has always been the full integration of women and underrepresented minorities into the mainstream of Ameri-can life. In "Separate Is Better," Susan Estrich argues that women and girls actually learn better when they are separated by gender. Girls' schools and private women's colleges, she reminds us, offer an abun-dance of same-sex role models and a support network that reinforces self-esteem, an indispensable ingredient in learning and personal growth.

Barbara Kantrowitz identifies computer culture as yet another world created, inhabited, and ruled by men in "Men, Women, and Computers." Whereas women are primarily attracted by what computers can do, men are attracted by the technology itself. The male love affair with automo-biles is mirrored in their desire to continually add accessories and in-crease the power and memory of their computers. And in listservs and bulletin boards, women contributors are routinely belittled and "flamed" (chased away by nasty messages).

In "Television Insults Men, Too," Bernard R. Goldberg points out that gender stereotypes hurt everyone, male and female alike. The efforts of television producers to reach out to female audiences (motivated largely by financial rather than moral interests) all too often result in male-bashing scripts that portray men as vain, lazy, beer-guzzling slobs.

Gender bias, homophobia, and racial prejudice are harmful because they deny a person's humanity. Although gender, sexual preference, and race are important cultural identifiers—perhaps even the most important aspect of a person's identity—we are, above all, human beings. The "per-son first" terminology that emerged with the passage of the Americans with Disabilities Act in 1990 offers a useful guide as we interact with peo-ple who are different from us. Just as we can learn to refer to the blind as "people with impaired vision," we can accustom ourselves to putting the *person* first, rather than the person's gender, sexual orientation, race, reli-gion, or other aspect of cultural identity.

Write Before You Read

A. After you've read the introduction, take a few minutes to survey the contents of this part. Then write three questions you expect will be answered in the course of your reading.

1. _____

    _____

2. _____

    _____

3. _____

    _____

B. Briefly reflect on each of the following topics. Then write freely and rapidly about what you already know about the topic, relevant experiences you have had, and any opinions you have formed about it.

1. How the opposite sex is different _____

    _____

    _____

    _____

    _____

    _____

2. Date rape_____

    _____

    _____

    _____

3. "Men only" or "women only" schools and organizations_____

Gendered Close Relationships
Julia T. Wood

PREVIEW

The field of gender studies has mushroomed over the past twenty years. Profound changes in work patterns and gender roles, a better understanding of the spectrum of sexual behavior and preference, increased awareness of the alarming extent of homophobia and violence against women, and recent studies of the human brain have prompted a growing body of research on gender and sex differences. In "Gendered Close Relationships," Julia T. Wood explains how these differences affect friendships and romantic relationships. Wood is Nelson R. Hairston Professor of Communication Studies at the University of North Carolina–Chapel Hill.

SOURCE: Adapted from Julia T. Wood, *Gendered Lives: Communication, Gender, and Culture* (Wadsworth, 1994), pp. 179–186; 188–189; 191; 201–203. Copyright © 1994 by Wadsworth Publishing Co. Reprinted by permission of Wadsworth Publishing Co. and the author.

PAIGE: Honestly, I almost left my boyfriend when we had our first fight after moving in together. It was really a big one about how to be committed to our relationship and also do all the other stuff that we have to do. It was major. And after we'd yelled and all for a while, there seemed to be nothing else to do—we were just at a stalemate in terms of conflict between what each of us wanted. So Ed walked away, and I sat fuming in the living room. When I finally moved out, I found him working away on a paper for one of his courses, and I was furious. I couldn't understand how he could concentrate on work when we were so messed up. How in the world could he just put us aside and get on with his work? I felt like it was a really clear message that he wasn't very committed.

MARK: Sometimes I just don't know what goes on in Ellen's head. We can have a minor problem—like an issue between us, and it's really not serious stuff. But can we let it go? No way with Ellen. She wants "to talk about it." And I mean talk and talk and talk and talk. There's no end to how long she can talk about stuff that really doesn't matter. I tell her that she's analyzing the relationship to death and I don't want to do that. She insists that we need "to talk things through." That may work for her, but, honestly, it makes no sense to me. Why can't we just have a relationship, instead of always having to talk about it?

Perhaps you have found yourself in situations such as those Mark and Paige describe. If you are a man, Mark's predicament may remind you of ones in your own life. If you are a woman, Paige's frustrations may be more familiar to you. What they describe reflects gendered orientations toward close relationships. For Mark, as with most people socialized into masculinity, the purpose of talking is to accomplish some goal or solve some problem; for his partner, talking about the relationship is a primary means to intimacy. Paige cannot understand how Ed could concentrate on his paper when there is a problem between them; for Ed, the paper is a way to distract himself from something that matters very much. If Paige and Ed and Mark and Ellen do not figure out that their gendered view-

141

points are creating misunderstandings, they will continue to find themselves at cross purposes.

Of the many relationships we form, only a few become close and personal. These are the ones that occupy a special place in our lives and affect us more than the other less important associations we have. Close relationships are ones that endure over time and in which participants depend on one another for various things from support to material assistance.

Gender and Closeness

There are notable differences in the ways women and men generally approach close relationships. Distinctive expectations, interaction patterns, and ways of interpreting others reflect gendered identities and communication styles. We know that masculine socialization emphasizes independence, instrumental activity, aggression and emotional reserve, and use of talk to gain status and control. In contrast, feminine socialization fosters interconnections with others, emotional disclosiveness, responsiveness and support of others, and use of communication to build and sustain relationships. What do these differences mean? While some scholars argue that men's interpersonal styles are inferior to women's, others think the two styles are distinct yet equally valid.

Based on a long-standing cultural definition of women as "relationship experts," our society tends to regard women as more interpersonally sensitive and competent than men. Because women are perceived as relationship experts, their ways of forming relationships and interacting with others are presumed to be "the right ways." Operating from this premise, a number of researchers consider men's ways of relating to be inadequate. This view, the **male deficit model,** maintains that men are not adept at intimacy because they are less interested and/or able than women to disclose emotions, reveal personal information, and engage in communication about intimate topics.

The **alternate paths model** agrees with the male deficit model that gendered socialization is the root of differences in women's and men's typical styles of interacting. It departs from the deficit model, however, in important ways. First, the alternate paths viewpoint does not presume that men lack feelings and emotional depth, nor that relationships and feelings are unimportant in men's lives. Rather, this explanation suggests that masculine socialization constrains men's comfort in verbally expressing feelings and, further, that it limits men's opportunities to practice emotional talk. A second important distinction is that the alternate paths model argues that men *do* express closeness in ways that they value and understand—ways that may differ from those of feminine individuals but that are nonetheless valid.

The safest conclusion may be that males generally do not express their feelings in feminine ways, just as women tend not to express theirs in masculine ways. This suggests some men may find that intimate talk doesn't make them feel close, just as some women feel that instrumental demonstrations of commitment are disappointing. This may be a case in which the genders really do have different languages. If so, then becoming bilingual is a necessity for healthy relationships. Understanding alternative ways of creating and sustaining intimacy empowers us to create and participate in a range of connections with others who matter to us.

Differences Between Men's and Women's Friendships

As early as 1982, Paul Wright pointed to interaction style as a key difference between women's and men's friendships. He noted that women tend to engage each other face to face, while men usually interact side by side. By this, Wright meant that women communicate directly and verbally with each other to share themselves and their feelings. Men more typically share activities and interests with friends. Wright suggested that what is central to friendship differs between the sexes: for men, it tends to be doing things together; for women, being and talking together is the essence of close, personal relationships.

The fact that women use talk as a primary way to develop relationships and men generally do not underlies four gender-linked patterns in friendship. First, communication is central to women friends, while ac-

> JANICE: One of the worst things about being female is not having permission to be selfish or jealous or *not* to care about a friend. Usually, I'm pretty nice and I feel good for my friends when good things happen to them, and I want to support them when things aren't going well. But sometimes I don't feel that way. Like right now, all my friends and I are interviewing for jobs, and my best friend just got a great offer. I've had 23 interviews and nothing so far. I felt good for Sally, but I also felt jealous. I couldn't talk about this with her, because I'm not supposed to feel jealous or be selfish like this. It's just not allowed, so my friends and I have to hide those feelings.

tivities are the primary focus of men's friendships. Second, talk between women friends tends to be expressive and disclosive, focusing on details of personal lives, people, relationships, and feelings; talk in men's friendships generally revolves around less personal topics such as sports, events, money, music, and politics. Third, in general, men assume a friendship's value and seldom discuss it, while women are likely to talk about the dynamics of their relationship. Finally, women's friendships generally appear to be broader in scope than those of men.

> JOEL: The best thing about guys' friendships is that you can just relax and hang out together. With women you have to be on—intense, talking all the time—but with guys you can just be comfortable. It's not like we're not close, but we don't have to talk about it or about our lives all the time like girls do. It's more laid back and easygoing. I don't know about other guys, but I feel a lot closer to guys than to *girls*.

> LEE: I don't know what girls get out of sitting around talking about problems all the time. What a downer. When something bad happens to me, like I blow a test or break up with a girl, the last thing I want is to talk about it. I already feel bad enough. What I want is something to distract me from how lousy I feel. That's where having buddies really matters. They know you feel bad and help you out by taking you out drinking or starting a pickup game or something that gets your mind off the problems. They give you breathing room and some escape from troubles; girls just wallow in troubles.

Gender and Intimacy

Nowhere else are cultural expectations of masculinity and femininity so salient as in romantic relationships. The cultural script for romance stipulates a number of "rules" that are well known to us. First, the romantic idea promoted by our culture is decidedly heterosexual, which excludes gay and lesbian couples, although they make up at least 10% of the population. The cultural script also specifies other things: women should be attracted to men, and men should be attracted to women; more feminine women and more masculine men are desirable; men should initiate, plan, and direct activities and have greater power within the relationship; women should facilitate conversation, generally defer to men, but control sexual behavior; men should excel in status and earning money, and women should assume primary responsibility for the relationship, the home, and the children; men should be autonomous, and women should depend on men. This heavily gendered cultural script is well understood by most people.

The conventional heterosexual dating script calls for women to be passive and men to take initiative. Although many people, especially women, claim not to believe in these gender stereotypes, research suggests that most heterosexuals conform to them. Conformity seems to reflect both our internalized sense of how we are supposed to be and the belief that the other sex expects us to meet cultural gender ideals. Thus, women tend to play feminine and men tend to play masculine, each reflecting and perpetuating established social views of gender.

Is one gender more romantic than the other? Contrary to folklore, research indicates men tend to fall in love sooner and harder than women do. The cultural gender script that calls for men to initiate may explain why they take the lead in declaring love. There are also differences in what love generally means to women and men. For men, it tends to be more active, impulsive, sexualized, and game playing than for women, whose styles of loving are more pragmatic and friendship focused. For instance, men may see love as taking trips to romantic places, spontaneously making love, and engaging in ploys to surprise a partner. Women might more typically think of quiet, extended conversation in front of a fire or a general comfort and security in each other's presence.

Relationships that continue and deepen—whether they are heterosexual, lesbian, or gay—typically progress through stages of initiating, intensifying (falling in love), working out problems, and making a commitment. Over time, couples work out norms for interacting, and they create private cultures. While each couple forms a unique private culture, generalizable gendered patterns are evident. Despite efforts to increase equality between the sexes, enduring heterosexual love relationships, in general, continue to reflect traditional gender roles endorsed by the culture. Men tend to be perceived as the "head of the family" and the major breadwinner; women tend to assume primary responsibility for domestic labor and child care; and men tend to have greater power.

Committed Relationships

Once two people commit to a future of intimacy, partners develop patterns of interaction that reflect their desires for a loving relationship.

Complicating their efforts are gendered identities, which incline women and men toward distinct understandings of how to create and communicate closeness.

SABRINA: To tell you the truth, even if my sexual preference were for men, I think I'd live with a woman. I've tried both sides of the track, and there's no comparison in the two kinds of relationship. When I used to date men and have relationships with them, I was always the one who had to do the caring. I had to prop them up emotionally and take care of them. They never did that for me. I had to point out when there was an issue in the relationship we needed to work out, and they still dragged their feet. By now I've had several serious relationships with women, and it's a different world. My partner right now is just as caring as I am. I don't get drained by doing it all, and neither does she. And relationship problems don't fester either, because both of us see them and want to do something about them.

Gendered modes of expressing care. As we have seen, women generally create and express closeness through personal talk, while men rely more on instrumental activities. This difference complicates heterosexual partners' efforts to achieve intimacy. A. W. Schaef has noted that "women are often hurt in relationships with men because they totally expose their beings and do not receive respect and exposure in return." Conversely, men may be threatened or resentful when women want them to be more emotionally expressive than they find comfortable. To many men, intensely personal talk feels more intrusive than loving.

For women, ongoing conversation about feelings and daily activities is a primary way to express and enrich connections between people. Communication processes are the core of the relationship. The masculine speech communities in which most men are socialized, however, regard the function of talk as solving problems and achieving goals. Thus, unless there is some problem, men often find talking about a relationship pointless, while women are more likely to feel that continuing conversation is the best way to keep problems from developing. These mismatched views of talking pave the way for misunderstandings, hurt, and dissatisfaction.

Modes of expressing closeness further reflect and reproduce gender by the different ways men and women tend to demonstrate they care.

C. K. Riessman maintains that, for women, closeness is identified with "communicating deeply and closely." The instrumental focus encouraged in men motivates them to show affection by doing things with or for others.

Not only are modes of expressing caring generally different for women and men, but there is a cultural bias favoring the feminine style. This goes back to the Industrial Revolution, which took men away from homes and bifurcated life into public and private spheres. According to F. Cancian, "With the split between home and work and the polarization of gender roles, love became a feminine quality." Since that time, love has been measured by a "feminine ruler," which assumes that women's ways of loving are *the right ways.*

Gay men, like their heterosexual counterparts, tend to engage in little emotional and intimate dialogue and do not process their relationship constantly. Lesbians, on the other hand, generally create the most expressive and nurturant communication climates of any type of couple, since both partners are socialized into feminine forms of interaction and, thus, value talk as a means of expressing feelings and creating closeness. Lesbian partners' mutual attentiveness to nurturing and emotional closeness may explain why, as a group, lesbian relationships are more satisfying than gay or heterosexual ones.

Gendered needs for autonomy and connection. Autonomy and connection are two basic needs of all humans. What may differ is how much of each of these we want and how partners coordinate preferences. Masculine individuals tend to want greater autonomy and less connection than feminine persons. It is not that men want *only* autonomy and women want *only* connection. Both genders tend to want both, yet the proportionate weights women and men assign to autonomy and connection generally differ.

Desires for different degrees of autonomy and connection frequently generate friction in close relationships, particularly heterosexual ones. Many couples are familiar with a pattern called "demand-withdraw" or "pursuer-distancer." The dynamic of this pattern is that one partner (usually the woman) seeks emotional closeness through disclosive, intimate communication, and the other partner (usually a man) withdraws from a degree of closeness that stifles his need for autonomy. The more one pursues, the more the other distances; the more one withdraws from interaction, the more the other demands talk and time together. Socialized toward independence, masculine individuals need some distance to feel comfortable, while feminine persons feel closeness is jeopardized and they are rejected when a partner retreats from intimate talk. While the pursuer-distancer pattern may persist in relationships, we may eliminate the poison of misinterpretation by respecting different needs for autonomy and connection.

Responsibility for relational health.   Sharing responsibility for safeguarding a relationship lessens the pressure on each partner and also reduces the potential for conflict over investing in the relationship. The expectation that one person should take care of relationships inequitably burdens one partner, while exempting the other person from responsibility. In addition, it is difficult for one person to meet relationship responsibilities if a partner does not acknowledge and work on matters that jeopardize relational health. What can happen is that the partner expected to safeguard the relationship is perceived as a nag by someone who fails to recognize problems until they become very serious. This can separate intimates into what J. Bernard (1972) years ago called "his marriage" and "her marriage," a situation in which spouses have different, often conflicting views of their relationship. Separation and the tension it generates are less likely when both partners take responsibility for the health of their commitment.

Gendered power dynamics.   All relationships involve power issues, and these particularly reflect gender patterns. The social view of women as less powerful than men carries over into intimacy. Even in the 1990s, traditional views of male dominance remain relatively intact in the perceptions of intimate partners. Both women and men believe that men should be more powerful, and this varies only slightly when a female partner's job equals a male's in prestige and salary.

Consistent with social prescriptions for masculinity, men are expected to have higher job status and earn greater salaries than women. When this expectation is not met, many heterosexual couples either experience dissatisfaction or engage in a variety of rationalizations to convince themselves the husbands are of greater status and value. The pressure for men to be primary breadwinners is especially arduous for African-Americans, since job discrimination makes it difficult for many African-American men to earn enough to support families.

Responsibility for domestic chores and care of children and other relatives, by and large, is still carried entirely or predominantly by women, regardless of whether they work outside of the home. In only 20% of dual-worker families do husbands contribute equally to homemaking and child care. Further, it is almost always women who assume responsibility for parents and in-laws who need assistance. The amount of housework and child care that husbands do has risen only 10% (from 20% to 30%) in nearly three decades. The inequity of the arrangement is a primary source of resentment and dissatisfaction, especially for women, and of marital instability. Marital stability is more closely tied to equitable divisions of housework and child care than to a couple's income.

Another clue to power dynamics is whose preferences prevail when partners differ. Research repeatedly finds that in both spouses' minds, husbands' preferences usually count more than those of wives on everything from how often to engage in sexual activity to who does the housework. Further, we know that masculine individuals (whether female or male) tend to use more unilateral strategies to engage in and to avoid conflicts. Feminine individuals more typically try to please, defer, submit, or compromise to reduce tension, and they employ indirect strategies when they do engage in conflict.

More than feminine or androgynous persons, individuals with masculine identities tend to deny problems or to exit situations of conflict, thus enacting the masculine tendency to maintain independence and protect the self. Feminine persons, in contrast, tend to initiate discussion of problems and stand by in times of trouble. As you might suspect, the tension between masculine and feminine ways of exerting influence is less pronounced in lesbian relationships, where equality is particularly high. For gay partners, power struggles are especially common, sometimes being a constant backdrop in the relationship.

Finally, gendered power dynamics underlie violence and abuse, which are means of exercising dominance over others. Mounting evidence demonstrates that violence and abuse are not rare but are fairly common in relationships. Not confined to any single group, violence cuts across race, ethnic, and class lines. Researchers estimate that at least 28% and possibly as many as 50% of women suffer physical abuse from partners, and even more suffer psychological abuse.

Violence is strongly linked to gender in two ways. First, it is inflicted primarily by those most frequently socialized into masculine identities: Less than 5% of violence against a partner is committed by women. In the United States, a women is beaten every 12 seconds by a man, and four women are beaten to death daily.

Cross-cultural research indicates that partner abuse, like rape, is lowest in societies that have ideologies of sexual equality and harmony among people and with nature; it is most frequent in cultures that are stratified by sex and that believe in male dominance of women. Like rape, battering and abuse seem to be promoted by cultural ideals linking masculinity with aggression, strength, control, and domination.

*   *   *

Close relationships reflect the distinctive expectations and interpersonal orientations encouraged by feminine and masculine socialization. In turn, these are evident in four processes central to intimacy: how partners express and experience caring, preferences for balances of autonomy and connection, responsibility for maintaining relationships, and power dynamics. Each of these dimensions of close relationships is deeply influenced by the gendered identities of participants in friendships and romantic commitments.

Social definitions of friendship and intimacy reflect traditional stereotypes of men's and women's roles so that men are expected to have more power and status, require more autonomy, and assume less responsibility for domestic and caretaking duties than women.

While these gendered patterns may work for some, they are not satisfying to growing numbers of people. As friends and committed partners discover the limits and disadvantages of traditional gender roles, they are experimenting with new ways to form and sustain relationships. For instance, men who are single fathers or who devote themselves to caring for their parents heighten their abilities to empathize and provide comfort, and they create rich, intimate relationships with others that traditional prescriptions for masculinity precluded. Women who pursue substantial careers develop senses of increased personal agency and confidence in their judgment and value. Illustrations such as these remind us that we can venture beyond conventional definitions of identity and relationships if we choose to. In so doing, we edit cultural scripts, using our own lives as examples of alternative visions of women, men, and the kinds of relationships they may form with each other. By contributing these to the cultural collage, we enrich our individual and interpersonal lives and the social fabric as a whole.

DIALOGUE

1. Julia T. Wood makes a number of generalized statements about close relationships. Do you agree with all her statements and conclusions? On which points do you agree or disagree? Why?
2. To what extent are Wood's insights about relationships reflected in American society? How are close relationships represented in movies, television, tabloid media, politics, sports, and the business world?
3. Do you have a stronger need for autonomy (independence, privacy) or for connection (talk, sharing)? Have you found ways to negotiate these needs in your close relationships, or are they a continuing source of conflict? Why?

WRITING TOPICS

1. What does Wood mean when she says "becoming bilingual is a necessity for healthy relationships"?
2. Wood suggests that each couple forms a "unique private culture" that responds to problems, develops patterns of intimacy, and evolves rules for interaction and communication. Describe the ideal components of the private culture that you would like to have in a close relationship. What roles would each of you play to achieve your idealized relationship?
3. Describe patterns you have observed in your parents' attitudes and behaviors with regard to:
   a. the expression and experience of caring
   b. preferences for autonomy and connection
   c. responsibility for maintaining the relationship
   d. power dynamics.

   Analyze how the attitudes of your own generation differ from those of your parents' generation in the preceding four areas.

INTERACTION

Working in groups, discuss the following dimensions of the cultural script for romance that Wood outlines in her section "Gender and Intimacy." Are these expectations and "rules" applicable to you? To a broad cross section of society? Draw conclusions about the general applicability and accuracy of the following cultural expectations for romantic relationships:

a. *The romantic idea promoted by our culture is decidedly heterosexual.*

b. *Women should be attracted to men, and men should be attracted to women.*

c. *More feminine women and more masculine men are desirable.*

d. *Men should initiate, plan, and direct activities within the relationship.*

e. *Women should facilitate conversation and generally defer to men but control sexual behavior.*

f. *Men should excel in status and earning money.*

g. *Women should assume primary responsibility for the relationship, the home, and the children.*

h. *Men should be autonomous, and women should depend on men.*

College Women Should Take Precautions Against Date Rape

Pamela Cantor

PREVIEW

During the past decade, there has been a heightened awareness on American college campuses of the frequency and seriousness of acquaintance rape or date rape. How serious is the problem? One study found that 7 percent of the women on thirty-two campuses had been sexually assaulted during the previous year. Other studies show figures as high as 40 percent. In all studies, a disproportionately high percentage of acquaintance rape cases involved first-year students.

Pamela Cantor is a health and fitness columnist for the Los Angeles Times. *In this column, she offers sensible advice to a young woman who described a rape that took place in a fraternity house on her campus and then asked, "How can I figure this out and protect myself?"*

Two-thirds of rapes occur with the victim knowing her attacker. Three-fourths of the victims live on a college campus and that means that about three-fourths of the attackers are educated young men. Rape is not something that only happens on desolate streets but more often happens in bars or at parties.

Women and girls under the age of twenty-four account for 83 percent of the rape victims, but the actual number of rapes is higher than the reported number because many young women are too frightened, too ashamed, or too concerned that they will be blamed and stigmatized.

In almost all of these episodes, alcohol is a factor. Alcohol, however, does not cause one person to rape another. A person who is not going to rape does not become a rapist because he drinks. Alcohol does loosen inhibitions and it does make self-control more difficult.

Peer pressure also contributes to the incidence of rape on campuses. Rape most often occurs when there is an all-male group, such as a fraternity or a sports team, and where alcohol is consumed in large quantities.

SOURCE: Pamela Cantor, "College Women Should Take Precautions Against Date Rape," Los Angeles Times as reprinted in *The Ann Arbor News*, June 13, 1995. Copyright, 1995, Los Angeles Times. Reprinted by permission.)

The root cause of rape is the attitudes toward women that still prevail because men have been socialized to believe they should have power over women and that they are entitled to sex.

Men who believe they have never raped a woman might readily admit they have forced someone to have sex. Men are taught to be "pushy" with women, to go as far as they are allowed and never to pass up an opportunity to have sex. The female is supposed to know when the situation has gone far enough and be responsible for stopping the guy.

How can one female stop four males or an entire sports team?

The stereotype that men must act like sex-starved animals and that they must take advantage of every opportunity is as absurd as the stereotype that women must be demure, controlled, and uninterested.

In relationships, both people have feelings. But gang rape or date rape does not involve consent; it involves conquest, or challenge, or violence. If a woman flirts, that does not mean she is asking for sex—she may just be letting a man know she likes him. Many women want to refrain from sex entirely, some until marriage and some until they have an important relationship. Wherever the line is drawn, for a woman, having sex against her wishes can mean a lifetime of shame, while for a man it is often just an event. Forcing a woman to have sex against her wishes is never, ever, excusable.

The best way to protect yourself is to remain in control. That means not drinking to excess. It means not hanging out in a fraternity house with a bunch of guys who are drinking with no other women around. Do not put yourself in a position of sitting around watching pornographic films with a bunch of guys. While you and I understand that watching videos does not mean you consent to sex, the guys might not understand or might not want to understand. You could end up suffering and justifying your behavior in front of a jury. Try to choose your dates wisely and be wary of anyone who wants to get you drunk or acts strangely.

I am not saying that date rape is a woman's responsibility, but I am saying that it is wise to take precautions to ensure your own safety.

When you say "no," do not coat it with sugar kisses. This is a mixed message that allows a man to justify his pursuit with the excuse of confusion. If you mean "yes," say "yes." Women have the need for affection and sexual expression just as men do. If women want to stop being "conquered" or seen as "conquests," they have to stop playing a game with sex. If you mean "no," say "no." And do not put yourself in a place where you will be alone or with a gang of men—or even one man—if you are uncomfortable with a sexual encounter.

It is a shame to think that our most educated young men are the ones who are perpetuating the most animal-like and least socialized behaviors on women and making them suffer for the rest of their lives.

DIALOGUE

1. In what ways is the root cause of rape related to prevailing attitudes that men have toward women?
2. Why do you think date rape is underreported?
3. Does American society show a special tolerance for certain groups of men (fraternity members, sports stars) who abuse women? Do you believe these individuals tend to be less sensitized than other populations to the crime of sexual assault? Or have they been unfairly singled out? Explain your answer.

WRITING TOPICS

1. Write a short definition of rape and consider whether your definition takes into account the feelings, perceptions, and reactions of the victim or restricts itself to the behaviors of the perpetrator.
2. Articles on date rape cite contradictory statistics on its frequency among college women: one in four, one in seven, one in ten. Reflect on how serious you think the problem is and why it is so difficult to get definitive statistics.
3. Design an effective program to address the problem of date rape on your campus. What steps should students and college officials take to ensure the personal safety of women on campus? Propose at least three constructive steps.

INTERACTION

Divide into groups and briefly debate each of the following statements:

a. *Most women on this campus are capable of taking care of themselves.*

b. *Most women on this campus are vulnerable, naive, and easily manipulated.*

c. *Women will always be in sexual danger.*

d. *The sexes are at war.*

e. *A girl who lets herself get dead drunk at a fraternity party is a fool.*

f. *Most college men have only one thing on their minds.*

g. *Today's young women don't know what they want.*

h. *The only solution to date rape is female self-awareness and self-control.*

Higher Education: Colder by Degrees
Myra and David Sadker

PREVIEW

Although girls routinely outperform boys in elementary school, their scores on standardized tests begin to decline in middle school, and by the time they graduate from high school, they trail well behind boys, a process that continues in college and beyond. Why? Myra and David Sadker, two distinguished social scientists from American University, devoted twenty years of research to finding an answer. In Failing at Fairness: How America's Schools Cheat Girls, *they provide a multitude of sobering answers, describing a deeply ingrained pattern of gender discrimination in American families, schools, and society. Girls are taught, often in subtle ways, to be quiet, passive, obedient, neat, and respectful of authority. They are gently urged into the humanities, education, and health fields, and away from math, science, engineering, and medicine—the "hard" sciences traditionally reserved for boys. The following passage, from Chapter 7 ("Higher Education: Colder by Degrees") of the Sadkers' book, describes how this pattern is perpetuated in college.*

The Divided Campus

Graduation day is a family milestone, official recognition of full and active partnership in the American Dream. Parents crowd the bookstore to buy sweatshirts and baseball caps emblazoned with school insignia.

SOURCE: Myra and David Sadker, "Higher Education: Colder by Degrees." Reprinted with the permission of Scribner, a Division of Simon & Schuster from *Failing at Fairness: How America's Schools Cheat Girls* by Myra & David Sadker. Copyright © 1994 Myra Sadker and David Sadker.

Even the car shows its colors with college decal affixed to the window, proclaiming to all the world previous accomplishments and future promise. Amid all this celebration it is easy to forget that little more than a century ago higher education was mainly a man's world.

In the late 1800s college was the place to be for rich young men; it was a source of social polish and a rollicking good time. Informal sporting events and athletic competitions were harbingers of today's lucrative college football and basketball seasons. Fraternities created a world without adult rules, a haven for males in their late teens and early twenties who drank, gambled, and talked about loose women. While a few focused on academics, most worked at fitting in and getting along, the marks of a successful student. In the vernacular of the 1800s, working to win the approval of the professor by class participation was ridiculed as "sticking your neck out" or "fishing." Cheaters were shielded by fraternities and secret societies, and peer loyalty was the measure of integrity.

The first women to enter this male-ordered campus were venturing into unmapped terrain. True pioneers who defied conventions to settle in hostile territory, they were not greeted with open arms or the hospitality accorded welcome guests. At the University of Michigan after the Civil War, women could not join the campus newspaper or college yearbook staffs. Michigaum, the prestigious honor society, closed its doors to females and kept the portals shut throughout the century. Cornell's response to the newcomers was undisguised disgust, and the school excluded them from clubs and social activities. Even speaking to women on campus was an infraction of fraternity rules. At Wesleyan, male students beat other men who talked to women.

When they graduated, these pioneering women cultivated new careers. Many worked in elementary schools or the recently created high schools. By 1918, 84 percent of the nation's teaching force were women, and in this profession they could earn more than unskilled men and could support themselves. Like Jane Addams and her Hull House colleagues, some women became settlement workers in the new profession of social work, while others studied to become doctors. As this wave of college women surged into emerging careers, they often abandoned the traditional life style of marriage and motherhood.

Many college administrators were not ecstatic about these new students. At Stanford, 102 men and 98 women graduated in 1901, but the women received more honors and awards. In 1904, Stanford corrected the problem by setting a quota for future enrollments of three males for every female admitted, a policy maintained until 1933. But the rate of women flooding the nation's colleges could not be halted. In 1870, two out of three postsecondary institutions turned women away; only thirty years later, more than two out of three admitted them; and by 1900, 19 percent of college graduates were female. But as their numbers increased, they became more conventional and less courageous.

The early twentieth century witnessed a second generation of college women who were wealthier, less serious, and more conforming. Rather than blaze new career trails, many of these women saw college as a four-year dating game, prelude to married life. Social activities became central as they formed their own clubs, originally called female fraternities. Barred from leadership positions in the main campus organizations, they created their own newspapers, honor societies, and athletic teams, although these lacked the power and prestige of male clubs and awards.

The choice of their academic major reinforced patterns of campus *apartheid*. Women enrolled in literature, the new social sciences, health courses and the liberal arts, which were particularly popular for those preparing to become teachers. The new field of home economics was created in the late 1800s and grew in popularity through the early part of the twentieth century. Although viewed as the epitome of the status quo, home economics included pioneering courses on the role of women in society, a precursor of today's women's studies programs. On the other side of the campus, men claimed the hard sciences and professions ranging from engineering to agriculture. The curricular lines were drawn, and men and women walked into different classrooms. In coeducational colleges, vocational goals dictated the courses that students chose, and social pressures channeled women and men into different careers.

Women began to realize that their organizations and academic pursuits were not as prestigious as the men's, and they therefore sought to gain prestige by dating the "right" men. Money fueled the dating game: the men financed the cars and entertainment while the women invested in appearance. So much was spent on clothes and makeup that in 1946 one campus reporter observed: "At coeducational colleges the girls generally dress to the teeth . . . [using] all the bait they can for the omnipresent man." College women were judged not by their academic achievements or career goals but by the number and quality of suitors. Wealthy men from the right families and the right fraternities were the most sought-after prizes.

Throughout much of the twentieth century, pursuing men rather than careers made good economic sense. In 1947, for example, 86 percent of male college graduates but only 36 percent of female graduates earned $3,000 or more a year. While 23 percent of college-educated men earned more than $7,750 a year, only 1 percent of women with college degrees earned that much. Most females graduated with teaching degrees and earned not only less than other professionals but also a third less than other teachers who happened to be born male.

From club to classroom, from social status to postgraduation economics, the signs of a second-class college education for women were everywhere. Some women found their limited higher education intolerable and rebelled. In 1919 a young woman arrived at DePauw College anticipating an "intellectual feast." She wrote: "I looked forward to studying fascinating subjects taught by people who understood what they were talking about. I imagined meeting brilliant students, students who would challenge me to stretch my mind and work. . . . In college, in some way that I devoutly believed in but could not explain, I expected to become a person." Instead she discovered fraternity life and football games. Margaret Mead had come up against her first anthropological insight: the male college culture.

After misspent efforts to join a sorority and fit in, Mead was transformed into a college rebel and transferred to Barnard. There she fought not to get into a sorority but to save Sacco and Vanzetti and to destroy the barriers that separated and subjugated women on campus. In the end she provided the college community with the intellectual feast she had so fervently sought.

The trickle of female pioneers fighting for admission to male universities in the 1870s eventually became a tidal wave. A century later most remaining holdouts, including many Ivy League schools, finally capitulated and opened their doors. Today, women are the majority, 53 percent of the nation's postsecondary students, and the barriers once separating the sexes seem to have been demolished. But appearances deceive. The brick walls have been replaced with those of glass; the partitions are so transparent that they are all but invisible. The campus remains a divided one; it channels women and men into different educations that lead to separate and unequal futures.

The "hard" sciences are still housed on the male side of the glass wall. Almost 70 percent of today's students who major in physics, chemistry, and computer science are male. Engineering tops all of these, however, with 85 percent of bachelor degrees going to men. The overwhelmingly male majority extends beyond the hard sciences and engineering to theology (75 percent male), philosophy (64 percent), agriculture (69 percent), and architecture (61 percent).

But it would be a mistake to view the male campus only in terms of academic courses because the heart of extracurricular life beats there, too. Male athletes enjoy an impressive array of "perks," including special meal allowances, exclusive living arrangements, lucrative scholarships, and at all too many institutions, academic dispensation when studies and game schedules conflict. This side of the campus also has valuable real estate, precious land that was turned over to fraternity row. In fact, this is the part of the campus where the lion's share of financial and educational resources are invested.

On the other side of the glass wall, the "soft" sciences and humanities are taught to classes populated mostly by women. On this second campus, females receive 90 percent of the bachelor degrees in home economics, 84 percent in health sciences, and 67 percent in general liberal arts. Here women are awarded three out of every four degrees in education and foreign language, and two out of three in psychology, communications, and the performing arts. On the women's side of the glass wall, class schedules are less likely to include advanced courses in mathematics, science, and technology. If graduation requirements insist on science courses, women typically opt for biology rather than physics or chemistry. Science, after all, is what many worked hard to avoid in high school. Although they pay the same tuition, study in the same libraries, reside in the same dorms, and receive diplomas with the name of the same college, the female students are less likely to take the courses that lead to lucrative and prestigious careers.

Women who move on to graduate and professional schools, where they earn half as many doctorates as men, also discover the divided campus: men receive 75 percent of the doctoral degrees in business and 91 percent of those in engineering, but women acquire more doctorates than men in education. Despite this, three out of every four professors are male, and nine out of ten are white and non-Hispanic. Even prestigious Ivy League schools, the ones with their pick of the most talented women, seem unable to find them. Only 10 percent to 13 percent of Ivy League faculties are female, and they earn on average almost $14,000 less annually than their male colleagues. Nationally, 68 percent of male faculty members have tenure, while only 45 percent of the women enjoy this lifetime job security. It is no secret among faculty members who is valued, vested, and rewarded. Through comments, attitudes, and behavior, the message is clear that female faculty members have second-class citizenship on campus; and this message filters down to the students.

If students somehow miss the salary and tenure subtleties, the power of numbers overwhelms. Ninety-eight percent of the engineering faculty is male. While this is the most extreme imbalance, in every field students see mainly male professors: more than 60 percent in the humanities, 75 percent in business, fine arts, and the social sciences, and 83 percent in the natural sciences. Again, women are best represented in education, but even here, where they claim almost 58 percent of the doctorates, they are only 45 percent of the faculty. Female students who are looking for role models, counselors, and mentors must search long and hard. With Hispanic and African-American women comprising only 1 percent of the faculty, students who are both minority and female receive an even stronger signal of their place on campus. Lacking role models and missing the mentoring connection, college women are less likely to pursue graduate work. The process becomes a continuing cycle: mainly male professors prepare men to become the faculty of the future, and the campus remains divided and unequal.

Every now and then the glass wall separating the two campuses is almost visible. For example, when we visited the school of education at one university, we entered a building and turned right. If we had turned left, we would have arrived at the physics department and met a faculty that was 100 percent male. As we observed students entering the building, it was like watching gender-segregated lines in elementary school: those who turned left for physics were male, those who turned right for the school of education were female.

Sometimes the differences between the two campuses is as simple as turning right or left in a building, but other differences can be observed in a different school: the community college. These two-year institutions offer a less expensive education, but they are also less prestigious. As the prestige factor dips, the proportion of women rises: women hold 47 percent of community college faculty positions and comprise 57 percent of the students.

While females are more likely to attend community colleges, they are less likely to find themselves at the most highly selective schools. Harvard may not be able to list by name the students who will be admitted next year, but it does know that only 40 percent of them will be women. Since females face occupational and income barriers, they will probably earn less than men and therefore will have less to donate to the university. From this perspective, admitting more men who will earn more money may be seen as good business practice. So economic discrimination becomes grounds for admissions discrimination, which in turn leads to further economic discrimination.

Although there are now more female applicants to college, most Ivy League schools also seem hard-pressed to locate acceptable female candidates. Only Columbia University accepts approximately equal numbers of female and male students. The frightening possibility of women comprising the majority of the student body can be reason enough to tinker with the admissions machinery. In 1987, officials at the University of North Carolina noted that more than half of their new students were women. They recommended placing more weight on SAT tests and less on high school grades in order to achieve the "desirable" balance.

Although sex segregation on campus has become a way of life, there are times when students attend classes in equal numbers. The glass walls come down in general subjects required of everybody, courses such as English and political science. In these classrooms, parallel campuses converge, and all students sit in the same rooms, read the same texts, and are taught by the same professors. But even as men and women share the same space, they receive substantially different teaching.

In a Silent Voice

At the highest educational level, where the instructors are the most credentialed and the students the most capable, teaching is the most biased. We discovered this during a two-year grant in which we and a staff of trained raters observed and coded postsecondary classrooms. When we analyzed the data, we discovered how hidden lessons, rooted in elementary school and exacerbated in high school, emerged full-blown in the college classroom. . . .

A visit to the typical college class, which is a stop on the campus tour that most parents never make, shows that students behave as if they, too, are visitors. While 80 percent of pupils in elementary and secondary classes contribute at least one comment in each of their classes, approximately half of the college class says nothing at all. One in two sits through an entire class without ever answering a question, asking one, or making a comment. Women's silence is loudest at college, with twice as many females voiceless. Considering the rising cost of college tuition, the female rule of speech seems to be: the more you pay, the less you say. . . .

At Iowa State, 65 percent of female students said they had been the target of sexist comments, and 43 percent said professors flirted with them. At Harvard University, almost half the women graduate students reported sexual harassment. This is how women described the incidents:

> He came into class, looked directly at me, and announced to everyone, "Your sweater is too tight." I felt terrible. The next week he whispered to me, "You look like you had a tough night." I just dropped this course and had to go to summer school.

> One day this professor requested that I come to his office to discuss a paper. When I arrived, he escorted me to a chair and closed the office door. He walked over to me, put his hands on either side of my face, and told me I was a very beautiful woman. Then he kissed my forehead. We never discussed any of my academic work. . . . I disregarded his constant requests to visit his office and hurriedly left his class. I received my lowest grade in his course.

Joseph Thorpe, a professor at the University of Missouri, knows just how bad it can get. He sent questionnaires to over one thousand women who were recent recipients of psychology doctorates and were members of the American Psychological Association. Thorpe found that many students had been propositioned by their professors. Most of these overtures were turned down, but almost half said they suffered academic penalties for refusing. The survey also revealed that one in every four or five women studying for their psychology doctorates was having sex with the teacher, adviser, or mentor responsible for her academic career. . . .

Out of Sight, Out of Mind

. . . Many college textbooks have withstood the winds of change. From philosophy to psychology, from history to the sciences, students may still learn about a world of male accomplishment and female invisibility. Centuries of recorded history parade before today's college students, but women continue to make only a rare appearance. For example, a classic text in English literature survey courses is the two-volume *Norton Anthology.* Here the culture's great works are collected, and the literary canon is offered to the next generation. Norton has introduced students to centuries of literature: Chaucer, Shakespeare, Milton, Byron, Shelley, Keats, Matthew Arnold, T. S. Eliot; the showcase of male literary accomplishment is extensive. The 3,450 pages of the initial 1962 edition were expanded to 5,000 pages in the 1986 (fifth) edition, where the preface discusses efforts to reflect "contemporary culture." Less than 15 percent of these new pages included women writers. In fact, the percentage of women in the *Norton Anthology* was greater in 1962 than in 1986.

Women in higher education are frequently aware that their lives are left out of books, and they feel excluded from a recorded culture that is not their own. As one student said: "In history we never talked about what women did; in geography it was always what was important to men; it was the same in our English class—we hardly ever studied women authors. I won't even talk about math and science . . . I always felt as though I didn't belong . . . Now I just deaden myself against it so I don't hear it anymore. But I really feel alienated."

We asked our students to analyze the content of their textbooks to see how widespread sex bias was in the books read at our own university. They found psychology, economics, and sociology textbooks that rarely even mentioned a woman's name. One art book included 245 photographs, but only 18 depicted women. Other studies have also noted the slow pace of textbook change, but not all textbooks are frozen in time;

several contain nonsexist language and include males and females in relatively equal numbers. Why such extremes? Unlike elementary and high schools, postsecondary schools do not have committees to evaluate and select books. At the college level, professors choose their own texts and call it academic freedom. For students, it's *caveat emptor*.

The Years of Living Dangerously

. . . Campus rape is more common than college officials care to admit, and they are far less well equipped to deal with it than most parents realize. According to national studies, approximately one in four college women says she has been forced into having sex, and one in six reports having been raped. While most people think of rape as an assault by a violent stranger, in nine out of ten college incidents, the sex is forced by a friend or acquaintance. Victims experience a maelstrom of emotions: shock, disbelief, fear, and depression. They also agonize over every nuance of their own behavior and are likely to find themselves at fault: "How could I have been so wrong about him?" "What did I do to lead him on?" When the perpetrator is a "friend," college women are not even sure they have a right to call the ordeal "rape."

While the victim is at a loss to figure out how it happened, the perpetrator fits a predictable profile. Socialized into the aggressive male role, he believes that women tease and lead him on, that they provoke and enjoy sexual encounters and later cry rape falsely. To these men it is not rape at all but part of a game men and women play. More than one in every three college men believes that a woman who says "no" to sex really means "yes," or at least "maybe." According to one study, a shocking 30 percent of men admitted they would rape a woman if they thought they could get away with it.

Drugs and alcohol trigger sexual violence. Intoxicated men are more likely to be violent, and intoxicated women are less able to resist. This dangerous situation is viewed very differently by females and males. When asked, 'If a woman is heavily intoxicated, is it okay to have sex with her?" only one in fifty women agreed. But one in four college men said that an intoxicated female was an appropriate target for sex. In addition to alcohol or drugs, location and date can be danger factors. Women who find themselves in a man's living quarters, at his party, or even in his car are more vulnerable. So are women who go out with athletes.

Basking in status and popularity, male athletes are like campus nobility. In athletic events and on television, their physical exploits garner glory, network dollars, and alumni contributions. But off the field, physical exploits of a different nature can bring disgrace. The National Institute of Mental Health found athletes involved in one out of every three sexual assaults nationally. At Maryland's Towson State, athletes are five times more likely than others to be involved in gang rapes. A major southern university found that 27 percent of its athletes had threatened women into having sex against their will. . . .

From the Classroom to the Boardroom

. . . While many college women envision compromised careers, others refuse to prepare for second-class employment. They are delaying romance, breaking glass walls, and taking aim at glass ceilings.

In 1970 women represented only 9 percent of medical students. Today they are 39 percent. Forty-three percent of today's law students are female, compared to less than 4 percent just thirty years ago. While these numbers suggest stunning progress, they tell only part of the story. Women entering professional schools may find a world more hostile than their undergraduate college or university campus. For women, higher education gets colder by degrees. . . .

The climate is chilly, to varying degrees, at many law schools around the country. Men still comprise 73 percent of law school faculty members and 85 percent of the full professors. Women are concentrated in the lowest ranks. Of the 178 law school deans, more than 93 percent are male. Gender differences in employment are also striking. In 1991, seven times as many male graduates as female graduates from Yale were scheduled to clerk for a federal appellate court, although women were 40 percent of the graduating class. The typical female lawyer in 1983 earned 89 percent of a male lawyer's income; by 1991 that had dropped to 75 percent. . . .

[In medical schools,] four out of every five professors are male, and at the highest level, full professor, more than 90 percent are men. While all women go about their studies in a distinctly male environment, minority women confront even more alien demographics. In addition to being overwhelmingly male, about 97 percent of medical school faculties are white and non-Hispanic. . . .

Business school enrollments exploded in the 1980s, ignited in large part by tens of thousands of women seeking new opportunities as entrepreneurs, managers, and executives. For many the shortest route to business success had three letters: MBA. But sometimes even the shortest route can be very long. A woman with a master of business administration degree from one of the nation's top twenty business schools in 1990 averaged $54,759 a year, which is a fine salary but still 12 percent less than the $61,400 earned by a man graduating with the same MBA. . . .

*   *   *

As graduation from college or professional school becomes but a memory, work too often turns into a sex-segregated reality. The gender divide begins immediately. During job interviews, women are rated as more qualified than men when they apply for traditionally female jobs, and males receive more favorable evaluations when they interview for "gender-appropriate" careers. Today, women are still only 17 percent of the nation's architects, 9 percent of the clergy, 8 percent of the engineers, 3 percent of the technicians, and 10 percent of the dentists (up approximately 3 percent during the past decade). On the women's side of the glass wall, females comprise 83 percent of librarians, 86 percent of elementary school teachers, 88 percent of speech therapists, 95 percent of registered nurses, and 99 percent of kindergarten and preschool teachers, dental hygienists, and secretaries.

But when glass walls break and women and men work alongside each other, it is like returning to school. The ordinary business meeting offers testimonial to how well lessons have been learned. If we could videotape the typical meeting, freeze it in time and record the dialogue, we would more likely hear the voices of men.

Men dominate workplace conversations just as they controlled classroom discussion. They speak with confidence in declarative sentences. They interrupt others, especially women. They jump in with answers to questions, even those that aren't addressed to them. As if in counterpoint, women speak less at meetings and defer to men, and the phrasing of their contributions is often tentative. And the more men there are at a meeting, the more uncertain and powerless the women become. At work they have mastered the fine art of the muted voice. This is not surprising: it is a lesson they have studied for twelve, sixteen, or more years at school.

There are other inequities as well. The videotape of our hypothetical meeting would likely show men, with their papers spread across the table, sprawled into women's space. By taking over territory, they make nonverbal statements about power, and these are reinforced by the use of touch. Men touch women more often than women touch men. A pat on the back on one level is a friendly gesture of camaraderie. But on another level it signifies power, for we touch things and people we think we can control.

Each of these gestures alone has little impact, but taken together and occurring repeatedly, they create a workplace culture of male dominance and one that is more likely to support and promote men. In a 1993 survey, six out of ten women who work for Congress reported they were taken less seriously than men and were paid less professional attention. Two out of three said they were paid less money, too. As one House aide put it, "Women start at the bottom and rise to the middle. . . . Men start in the middle and rise to the top." And on Capitol Hill as in the workplace nationally, 34 percent of women are affected by sexual harassment. But just like girls at school who face repercussions when they report an incident, women at work, fearing retaliation, often do not come forward.

Sexist lessons transform girls into second-class students. These same lessons resurface at work, where women are listened to less, promoted less, and paid less. Only when their silence is broken in the classroom will women be heard in the boardroom.

DIALOGUE

1. According to the authors, women tend to be less assertive in class than men. Have you found this to be true at your school? Share with your group your observations about male and female classroom behavior.

2. Scan the faculty roster in the mathematics, computing, engineering, and science departments at your college. What is the ratio of men to women? What explanations does the author provide for male dominance in the sciences? What additional reasons can you think of? What can be done to make careers in math and science more attractive to girls and women?

3. How would you design an experiment to prove or disprove the following claims:
   a. Women are featured less prominently than men in college textbooks.
   b. Male professors pay more attention to male students than to female students.
   c. Fraternities occupy more valuable real estate than sororities.
   d. Nine out of ten campus rapes are perpetrated by friends or acquaintances.
   e. Academic advisers and career counselors steer students into "gender-appropriate" majors and careers.
   f. Male students are more vocal in the classroom than female students.

WRITING TOPICS

1. The authors provide several examples of "glass walls" and "glass ceilings." Define each of these terms and clarify how these concepts are similar and different in their application to the workplace.

2. Assume the role of a futurist. Write an essay that projects the status of women in relation to men in higher education, business, and the professions in the year 2020. What kind of social progress would you ex-

pect to observe? Will there be significant and meaningful change for women? What factors will lead to such change? If you do not foresee measurable change in this area, why not?

3. Describe an incident or pattern of gender discrimination that you have noticed since you arrived at college.

INTERACTION

Working in groups, propose three fundamental ways that colleges could be changed to reduce the pressures and inequalities that the authors cite in this essay. Then share and critique your results with the other groups.

Separate Is Better
Susan Estrich

PREVIEW

A popular and rarely challenged assumption in American public education is that the classroom should, in President Bill Clinton's words, "look like America." Different races, genders, and cultures; rich and poor; and students with and without disabilities—all should be mingled together so that all will be prepared to function successfully in a diverse world. In "Separate Is Better," Susan Estrich, professor of law and political science at the University of Southern California, challenges this assumption by claiming that female students who choose single-sex schools not only do disproportionately well in the traditionally male-dominated fields of math and science but also function more comfortably and successfully later in life.

Twenty years ago, when I attended Wellesley College, an all-women's college, coeducation fever was gripping America. Yale and Princeton had just "gone"; Dartmouth "went" next. My freshman year, we were polled

SOURCE: "For Girls' Schools and Women's Colleges; Separate Is Better," by Susan Estrich, *New York Times*, May 22, 1994. Copyright © 1994 by The New York Times Co. Reprinted by permission.

on whether we thought Wellesley should join the stampede. What did I know? I said yes. But now I know I was wrong, and I'm glad my vote didn't change anything.

This year, 60 percent of the National Merit Scholarship finalists are boys, because boys out scored girls on the Preliminary Scholastic Assessment Test (P.S.A.T.), which determines eligibility for the scholarships. The test doesn't ask about sports; it does ask about math and science, though, and that's where the differences between boys and girls are most pronounced. The American Civil Liberties Union and the National Center for Fair and Open Testing filed a federal civil rights suit in February charging that the test discriminates against women. The plaintiffs want more girls to get National Merit Scholarships. So do I. But I want to see the girls earn them, in schools that give them a fair chance.

I didn't win a Merit Scholarship either, although if the Fair Test people had their way, I might have. My grades were near perfect. But I didn't take the tough math and science courses. I had different priorities. I started junior high as the only girl on the math team. By high school, I'd long since quit. Instead, I learned to twirl a baton, toss it in the air and catch it while doing a split in the mud or the ice. The problem wasn't the P.S.A.T., but me, and my school.

Things have changed since then, but not as much as one would hope. The American Association of University Women did a major study in 1992 about how schools shortchange girls and concluded that even though girls get better grades (except in math), they get less from school. Teachers pay less attention to girls and give them less encouragement. Two American University researchers, Myra and David Sadker, reached a similar conclusion after 20 years of study. Girls are the invisible students; boys get the bulk of the teachers' time. Boys call out eight times as often as girls do. When the boys call out, they get answers; when the girls do, they're often admonished for speaking out. And that's true whether the teacher is a man or a woman. Even the new history textbooks devote only about 2 percent of their pages to women. What is happening, says Elisabeth Griffith, a historian and headmistress of the Madeira School in McLean, Va., is that "boys learn competence, girls lose it."

If schools shortchange girls, why is it surprising when the tests show that they're doing less well? It isn't just the P.S.A.T.'s, where 18,000 boys generally reach the top categories and only 8,000 girls do. While the gap has narrowed, boys also outscore girls on 11 of the College Board Achievement tests, and on the A.C.T. exams and on the S.A.T.'s. It is possible to jimmy selection standards to make sure girls win more scholarships, but equal results don't count for much if those results are forced. Instead of declaring equality, society should be advancing it. The challenge isn't to get more scholarships for baton twirlers but to get more baton twirlers to take up advanced mathematics.

One place that happens is in girls' schools and women's colleges. Sometimes separate isn't equal; it's better. Changing the way teachers teach in coed schools, changing the textbooks to make sure they talk about women as well as men, educating parents about raising daughters—all of these things make sense, since most girls will be educated in coed classrooms. But we've been talking about them for a decade, and the problems of gender bias stubbornly persist. In the meantime, for many girls, single-sex education is working.

In girls' schools, 80 percent of the girls take four years of science and math, compared with the national average of two years in a coed environment. Elizabeth Tidball, a George Washington University researcher, found that graduates of women's colleges did better than female graduates of coed colleges in terms of test scores, graduate school admissions, number of earned doctorates, salaries and personal satisfaction. One-third of the female board members of Fortune 1000 companies are graduates of women's colleges, even though those colleges contribute less than 4 percent of total graduates. Forty-three percent of the math doctorates and 50 percent of engineering doctorates earned by female liberal-arts college students go to graduates of Barnard, Bryn Mawr, Mount Holyoke, Smith, or Wellesley—all women's colleges. Graduates of women's colleges outnumber all other female entries in Who's Who.

I stopped twirling my baton when I got to Wellesley. I'd like to say that I knew I needed a women's college after all those years in the mud at football games, but it doesn't always work that way. I went to Wellesley because they gave me a generous scholarship, and because Radcliffe rejected me (the test scores, maybe). I was actually miserable a good deal of the time I was there, particularly during the long winters when the janitor was the only man around. But what I learned was worth it. I spent the better part of four years in a world in which women could do anything, because no one told us we couldn't. I even took some math courses. By senior year, somehow, I'd become an accomplished test-taker. When I got to Harvard Law School, where men vastly outnumbered women and sexism was the rule, a professor told me on the first day that women didn't do very well. I laughed and decided to prove he was wrong. That's a Wellesley education.

I'm not proposing that coed public schools be replaced with a network of single-sex academies. But if the problem is that women don't do well in math or science, then single-sex classes, and single-sex schools, may be part of the answer.

The evidence, though scant, is promising. In Ventura, California, the public high school has begun offering an all-girls Algebra II course. The girls, one teacher says, think so little of their ability that the teacher spends her time not only teaching math but also building self-confidence, repeatedly telling the girls that they're smart and that they can do it. The Illinois Math and Science Academy in Aurora is experimenting with a girls-only calculus-based physics class for the first semester, with the girls joining the coed class at midyear. In the girls-only class, the students report that they are jumping up to ask and answer questions instead of sitting back, hoping that the teacher doesn't call on them. One student said she was worried about the transition to a coed classroom: "We need to make sure we don't lose our newfound physics freedom." "Physics freedom" for girls—what a wonderful concept.

The biggest obstacles to such classes, or even to all-girls public schools, are erected by lawyers bent on enforcing legal equality. In the 1954 case of Brown v. Board of Education, the Supreme Court declared that "separate but equal" was inherently unequal. That was certainly true in Topeka, Kansas, whose school system was challenged. It was true of the black-only law school established to keep blacks out of the University of Texas law school. It is not necessarily true of the Ventura High School math class for girls or the Aurora Academy calculus-based physics class, whose futures are in jeopardy because of the knee-jerk application of Brown.

Classes like those in Ventura County or Aurora, Illinois, survive constitutional challenge by formally opening their doors to men, with a wink and a nod to keep them from coming in. Otherwise, the schools could be stripped of federal support, and even enjoined under the Constitution by federal court order, because they are "discriminating." Private schools may open their doors only to boys or girls under an exemption from federal laws mandating "equality." But public schools enjoy no such freedom. The reality is that if you need a Wellesley education in America, you have to pay for it. That's the price of committing to real opportunity.

Boys may pay the price as well. Some educators in the African-American community believe that all-boys classes may be part of the solution to the dismal failure and dropout rates of African-American boys in school. But the courts prevented the Detroit school district from establishing three public all-boys schools, effectively stopping similar projects planned in other cities. Nonetheless, all-boys classes are being held quietly in as many as two dozen schools around the country, mostly in inner cities.

Such programs may or may not succeed in the long run. Research and careful study are plainly needed. But research and careful study are difficult when classes are held in near secrecy for fear of discovery by lawyers and government officials intent on shutting them down in the name of equality.

If girls don't want to go to all-girls schools, or if parents don't want to send them, that's their choice. If the experiments with girls-only math classes or boys-only classes should fail, then educators can be trusted to abandon them. But short of that, let the educators and the parents and the students decide, and leave the lawyers and judges out of it.

DIALOGUE

1. What explanation does the author provide or imply for the success of same-sex classrooms? Can you think of additional reasons for their success?
2. Self-segregation—the tendency of groups of students to band together by gender, race, religion, sexual preference, ethnicity, national origin, and other shared identities—has been a source of anxiety to administrators who want to encourage cultural interaction as an important part of the learning process. Do you think self-segregation inhibits the learning process or helps it? Explain your answer. Is it important to distinguish between voluntary and involuntary segregation?
3. Are you satisfied with the author's challenge to the U.S. Supreme Court's 1954 ruling in *Brown* v. *Board of Education* that "separate but equal" facilities are unconstitutional? What do you think of the practice of formally allowing the participation of an undesirable group but then ostracizing that group "with a wink and a nod"?

WRITING TOPICS

1. In a paragraph, agree or disagree with Susan Estrich's statement that "sometimes separate isn't equal; it's better."
2. Define the author's concept of "physics freedom."
3. Consider the question of whether there is a place in our society for "men only" and "women only" organizations (clubs, apartments, dorms). Develop three arguments supporting or opposing sexually segregated organizations.

INTERACTION

Reflect on your own experience with standardized tests. Working in groups, discuss the author's assertion that the PSAT test that determines

National Merit Scholarship finalists discriminates against women. Propose at least three steps that could be taken by test makers to ensure that there is no gender bias in such a standardized test. Critique the effectiveness of each group's suggestions.

Men, Women, and Computers
Barbara Kantrowitz

PREVIEW

How goes the gender conflict in cyberspace? In the brave new world of computers and the Internet, Barbara Kantrowitz finds that men and women are "like two chips that pass in the night." Computer culture appears to be dominated by men, but who or what is to blame for this situation? The answers have a familiar ring.

As a longtime *Star Trek* devotee, Janis Cortese was eager to be part of the Trekkie discussion group on the Internet. But when she first logged on, Cortese noticed that these fans of the final frontier devoted megabytes to such profound topics as whether Troi or Crusher had bigger breasts. In other words, the purveyors of this *Trek* dreck were all *guys*. Undeterred, Cortese, a physicist at California's Loma Linda University, figured she'd add perspective to the electronic gathering place with her own momentous questions. Why was the male cast racially diverse while almost all the females were young, white and skinny? Then, she tossed in a few lustful thoughts about the male crew members.

After those seemingly innocuous observations, "I was chased off the net by rabid hounds," recalls Cortese. Before she could say "Fire phasers," the Trekkies had flooded her electronic mailbox with nasty messages—a practice called "flaming." Cortese retreated into her own galaxy by starting the all-female Starfleet Ladies Auxiliary and Embroidery/Baking Society. The private electronic forum, based in Houston, now has more than 40 members, including psychologists, physicians, students and secretaries. They started with Trek-talk, but often chose to

---

SOURCE: Barbara Kantrowitz, "Men, Women, and Computers," From *Newsweek*, May 16, 1994, © 1994, Newsweek, Inc. All rights reserved. Reprinted by permission.

beam down and go where no man had ever wandered before—into the personal mode. When Julia Kosatka, a Houston computer scientist, got pregnant last year, she shared her thoughts with the group on weight gain, sex while expecting and everything else on her mind. Says Kosatka: "I'm part of one of the longest-running slumber parties in history."

From the Internet to Silicon Valley to the PC sitting in the family room, men and women often seem like two chips that pass in the night. Sure, there are women who spout techno-speak in their sleep and plenty of men who think a hard drive means four hours on the freeway. But in general, computer culture is created, defined and controlled by men. Women often feel about as welcome as a system crash.

About a third of American families have at least one computer, but most of those are purchased and used by males. It may be new technology, but the old rules still apply. In part, it's that male-machine bonding thing, reincarnated in the digital age. "Men tend to be seduced by the technology itself," says Oliver Strimpel, executive director of The Computer Museum in Boston. "They tend to get into the faster-race-car syndrome," bragging about the size of their discs or the speed of their microprocessors. To the truly besotted, computers are a virtual religion, complete with icons (on-screen graphics), relics (obsolete programs and machines) and prophets (Microsoft's Bill Gates, outlaw hackers). This is not something to be trifled with by mere . . . females, who seem to think that machines were meant to be *used*, like the microwave oven or the dishwasher. Interesting and convenient on the job but not worthy of obsession. Esther Dyson, editor of *Release 1.0*, an influential software-industry newsletter, has been following the computer field for two decades. Yet when she looks at her own computer, Dyson says she still doesn't "really care about its innards. I just want it to work."

Blame (a) culture (b) family (c) schools (d) all of the above. Little boys are expected to roll around in the dirt and explore. Perfect training for learning to use computers, which often requires hours in front of the screen trying to figure out the messy arcanum of a particular program. Girls get subtle messages—from society if not from their parents—that they should keep their hands clean and play with their dolls. Too often, they're discouraged from taking science and math—not just by their schools but by parents as well (how many mothers have patted their daughters on the head and reassured them: "Oh, I wasn't good at math, either").

The gender gap is real and takes many forms.

Barbie vs. Nintendo

Girls' technophobia begins early. Last summer, Sarah Douglas, a University of Oregon computer-science professor, took part in a job fair for teenage girls that was supposed to introduce them to nontraditional occupations. With great expectations, she set up her computer and loaded it with interesting programs. Not a single girl stopped by. When she asked why, the girls "told me computers were something their dads and their brothers used," Douglas sadly recalls. "Computer science is a very male profession. . . . When girls get involved in that male world, they are pushed away and belittled. Pretty soon, the girls get frustrated and drop out."

Computer games usually involve lots of shooting and dying. Boy stuff. What's out there for girls? "If you walk down the street and look in the computer store, you will see primarily male people as sales staff and as customers," says Jo Sanders, director of the gender-equity program at the Center for Advanced Study in Education at the City University of New York Graduate Center.

Boys and girls are equally interested in computers until about the fifth grade, says University of Minnesota sociologist Ronald Anderson, who coauthored the recent report "Computers in American Schools." At that point, boys' use rises significantly and girls' use drops, Anderson says, probably because sex-role identification really kicks in. Many girls quickly put computers on the list of not-quite-feminine topics, like car engines and baseball batting averages. It didn't have to be this way. The very first computer programmer was a woman, Ada Lovelace, who worked with Charles Babbage on his mechanical computing machines in the mid-1800s. If she had become a role model, maybe hundreds of thousands of girls would have spent their teenage years locked in their bedrooms staring at screens. Instead, too many are doing their nails or worrying about their hair, says Marcelline Barron, an administrator at the Illinois Mathematics and Science Academy, a publicly funded coed boarding school for gifted students. "You're not thinking about calculus or physics when you're thinking about that," says Barron. "We have these kinds of expectations for young girls. They must be neat, they must be clean, they must be quiet."

Despite great strides by women in other formerly male fields, such as law and medicine, women are turning away from the computer industry. Men earning computer-science degrees outnumber women 3 to 1 and the gap is growing, according to the National Science Foundation. Fifteen years ago, when computers were still new in schools, they hadn't yet been defined as so exclusively male. But now girls have gotten the message. It's not just the technical and cultural barrier. Sherry Turkle, a Massachusetts Institute of Technology sociologist who teaches a course on women and computers, says that computers have come to stand for "a world without emotion," an image that seems to scare off girls more than boys.

In the past decade, videogames have become a gateway to technology for many boys, but game manufacturers say few girls are attracted to these small-screen shoot-'em-ups. It's not surprising that the vast majority of videogame designers are men. They don't call it Game *Boy* for nothing. Now some manufacturers are trying to lure girls. In the next few months, Sega plans to introduce "Berenstein Bears," which will offer players a choice of boy or girl characters. A second game, "Crystal's Pony Tale," involves coloring (there's lots of pink in the background). Neither game requires players to "die," a common videogame device that researchers say girls dislike. Girls also tend to prefer nonlinear games, where there is more than one way to proceed. "There's a whole issue with speaking girls' language," says Michealene Cristini Risley, group director of licensing and character development for Sega. The company would like to hook girls at the age of 4, before they've developed fears of technology.

Girls need freedom to explore and make mistakes. Betsy Zeller, a 37-year-old engineering manager at Silicon Graphics, says that when she discovered computers in college, "I swear I thought I'd seen the face of God." Yet she had to fend off guys who would come into the lab and want to help her work through problems or, worse yet, do them for her. "I would tell them to get lost," she says. "I wanted to do it myself." Most women either asked for or accepted proffered help, just as they are more likely to ask for directions when lost in a strange city. That may be the best way to avoid driving in circles for hours, but it's not the best way to learn technical subjects.

Schools are trying a number of approaches to interest girls in computers. Douglas and her colleagues are participating in a mentorship program where undergraduate girls spend a summer working with female computer scientists. Studies have shown that girls are more attracted to technology if they can work in groups: some schools are experimenting with team projects that require computers but are focused on putting out a product, like a newspaper or pamphlet. At the middle and high-school level, girls-only computer classes are increasingly popular. Two months ago Roosevelt Middle School in Eugene, Ore., set up girls-only hours at the computer lab. Games were prohibited and artists were brought in to teach girls how to be more creative with the computer. Students are also learning to use e-mail, which many girls love. Says Debbie Nehl, the computer-lab supervisor: "They see it as high-tech note-passing."

Power Networks

As a relatively new industry, the leadership of computerdom might be expected to be more gender-diverse. Wrong: few women have advanced beyond middle-management ranks. According to a study conducted last year by the *San Jose Mercury News,* there are no women CEOs running major computer-manufacturing firms and only a handful running software companies. Even women who have succeeded say they are acutely conscious of the differences between them and their male coworkers. "I don't talk the same as men," says Paula Hawthorn, an executive at Montage Software, in Oakland, California. "I don't get the same credibility." The difference, she says, "is with you all the time."

Women who work in very technical areas, such as programming, are often the loneliest. Anita Borg, a computer-systems researcher, remembers attending a 1987 conference where there were so few women that the only time they ran into each other was in the restroom. Their main topic of discussion: why there were so few women at the conference. That bathroom cabal grew into Systers, an on-line network for women with technical careers. There are now 1,740 women members from 19 countries representing 200 colleges and universities and 150 companies. Systers is part mentoring and part consciousness-raising. One graduate student, for example, talked about how uncomfortable she felt sitting in her shared office when a male graduate student and a professor put a picture of a nude woman on a computer. The problem was resolved when a couple of female faculty members, also on the Systers network, told their offending colleagues that the image was not acceptable.

Women have been more successful in developing software, especially when their focus is products used by children. Jan Davidson, a former teacher, started Davidson & Associates, in Torrance, California, with three programs in 1982. Now it's one of the country's biggest developers of kids' software, with 350 employees and $58.6 million in revenues. Multimedia will bring new opportunities for women. The technology is so specialized that it requires a team—animators, producers, scriptwriters, 3-D modelers—to create state-of-the art-products. It's a far cry from the stereotype of the solitary male programmer, laboring long into the night with only takeout Chinese food for company. At Mary Cron's Rymel Design Group in Palos Verdes, California, most of the software artists and designers are women, Cron says. "It's like a giant puzzle," she adds. "We like stuff we can work on together."

As more women develop software, they may also help create products that will attract women consumers—a huge untapped market. Heidi Roizen, a college English major, cofounded T/Maker Co. in Mountain View, California, a decade ago. She says that because women are often in charge of the family's budget, they are potential consumers of personal-finance programs. Women are also the most likely buyers of education and family-entertainment products, a fast-growing segment of the industry. "Women are more typically the household shopper," Roizen says. "They have tremendous buying power."

Wired Women

The Infobahn—a.k.a. the Information Superhighway—may be the most hyped phenomenon in history—or it could be the road to the future. In any case, women want to get on. But the sign over the access road says CAUTION. MEN WORKING. WOMEN BEWARE. Despite hundreds of thousands of new users in the last year, men still dominate the Internet and commercial services such as Prodigy or CompuServe. The typical male conversation on line turns off many women. "A lot of time, to be crude, it's a pissing contest," says Lisa Kimball, a partner in the Meta Network, a Washington, D.C., on-line service that is 40 percent female. Put-downs are an art form. When one woman complained recently in an Internet forum that she didn't like participating because she didn't have time to answer all her e-mail, she was swamped with angry responses, including this one (from a man): "Would you like some cheese with your whine?"

Some men say the on-line hostility comes from resentment over women's slowly entering what has been an almost exclusively male domain. Many male techno-jocks "feel women are intruding into their inner sanctum," says André Bacard, a Silicon Valley, California, technology writer. They're not out to win sensitivity contests. "In the computer world, it's 'Listen baby, if you don't like it, drop dead'," says Bacard. "It's the way men talk to guys. Women aren't used to that."

Even under more civilized circumstances, men and women have different conversational styles, says Susan Herring, a University of Texas at Arlington professor who has studied women's participation on computer networks. Herring found that violations of long-established net etiquette—asking too many basic questions, for example—angered men. "The women were much more tolerant of people who didn't know what they were doing," Herring says. "What really annoyed women was the flaming and people boasting. The things that annoy women are things men do all the time."

Like hitting on women. Women have learned to tread their keyboards carefully in chat forums because they often have to fend off sexual advances that would make Bob Packwood blush. When subscribers to America Online enter one of the service's forums, their computer names appear at the top of the screen as a kind of welcome. If they've chosen an obviously female name, chances are they'll soon be bombarded with private messages seeking detailed descriptions of their appearance or sexual preferences. "I couldn't believe it," recalls 55-year-old Eva S. "I said, 'Come on, I'm a grandmother'."

More and more women are signing on to networks that are either coed and run by women, or are exclusively for women. Stacy Horn started ECHO (for East Coast Hang Out) four years ago because she was frustrated with the hostility on line. About 60 percent of ECHO's 2,000 subscribers are men; among ECHO's 50 forums, only two are strictly for women. "Flaming is nonexistent on ECHO," Horn says. "New women get on line and they see that. And then they're much more likely to jump in." Women's Wire in San Francisco, started in January, has 850 subscribers, only 10 percent of them men—the reverse of most on-line services. "We wanted to design a system in which women would help shape the community from the floor up," says cofounder Ellen Pack. The official policy is that there is no such thing as a dumb question—and no flaming.

Male subscribers say Women's Wire has been a learning experience for them, too. Maxwell Hoffmann, a 41-year-old computer-company manager, says that many men think that only women are overly emotional. But men lose it, too. A typical on-line fight starts with two guys sending "emotionally charged flames going back and forth" through cyberspace (not on Women's Wire). Then it expands and "everybody starts flaming the guy. They scream at each other and they're not listening."

If only men weren't so *emotional,* so *irrational,* could we all get along on the net?

Toys and Tools

In one intriguing study by the Center for Children and Technology, a New York think tank, men and women in technical fields were asked to dream up machines of the future. Men typically imagined devices that could help them "conquer the universe," says Jan Hawkins, director of the center. She says women wanted machines that met people's needs, "the perfect mother."

Someday, gender-blind education and socialization may render those differences obsolete. But in the meantime, researchers say both visions are useful. If everyone approached technology the way women do now, "we wouldn't be pushing envelopes," says Cornelia Bruner, associate director of the center. "Most women, even those who are technologically sophisticated, think of machines as a means to an end." Men think of the machines as an extension of their own power, as a way to "transcend physical limitations." That may be why they are more likely to come up with great leaps in technology, researchers say. Without that vision, the computer and its attendant industry would not exist.

Ironically, gender differences could help women. "We're at a cultural turning point," says MIT's Turkle. "There's an opportunity to remake the culture around the machine." Practicality is now as valued as invention. If the computer industry wants to put machines in the hands of the masses, that means women—along with the great many men who have no interest in hot-rod computing. An ad campaign for Compaq's popular Presario line emphasizes the machine's utility. After kissing her child good night, the mother in the ad sits down at her Presario to work. As people start to view their machines as creative tools, someday women may be just as comfortable with computers as men are.

DIALOGUE

1. "Computer science is a very male profession." Is this an accurate statement based on your experiences with friends, family, and fellow students? If so, what reasons can you offer for the male dominance in this arena?
2. In what ways is the miscommunication between the sexes in cyberspace a reflection of today's man-woman social interaction?
3. What hope, if any, does the author offer for resolving the problem? What positive outcomes are projected?

WRITING TOPICS

1. Reflect on your personal interaction with computers. How and why have your attitudes changed over the years? Of the behaviors described in the essay, which ones do you exhibit?
2. Write an essay in which you speculate on the future implications of computer culture and the chances of its technological outreach remaining a male-dominated phenomenon. What kind of power is represented by control of cyberspace?

3. Is the author guilty of stereotyping both men and women in this essay? Locate elements of her argument and examples of behaviors by both sexes that overstate the case or generalize without sufficient support. Critique the overall effectiveness of the author's argument.

INTERACTION

Barbara Kantrowitz suggests that educational institutions can play a significant role in promoting computer use for girls and women. In small groups, brainstorm specific strategies that schools and universities can adopt to make computer technology and use more attractive to women.

Television Insults Men, Too
Bernard R. Goldberg

PREVIEW

In the past decade, commercial television has been reaching out to a newly affluent and independent group of consumers—women. In so doing, television has systematically cleaned up its act in its dramatic portrayals of women. Men, meanwhile, continue to be portrayed in sitcoms and commercials as vain, lazy, clumsy, insensitive, and worse. In this New York Times *editorial, columnist Bernard R. Goldberg describes this new version of the old double standard.*

It was front page news and it made the TV networks. A mother from Michigan single-handedly convinces some of America's biggest advertisers to cancel their sponsorship of the Fox Broadcasting Company's "Married . . . With Children" because, as she put it, the show blatantly exploits women and the family.

The program is about a blue collar family in which the husband is a chauvinist pig and his wife is—excuse the expression—a bimbo.

These are the late 1980s, and making fun of people because of their gender—on TV, no less, in front of millions of people—is déclassé. Un-

SOURCE: Bernard R. Goldberg, "Television Insults Men, Too," *New York Times* (March 14, 1989). Copyright © 1989 by The New York Time Co. Reprinted by permission.

less, of course, the gender we're ridiculing is the male gender. Then it's O.K.

Take "Roseanne." (Please!) It's the season's biggest new hit show, which happens to be about another blue collar family. In this one, the wife calls her husband and kids names.

"Roseanne" is Roseanne Barr, who has made a career saying such cute things as: "You may marry the man of your dreams, ladies, but 15 years later you are married to a reclining chair that burps." Or to her TV show son: "You're not stupid. You're just clumsy like your daddy."

The producer of "Roseanne" does not mince words either: "Men are slime. They say they're going to do 50 percent of the work around the house, but they never do."

I will tell you that the producer is a man, which does not lessen the ugliness of the remark. But because his target is men, it becomes acceptable. No one, to my knowledge, is pulling commercials from "Roseanne."

In matters of gender discrimination, it has become part of the accepted orthodoxy—of many feminists and a lot of the media anyway—that only women have the right to complain. Men have no such right. Which helps explain why there have been so many commercials ridiculing men—and getting away with it.

In the past year or so, I have seen a breakfast cereal commercial showing a husband and wife playing tennis. She is perky and he is jerky.

She is a regular Martina Navratilova of the suburbs and he is virtually dead (because he wasn't smart enough to eat the right cereal).

She doesn't miss a shot. He lets the ball hit him in the head. If he were black, his name would be Stepin Fetchitt.

I have seen a commercial for razor blades that shows a woman in an evening gown smacking a man in a tuxedo across the face, suggesting, I suppose, that the male face takes enough punishment to deserve a nice, smooth shave. If he hit her (an absolutely inconceivable notion, if a sponsor is trying to sell a woman something) he would be a batterer.

I have seen an airline commercial showing two reporters from competing newspapers. She's strong and smart. He's a nerd. He says to her: I read your story this morning; you scooped me again. She replies to him: I didn't know you could read.

I have seen a magazine ad for perfume showing a businesswoman patting a businessman's behind as they walk down the street. *Ms.* magazine, the Journal of American Feminism, ran the ad. The publisher told me there was nothing sexist about it.

A colleague who writes about advertising and the media says advertisers are afraid to fool around with women's roles. They know, as she puts it, they'll "set off the feminist emergency broadcast system" if they do. So, she concludes, men are fair game.

In 1987, Fred Hayward, who is one of the pioneers of the men's rights movement (yes, there is a men's rights movement) studied thousands of TV and print ads and concluded: "If there's a sleazy character in an ad, 100 percent of the ones that we found were male. If there's an incompetent character, 100 percent of them in the ads are male."

I once interviewed Garrett Epps, a scholar who has written on these matters, who told me: "The female executive who is driven, who is strong, who lives for her work, that's a very positive symbol in our culture now. The male who has the same traits—that guy is a disaster: He harms everybody around him; he's cold, he's unfeeling; he's hurtful."

The crusading mother from Michigan hit on a legitimate issue. No more cheap shots, she seems to have said. And the advertisers listened. No more cheap shots is what a lot of men are saying also. Too bad nobody is listening to *them*.

DIALOGUE

1. Is the author overreacting? Could his views be regarded as antifeminist? Explain your answer.
2. To what extent do you think commercial television programs and ads reflect the lives of real people in our society?
3. Is there a need for a men's rights movement in this country? If so, what specific male rights need to be protected?

WRITING TOPICS

1. Have you noticed evidence of antimale prejudice or stereotyping of men at your college? In the classroom? In campus publications? In the residence hall or other campus facilities? At social events? Is the behavior the same in all these settings? Explain in three short paragraphs.
2. Evaluate the following argument in an essay: *Women have suffered systematic discrimination for centuries at the hands of men. To remedy the situation, it is important for the popular media to show that women can be strong and men can be weak.*
3. Compose a letter to a television network executive in which you offer specific suggestions on how to reduce gender discrimination in TV programs and ads and achieve a balanced portrayal of both men and women.

INTERACTION

In small groups, make a list of four or five dramatic TV shows with which most of you are familiar. Discuss to what extent males and females are portrayed stereotypically in these shows. Make a list of the dominant characteristics of the males and females. Is there any noticeable pattern of discrimination by gender? Are men portrayed negatively more often than women? Work toward some general conclusions to share with the other groups.

Part IV Reflections

Review the ideas you expressed at the beginning of this part in "Write Before You Read." How have your ideas changed as a result of reading the articles in this part? Explain in the space below.

1. How the opposite sex is different _____

_____

_____

_____

_____

_____

2. Date rape _____

_____

_____

_____

_____

_____

3. "Men only" or "women only" schools and organizations_____

_____

_____

_____

_____

_____

Part IV Writing Assignment

Write a first-person narrative about an event in your life in which you:

   a. acquired a new understanding of the opposite sex.

OR

   b. became aware of your own sexual identity.

Try to go beyond merely describing the sequence of events; place them in a context of meaning. How were you affected by the event? What meaning did it have for your life? Describe the outcomes, both negative and positive.

CAMPUS SKETCH

Now that you're better acquainted with your campus, draw another sketch of it. Then compare it with your first sketch on page 111. Show both sketches to your group and describe how you came to know your campus better since your arrival.

Part V

Living with Diversity

INTRODUCTION

Perhaps the greatest democratizing force of the twentieth century has been the electronic media. After World War II, Radio Free Europe was instrumental in the popular revolts against communist rule in Hungary and Czechoslovakia. In the 1960s and 1970s, television instantly captured and transmitted around the world the images of brutality in Vietnam, racist violence and freedom marchers in Selma and Montgomery, and the massacre of Israeli athletes at the Olympic Village in Munich. Soviet dissident writers, forbidden to publish, used illegal electronic copiers to circulate their work. Chinese students imprisoned for facing down tanks in Beijing's Tiananmen Square maintained contact with supporters around the world by fax and Internet messages. And Iranian housewives returning home from the market remove the veils and long gowns prescribed by the mullahs and turn on Oprah Winfrey or Larry King, beamed into their homes by forbidden satellite dishes. The electronic media were responsible, more than any other single force, for the breakdown of political and cultural barriers that led to the destruction of the Berlin Wall and the death of Soviet Marxism in 1990.

The movement toward multiculturalism has been inexorable in the second half of the twentieth century. Twenty-first-century life will be multicultural life. College students who learn to understand and appreciate cultural diversity are likely to prosper in tomorrow's work force. Those who cling rigidly to cultural stereotypes will be left by the wayside. Although the essays in this section by no means encompass the vast tapestry of cultures that represent contemporary America, they do provide insight into the current status of a few of the minority groups on today's college campuses.

In "Separate by Choice," Mary Jordan, a reporter for the *Washington Post*, examines the phenomenon of self-segregation—groups of common-culture students banding together in cafeterias, classrooms, and dormitories. Is this a good thing or a bad thing? Does multiculturalism require the full integration of racial, gender, and ethnic groups? Or should students be encouraged to affirm their cultural identities through their living arrangements and seating choices?

The next four essays focus on specific minority groups—Hispanics, Asian Americans, Native Americans, and African Americans—each of which experiences a unique form of racial prejudice. In "The Undergraduate Hispanic Experience," Edward B. Fiske explores what he calls "A Case of Juggling Two Cultures." For many, the shock of transplantation from an urban barrio or a rural farm to a college campus creates a profound sense of alienation that disrupts the learning experience. In "The

Harmful Myth of Asian Superiority," Ronald Takaki addresses the stereotypes of Asian American students as the "model minority." And Arlene B. Hirschfelder urges us to "stop playing Indians"—the persistent habit of white Americans to trivialize and insult an ancient culture by sports team names, logos, and mascots; headdresses; and cigar-store Indians.

Finally, Shelby Steele's extended essay "The Recoloring of Campus Life: Student Racism, Academic Pluralism, and the End of a Dream" is one of a series originally written for *Harper's* magazine and later reprinted in Steele's 1990 book *The Content of Our Character: A New Vision of Race in America*. Writing from a conservative perspective, Steele questions many of the reforms intended to correct racial inequities in higher education, including affirmative action, African American studies departments, and voluntarily segregated fraternities and student organizations. He argues that racial tensions on America's campuses are caused by racial equality rather than by racism. American colleges have historically assumed a leadership role in promoting racial equality and cultural diversity. But this very attempt to achieve fairness and freedom creates an atmosphere of tension. Inherited guilt in white students and ancient wounds and a residue of anger and resentment in black students are sources of anxiety that require outlets and scapegoats.

What can college students do to confront and counteract instances of discrimination and stereotyping? In "Don't Just Stand There," Diane Cole tells readers to take a stand. She offers practical tips on how to do this without appearing sanctimonious and morally superior but by using tact, compassion, and a sense of humor.

Write Before You Read

A. After you've read the introduction, take a few minutes to survey the contents of this part. Then write three questions you expect will be answered in the course of your reading.

1. _____

_____

2. _____

_____

3. _____

_____

B. Briefly reflect on each of the following topics. Then write freely and rapidly about what you already know about the topic, relevant experiences you have had, and any opinions you have formed about it.

1. Self-segregation on your campus _____

_____

_____

_____

_____

_____

2. Difficulties you have had understanding or accepting another

culture _____

_____

_____

_____

_____

_____

3. Difficulties you have had being accepted by others _____

_____

_____

_____

Separate by Choice
Mary Jordan

PREVIEW

Thirty years ago, segregation was the principal target of the civil rights movement. Today a person visiting the classrooms and cafeterias on America's campuses might conclude that segregation is still in force: students continue to cluster together by race in like-minded groups. Today's student community looks less like a melting pot than a mosaic, with different-colored tiles each maintaining its own distinct quality.

Some college administrators are frustrated by the practice of self-segregation and seek ways for students to assimilate. But many minority students who feel alienated by the mainstream community find in ethnic dorms, fraternities, and social organizations a means of affirming their individuality and a safe harbor in a turbulent racist sea. Mary Jordan, a reporter for the Washington Post *and an adjunct professor of journalism at Georgetown University, writes about this phenomenon.*

The newest dormitory at Brown University, one set aside chiefly for African Americans, is called "Harambee House," Swahili for "the coming together of community."

Already on Brown's hilltop campus overlooking downtown are Hispanic House, French House, Slavic House, East Asian House, and German House. Many other universities are acceding to students' demands and organizing dormitories by race, ethnicity, sexual orientation—even by drinkers and teetotalers.

But as they do, educators question whether these specialized living arrangements are bringing people together, as the name "Harambee" suggests, or driving them farther apart. *Doonesbury* and other comic

SOURCE: Mary Jordan, "Separate by Choice," © 1994, *The Washington Post*. Reprinted with permission.

strips have even parodied what some call the "separatist movement," depicting scenes such as campus drinking fountains labeled for blacks and whites.

In a sign of concern, Brown has halted opening any more "theme" houses until their effects can be studied. "We don't want to have a Balkanization of the campus," says Executive Vice President Robert A. Reichley.

Reichley says the idea of a university is to have diverse people living and learning together in one community, not "small enclaves."

The separatist movement is a hot issue well beyond Providence. Last month at the University of Pennsylvania, a special commission studying the "key aspects of campus life" recommended that first-year students be assigned housing to avoid what it called "self-segregation."

Under the current system, students may choose where they will live. The commission found that they often "self-segregate and lose opportunities for wider interaction among diverse groups of students."

Claire Fagin, Penn's interim president, says she is considering a pilot program next year in which students would agree to be randomly assigned to dorms.

"In general, what we are seeing is a much more divided population on our college campuses," Fagin says. "We are moving into a very, very hyphenated world: it's Asian-American, African-American; it's so contrary to everything I grew up with when everyone fought to just be American.

"For many of us who stress pluralism, these are not easy times," she says.

While separate housing is perhaps the most controversial part of recent demands from student groups, it is not the only one. On many campuses, African Americans, Asians, Latinos, gay students, and others have demanded their own lounges, activities, even their own curriculum.

Nothing, however, seems to unnerve people as much as separate housing, especially when it involves African Americans. Some see it as a painful slap at the 1950s and '60s fight for integration.

"The goal of the civil rights movement was to be color-blind," says Robin Rose, Brown's dean of student life. "There was a high value on integration, integration at any cost. Now these students are saying any cost is too high. They want to live together. And who can blame them?"

Abigail Ramsay, for one, says she is glad she can live in Harambee House, after living on a floor with all white students last year. "All of a sudden I can talk to people going through the same things," says Ramsay, a New Yorker who aspires to be a doctor. "It feels more like home."

Proponents say there are small comforts that help them in their studies, such as shared tastes in music and food, and more important ones, such as living with people who have felt the sting of the same racial or ethnic insults. College officials at many campuses agree that black students often earn better grades when they are living in exclusively African American dorms.

Ramsay says that because she is black, in a city with a small percentage of black residents, Providence natives have assumed that she couldn't be a Brown student. She says some have even approached her "thinking I am a prostitute because I am a black woman."

On a campus where 7 percent of undergraduates are African American, Ramsay says she is always in the minority, except when she comes back to Harambee. In its first year, Harambee has seventeen students who fill two floors of a brick building in Wriston Quad. Sixteen are African American and one is white. The house, "open to all students who identify with their African descent, speak an African language, or major solely in Pan-African studies," is expected to attract more African American students next year.

Joshua Lehrer, a Brown sophomore who is white, is one of the students who doesn't think separate dorms are a good idea. He says he had more black friends when he attended high school in Philadelphia than he does at Brown, even though he is around many more African Americans there.

Of Brown's 5,600 undergraduates, 390 are African Americans, 300 are Hispanic, and 660 are Asian.

Lehrer says students naturally tend to eat, go to movies and parties, and become friendly with the people they live with. So, he says, separate housing inhibits the mixing of different groups of people.

As Lehrer spoke in the cavernous dining hall called the "Ratty," most of the Hispanics, Asians, and blacks ate lunch in small separate groups.

Several white students said they understood why there were Spanish and German houses, because students practiced new languages there. But they said they didn't understand how there could be an "African American house," because they doubted they would be allowed to have a "White House." Many white students were uncomfortable discussing the issue and did not want to be identified.

Various racial and ethnic groups "are separating themselves from everybody else, yet complain when society separates them," Lehrer says. "Can you really have it both ways?"

Supporters of separate dorms say that for as long as there have been fraternities and sororities, students have been seeking out ways to live with other people like themselves.

They say jocks room together, people from New Jersey room together, rich people with summer homes in Long Island room together. Because there are so few minority students on major campuses, every dormitory is essentially a "white dorm," they say.

William H. Gray III, president of the United Negro College Fund, says colleges should be doing everything they can to make minority students feel welcome and accepted. Both black students and Hispanic students drop out of college at much higher rates than white students. "What is important is they have got to survive," he says, adding that he believes "these students are looking to black cultural expression as a way of feeling refuge for what they perceive as hostile, nonnurturing environments."

"We say it's acceptable to have a Hillel House, a Newman [Catholic] House, and Lutheran House, but as soon as we have a Harambee House, it's bad," Gray says. "Instead of asking why are black students separating from whites at white college campuses, we should be asking what is wrong with white America and its institutions that blacks don't feel welcome."

John O'Brien, twenty-one, of Washington, D.C., is the sole white student in Harambee. After taking a trip to Kenya and taking African studies, he decided to move in.

"I get to meet people I wouldn't otherwise," says O'Brien. He believes Brown is right to give students an option of where they want to live. "Obviously we want to live in a world where everyone is mixed together," he says. "But we are not there yet."

DIALOGUE

1. Is self-segregation commonly practiced at your institution? How does it manifest itself, and how extensive is it?
2. How is the segregation practiced on America's campuses today different from the segregation in American society prior to the civil rights movement?
3. Is the separatist movement a good thing or a bad thing? What's good or bad about it? Should student government look for ways to bring students together or facilitate the efforts of groups to separate themselves on the basis of shared identity? Is it possible or desirable to do both at the same time?

WRITING TOPICS

1. In a paragraph, explain the phrase "Balkanization of the campus."
2. In an essay, argue for or against the establishment of a "White House" on your campus.
3. Place yourself in the role of a college administrator who is assessing the influence on campus life of theme houses (German House, Hispanic House, and so on). Through interviews, informal surveys, and other research, prepare a list of five findings that reflect various attitudes and positions on the issue. Based on these findings, make a formal recommendation about the future of theme houses on campus.

INTERACTION

In small groups, list the virtues and benefits of an integrated campus as opposed to a campus that is self-segregated on the basis of race, ethnicity, or sexual orientation.

The Undergraduate Hispanic Experience: A Case of Juggling Two Cultures
Edward B. Fiske

PREVIEW

"Cold and impersonal" is how many minority students describe their campuses shortly after they arrive. For Hispanic students coming from small towns or a close-knit barrio family, this feeling of estrangement is especially intense. Finding a community of like-minded souls often becomes a higher priority than succeeding academically: the soul must be fed before the mind can be clothed.

In this article, Edward B. Fiske describes the ambivalent feelings of Hispanic, Latino, and Chicano college students who find themselves torn between two cultures. He describes "the anxiety of breaking close family ties," the homesickness, and "the loneliness and tensions inherent in finding their way in institutions built around an alien culture."

SOURCE: Edward B. Fiske, "The Undergraduate Hispanic Experience: A Case of Juggling Two Cultures," Reprinted by permission of Sterling Lord Literistic, Inc. Copyright © 1988 by Edward B. Fiske.

Many who were academic stars in high school find themselves struggling to compete in college. At the same time, most cope remarkably well with the pressure they face—from both themselves and their family's expectations of them—to achieve academic, social, and economic success.

Michael Sanchez grew up in Coolidge, Arizona, a community of 6,800 persons 52 miles southwest of Phoenix. A good student in high school, he enrolled in Arizona State University in 1983 as a business major with the dream of becoming the first member of his family to earn a college degree.

Two years later Mr. Sanchez put his dream on hold. He found the university, where the student population is more than six times that of his hometown, to be "cold and impersonal." He couldn't find an advisor to help him sort out his academic program, or a group that would make him feel he belonged at Tempe; the lack of Hispanic professors left him without reason to believe that Hispanics could advance to become academic leaders.

"I was really overwhelmed," he confesses. Mr. Sanchez returned home and enrolled in a nearby community college, which he likes because it is smaller and more personal. Soon, he hopes to transfer to Arizona State to try again.

For many Hispanic students the most serious problems are not those they confront getting into college but those they face once they get there. The problems range from the anxiety of breaking close family ties to the loneliness and tensions inherent in finding their way in institutions built around an alien culture. Some Hispanic undergraduates complain of subtle or not-so-subtle discrimination. Even those from secure and privileged backgrounds are often thrown off-balance by finding themselves identified as belonging to a "minority" group for the first time.

Culture shock is a reality for many, if not most, Hispanic college students when they first set foot on an American college campus. For some the shock comes simply from being thrown on their own in a large institution. Ron Lopez grew up in Pacific Palisades, a middle-class suburb of Los Angeles, where his father is a high school teacher and his mother a counselor at a local community college. He set his sights on the University of California at Los Angeles.

"UCLA was overwhelming," he says. "It was just big. I had to work and live on my own. It was a real shock: My first two years were outrageous. I was working so hard at the academics and at my job—I was spending at least twenty hours a week at the job—that was just hardship, serious hardship."

Add to that the cultural differences. Angelina Medina, a 21-year-old marketing major at the University of Texas at San Antonio, observes that Hispanics from the barrios on the south and west sides of the city are readily identifiable in a university where most students are middle-class whites. "They dress differently," she says. "They drive different cars, low to the flow."

Since curricula rarely reflect Hispanic interests, even the classroom can contribute to a sense of alienation. "We validate other cultures by studying them but we don't extend that same validation to Chicanos," observes Maria Meier, a senior international relations major at Stanford University who would like to see aspects of Latino culture worked into that university's controversial general education program.

Since Hispanics often come from weaker high schools, failure in the classroom is a frequent occurrence. Vladimir Garcia grew up in New York City and was recruited by Boston University because of high math scores on standardized admissions tests. But when he got there he found that he wasn't prepared for a fast-paced urban university. "A lot of people were shocked that I was Hispanic and was from New York, and here I was an engineering student," he says. "My first month was my loneliest month ever. I felt like I was alone. But once I failed, I found I wasn't alone." Mr. Garcia eventually switched from engineering to economics and, thanks to a stint at Lehman College in New York City, expects to get his BU diploma.

Academic disillusionment can come in other forms. Hispanics who reach colleges are used to being considered part of an elite—which they are. "The Mexican-American students that come to the University of Texas think that they have it made, because they were stars in high school," says Consuelo Trevino, a counselor in the dean's office at UT. "When they start competing, they realize that they're competing with stars. It's a big shock."

Hispanic college students say that discrimination is pervasive in American colleges and universities, sometimes in subtle ways, sometimes overtly. The stereotypes of Hispanics fed by television and the movies persist—Latinos as dope peddlers and pimps, people who wear their pants low and just arrived by swimming across some river.

"I've been stereotyped out the wazoo," says Jake Foley, a 22-year-old Mexican-American accounting student at the University of Texas who grew up in the Rio Grande Valley. "People will joke around—at least, I hope they're joking—and say, 'Oh, he's Mexican, hide your wallet.' Or,

'Do you have a switchblade?' Or, 'Do you go out and buy velvet posters of Elvis?' They're insulting you in a public setting without knowing who you are, what you've done, what you've accomplished. You grow up around 4,400 Mexican-Americans, and you don't think you're different. You don't know you're different until people point it out."

Efrain Ramos, a 21-year-old government major at Notre Dame, recalls his freshman year when students on his dormitory floor decided to adopt a Mexican theme for a dance. "They were talking about putting a stream down the hall and distributing green cards," he said. "That got me really mad. I get very offended by that kind of stuff." Now that his feelings are known on such matters, he added, "people are cautious around me."

Cynthia Salinas, who graduated from Indiana University last year, chalks such incidents up mainly to ignorance. "I never really came across any prejudice or racial slurs—just some misunderstanding of who I was," she says. "Was I from another country? They asked me if I was from Spain."

Other Hispanic undergraduates, however, have other tales to tell. "I never really experienced racism until I got to this university," says Raul Mendez, a senior English major at UCLA who is from New Orleans. "I was very ignorant." When he went to apply for California residency, a move that would mean considerably lower tuition bills, he encountered a "very antagonistic" clerk who turned him down.

"I have a friend who arrived at the same time I did, lived in the same dorm I did, and applied for residency when I did, but she was white," Mr. Mendez reports. Even though he had a California driver's license and a part-time job, he said, "She got residency, and I didn't. All the clerk would say was, 'Your papers are not qualified.'" Eventually, by appealing the decision, he got his residency.

Many Hispanic students feel themselves under pressure to continually justify their presence on a college campus, in part because of the existence of affirmative action programs. "We carry a stigma in a sense," said Irma Rodriguez, a 21-year-old senior at the University of California at Berkeley. "When I first came here as a freshman, a white undergraduate said to me, 'You're here, and my friend, who is better qualified, is not.'"

Mr. Mendez of UCLA says that he has heard the arguments against affirmative action over and over and takes the position that majority students just don't understand the situation. "What they don't realize is that we have to fight other barriers than they do," he observes. "We're from a different culture. We have pressures on us not to lose our culture, while maintaining a status quo in this culture. That's a big pressure. Some people don't think it is, but it is. You lose your culture. You get branded as a sellout. People who argue against affirmative action often aren't aware of our backgrounds or how we feel. They don't understand where we're coming from. If they did, they'd realize that affirmative action has helped a lot of people."

The problem of how to balance participation in two cultures is a continuing one, and each Hispanic student must make his or her own decision. Some join Hispanic social or political groups and affirm their heritage as overtly as possible. Others become "coconuts"—brown on the outside, white on the inside—but this leads to charges of "selling out."

Juggling two cultures is never an easy task. "I think I'm always swimming against the current," says Lupe Gallegos-Diaz, a 26-year-old graduate student at Berkeley. "I feel as a Chicana that I always have to perform. I have to know my material, then deliver it in a forceful, articulate manner. Otherwise, you're stereotyped as not being able to cope." Even the most successful students are not immune from subtle forms of racism, says Mr. Lopez. "Sometimes that will take the form of someone's saying, 'You say you're Chicano, but you're not really like them. You're not the way they are.'"

Scratch a Hispanic college student, and you'll probably find someone in his or her background who showed a special interest in them, who took them aside and gave them the aspiration and encouragement to go on to higher education. For Jorge A. Ontiveros, a student at Our Lady of the Lake College in San Antonio, it was the Hispanic doctor down the street where he grew up in Dallas. "He told me that I had to go to college," he says, "It was his way of putting back what he himself got."

Eusebia Aquino, a 1983 graduate of Wayne State University who is now a nurse, arrived in this country from Puerto Rico at the age of six. She grew up in Detroit in a single-parent family and had to drop out of school for four years to help raise her eight brothers and sisters, but she was encouraged by the local priest to fulfill her academic promise. "I used to steal books from Holy Trinity Church," she says. "I couldn't read English, but I had a hunger to learn, so I would take them. I found out many years later that Father Kern would leave books out for me to take that he thought I'd like." The priest turned out to be more supportive than her high school counselor, who refused to give her application forms for Wayne State or the University of Michigan. "Instead, she said I should take a housekeeping job at the K-Mart downtown because that's what Hispanic women are supposed to do," she recalls.

Hispanic students say that they feel the absence of "role models" once they get to predominantly Anglo colleges and universities. Julie Martinez, a senior at Stanford who is from a predominantly Hispanic working-class high school in San Antonio, wants to become an anthropology professor and says that the biggest improvement Stanford could make would be to have more Latino faculty members. "Just having them here makes a big difference," she observes. "They serve as role models. Before I came here, I had never seen a Mexican-American in a position where I wanted to be in ten years."

Not surprisingly, Hispanic college students are conscious that they, too, become role models for their siblings or other younger Hispanics. Miss Aquino encouraged four of her brothers and sisters to get their high school equivalency diplomas, and three of them are now in college. Miss Martinez knows that her progress at Stanford is being watched closely by people in her hometown.

"Coming here was a really big deal," she says. "Everyone from my community is watching me. If I do well, people will encourage their children to do well in school and go to college." Her status as a role model is complex, though, because of her aspirations to become an anthropology professor. "If I drive back in a beat-up little car in 15 years—even if I'm a university professor—they'll say, 'What good did it do her? All that money, all that work and time? That guy down the street who got a job at the grocery store was more successful.'"

A universal theme among Hispanics in American colleges is the need for adequate support systems. This starts, of course, well before college. "Many Hispanics are first-generation college students with very little knowledge of exactly what the heck they are getting into," says Jose Anaya, a Mexican-born student from East Chicago at Indiana University and president of Latinos Unidos, a campus Hispanic group.

Mr. Anaya came to Indiana through the Groups Special Services Program that takes students who might not be considered college material and puts them through a summer program to help shore up their academic and nonacademic skills. "I was scared and a little timid," he recalls. "I decided to find out if I could survive a large campus. The Groups Program offered me an opportunity without throwing me in the waters and saying 'swim or drown.'"

Miss Aquino found help in the Chicano-Boricua Studies Program (CBS). "When I came to Wayne State, I felt totally isolated," she recalled. "There was no one who cared outside of CBS. I wasn't white enough to join white groups or black enough to join black groups, so I hibernated at the CBS offices." Without this backing, she added, "I would be barefoot and pregnant somewhere in the city."

This tendency to stick close to other Hispanics and to Hispanic campus organizations is not unusual. "It's taken this long to establish the ethnic organizations, and students see that as being their thing," says Miss Meier of Stanford.

This may be one reason why Hispanics typically end up majoring in the humanities and social sciences. "It might have to do with the fact that there are already more Latinos in social science or that are interested in literature," suggests Mr. Lopez of UCLA. "One thing that has characterized the Chicano movement in general is a great deal of continuity." Being part of a minority group can also have a profound effect on academic choices. "Perhaps it has something to do with growing up in a marginalized cultural group," he comments. "Maybe we study cultural things as a consequence of that. When you grow up in a marginalized group, even if you're becoming an intellectual, you're interested in understanding that."

One of the great strengths of Hispanic culture is the close family relationships that it fosters, and these have a profound influence on the experience of Hispanic college students. Many will tell you how hard it was to break away from their families to come in the first place. "I have a lot of friends back home who are smart enough to be here and who could afford it through scholarships and their parents," says Alicia Estes, a 19-year-old Mexican-American at the University of Texas. "But because of the close family ties they have, their parents didn't want them to come."

Given the strength of family bonds, the first weeks and months of the freshman year can be difficult. Mr. Ramos at Notre Dame says that at first he "couldn't control" his homesickness. "I couldn't concentrate when I was studying," he recalls. "We hold family very important. We're very attached to our families. I've heard it causes a great deal of drop-outs because they can't deal with homesickness."

University administrators tell stories of students going home for Christmas vacation and not coming back, and Hispanic students seem more willing than students in similar economic situations to put aside their academic plans to help earn money for their family. "We are brought up to do things for the good of the family," says Antoinette Garza, director of library services at Our Lady of the Lake. "It is difficult for us to put ourselves first, even as an adult."

Hispanic cultural values sometimes come into conflict with those that make for academic success. For Hispanics, looking someone in the eye is seen as a sign of disrespect, even if that person is standing in front of you in a classroom. "You're taught to be more humble and not to question authority," says Sylvia Garza at the University of Texas at San Antonio. "It's real hard to ask questions."

This can translate into a tendency not to make use of the academic resources available. "Minority students, and Hispanics in particular, are not prepared by high schools to be assertive enough, to make use of all the services this university has," says Alberto Torchinsky, dean of Latino Affairs at Indiana University. "Indiana University doesn't extend a welcome mat to the Hispanic students. I'm sure other universities don't either."

But Hispanic college students are, almost by definition, resilient. Mr. Lopez of UCLA is managing editor of *La Gente*, the Hispanic student newspaper, and he sees such activities as providing a higher sense of loyalty to his people. "To be a politically conscious Chicano gives me a sense of profound responsibility," he says. "We're working for better lives for our raza, which to me means access to socioeconomic mobility and to social justice. To me, being a Chicano student and activist just means pursuing fairness. Today, in this society, that's asking a lot."

Hispanic students are also increasingly conscious that, for all the obstacles they face—inferior schools, insensitive high school counselors, stereotyping, and the like—a college education is worth the effort. "To me, being a Latino student means trying to succeed, using all the resources within my grasp," says Mr. Mendez of UCLA. "It means meeting others' expectations—peers and family members—to achieve what other Latinos were unable to achieve."

Miss Medina of the University of Texas at San Antonio, the youngest of four children, all of whom have gone to college, put it best. "Our family doesn't have money or a business to pass down to our children," she says. "All we have is education. And that's something that no one can ever take from you."

DIALOGUE

1. In what ways is the college experience of Hispanic students different from that of other minority students? How is it similar?
2. Why is failure in the classroom such a frequent occurrence for Hispanic students?
3. Edward B. Fiske points out that many Hispanic students are the first members of their families to attend college. What are some of the consequences for Hispanic students who find themselves in this situation? How might this factor influence their chances for success or failure?

WRITING TOPICS

1. Define the term *coconut* as it is sometimes applied to Hispanic students.
2. The experiences of all first-year college students are similar as they confront new freedoms and challenges. Describe the culture shock that you have felt in moving from your former situation to your first semester in college. Are there aspects of the transition that have been made more difficult because of racial, ethnic, socioeconomic, cultural, or family issues?
3. In an essay, argue against one of the following statements:

   Affirmative action programs place unfair pressure on Hispanic students, allow marginally qualified Hispanic students to enter college, and stigmatize the achievements of those who receive affirmative action benefits.

   OR

   Affirmative action programs are essential to the success of Hispanic students in college. They encourage greater numbers of Hispanic students to enroll in college, help them overcome cultural and educational barriers, and facilitate academic achievement that leads to social progress.

INTERACTION

Fiske suggests that if there were more Hispanic faculty members, they could serve as role models and help ensure greater academic success for Hispanic students. Working in groups, brainstorm creative strategies that your college could implement to recruit and hire more Hispanic faculty.

The Harmful Myth of Asian Superiority
Ronald Takaki

PREVIEW

When compared to other minority groups, Asian-Americans are some-times called the "model minority." According to this popular view, Asian-Americans are viewed as more industrious, law-abiding, and in-telligent than other ethnic minority groups in the United States. Ac-cording to Ronald Takaki, a third-generation Japanese-American who teaches ethnic studies at the University of California–Berkeley, such a view distorts the reality of the lives of Asian-Americans. In his 1989 book Strangers from a Different Shore, *Professor Takaki chronicles the turbulent history of Asian immigrants to the United States and the discrimination they suffered upon their arrival. In this* New York Times *article, he offers a reality check to those who continue to pro-mulgate the myth of Asian-American prosperity.*

Asian-Americans have increasingly come to be viewed as a "model mi-nority." But are they as successful as claimed? And for whom are they supposed to be a model?

Asian-Americans have been described in the media as "excessively, even provocatively" successful in gaining admission to universities. Asian-American shopkeepers have been congratulated, as well as criti-cized, for their ubiquity and entrepreneurial effectiveness.

If Asian-Americans can make it, many politicians and pundits ask, why can't African-Americans? Such comparisons pit minorities against each other and generate African-American resentment toward Asian-Americans. The victims are blamed for their plight, rather than racism and an economy that has made many young African-American workers superfluous.

The celebration of Asian-Americans has obscured reality. For exam-ple, figures on the high earnings of Asian-Americans relative to Cau-casians are misleading. Most Asian-Americans live in California, Hawaii, and New York—states with higher incomes and higher costs of living than the national average.

SOURCE: Ronald Takaki, "The Harmful Myth of Asian Superiority," *New York Times* (June 16, 1990). Copyright © 1990 by The New York Times Co. Reprinted by permission.

Even Japanese-Americans, often touted for their upward mobility, have not reached equality. While Japanese-American men in California earned an average income comparable to Caucasian men in 1980, they did so only by acquiring more education and working more hours.

Comparing family incomes is even more deceptive. Some Asian-American groups do have higher family incomes than Caucasians. But they have more workers per family.

The "model minority" image homogenizes Asian-Americans and hides their differences. For example, while thousands of Vietnamese-American young people attend universities, others are on the streets. They live in motels and hang out in pool halls in places like East Los Angeles; some join gangs.

Twenty-five percent of the people in New York City's Chinatown lived below the poverty level in 1980, compared with 17 percent of the city's population. Some 60 percent of the workers in the Chinatowns of Los Angeles and San Francisco are crowded into low-paying jobs in garment factories and restaurants.

"Most immigrants coming into Chinatown with a language barrier cannot go outside this confined area into the mainstream of American industry," a Chinese immigrant said. "Before, I was a painter in Hong Kong, but I can't do it here. I got no license, no education. I want a living; so it's dishwasher, janitor, or cook."

Hmong and Mien refugees from Laos have unemployment rates that reach as high as 80 percent. A 1987 California study showed that 3 out of 10 Southeast Asian refugee families had been on welfare for 4 to 10 years.

Although college-educated Asian-Americans are entering the professions and earning good salaries, many hit the "glass ceiling"—the barrier through which high management positions can be seen but not reached. In 1988, only 8 percent of Asian-Americans were "officials" and "managers," compared with 12 percent for all groups.

Finally, the triumph of Korean immigrants has been exaggerated. In 1988, Koreans in the New York metropolitan area earned only 68 percent of the median income of non-Asians. More than three-quarters of Korean greengrocers, those so-called paragons of bootstrap entrepreneurialism, came to America with a college education. Engineers, teachers, or administrators while in Korea, they became shopkeepers after their arrival. For many of them, the greengrocery represents dashed dreams, a step downward in status.

For all their hard work and long hours, most Korean shopkeepers do not actually earn very much: $17,000 to $35,000 a year, usually representing the income from the labor of an entire family.

But most Korean immigrants do not become shopkeepers. Instead, many find themselves trapped as clerks in grocery stores, service workers in restaurants, seamstresses in garment factories, and janitors in hotels.

Most Asian-Americans know their "success" is largely a myth. They also see how the celebration of Asian-Americans as a "model minority" perpetuates their inequality and exacerbates relations between them and African-Americans.

DIALOGUE

1. How does the Asian American image as a "model minority" actually work to perpetuate their inequality in relation to other minority groups?
2. In what ways are myths and stereotypes about one group of people harmful to other groups of people?
3. What can college students do to counteract ethnic myths and stereotypes?

WRITING TOPICS

1. If there were such a thing as a model minority, what characteristics would this group possess? Is there such a group in American society? On college campuses? Why or why not would such a group exist? Compare and contrast the experience of Asian Americans with that of another cultural minority in America. What do these similarities and differences tell us about each group?
2. Describe a particular relationship or encounter that changed your thinking about another culture or ethnic group. Was it a positive or negative experience? Explain.
3. List ways that the Asian American experience directly parallels the circumstances of Hispanics, Native Americans, African Americans, and other minority groups. What can be learned by establishing such parallels?

INTERACTION

In small groups, make a list of ethnic minority groups in the United States. What myths and stereotypes are associated with each group? Discuss the extent to which these stereotypical views are accurate or inaccurate.

It's Time to Stop Playing Indians
Arlene B. Hirschfelder

PREVIEW

Some white Americans justify the stereotyping of Native Americans as harmless fun or even as a sincere effort to memorialize a noble race of people. In this article, Arlene B. Hirschfelder, an expert on Native American history and culture, argues that Indian iconography, as it is manifested in Thanksgiving pageants, Halloween costumes, and sports team nicknames and mascots, insults the race and trivializes their miseries. Hirschfelder is the author of the award-winning book Happily May I Walk: American Indians and Alaska Natives. *She works for the Association on American Indian Affairs.*

It is predictable. At Halloween, thousands of children trick-or-treat in Indian costumes. At Thanksgiving, thousands of children parade in school pageants wearing plastic headdresses and pseudo-buckskin clothing. Thousands of card shops stock Thanksgiving greeting cards with images of cartoon animals wearing feathered headbands. Thousands of teachers and librarians trim bulletin boards with Anglo-featured, feathered Indian boys and girls. Thousands of gift shops load their shelves with Indian figurines and jewelry.

Fall and winter are also the seasons when hundreds of thousands of sports fans root for professional, college and public school teams with names that summon up Indians—"Braves," "Redskins," "Chiefs." (In New York State, one out of eight junior and senior high school teams call themselves "Indians," "Tomahawks" and the like.) War-whooping team mascots are imprinted on school uniforms, postcards, notebooks, tote bags and car floor mats.

All of this seems innocuous; why make a fuss about it? Because these trappings and holiday symbols offend tens of thousands of other Americans—the Native American people. Because these invented images prevent millions of us from understanding the authentic Indian America, both long ago and today. Because this image-making prevents Indians from being a relevant part of the nation's social fabric.

Halloween costumes mask the reality of high mortality rates, high di-

SOURCE: Arlene B. Hirschfelder, "It's Time to Stop Playing Indians," *Los Angeles Times* (November 25, 1987). Copyright, 1987, Los Angeles Times. Reprinted by permission.

abetes rates, high unemployment rates. They hide low average life spans, low per capita incomes and low educational levels. Plastic war bonnets and ersatz buckskin deprive people from knowing the complexity of Native American heritage—that Indians belong to hundreds of nations that have intricate social organizations, governments, languages, religions and sacred rituals, ancient stories, unique arts and music forms.

Thanksgiving school units and plays mask history. They do not tell how Europeans mistreated Wampanoags and other East Coast Indian peoples during the 17th century. Social studies units don't mention that, to many Indians, Thanksgiving is a day of mourning, the beginning of broken promises, land theft, near extinction of their religions and languages at the hands of invading Europeans.

Athletic team nicknames and mascots disguise real people. War-painted, buckskin-clad, feathered characters keep the fictitious Indian circulating on decals, pennants and team clothing. Toy companies mask Indian identity and trivialize sacred beliefs by manufacturing Indian costumes and headdresses, peace pipes and trick-arrow-through-the-head gags that equate Indianness with playtime. Indian figures equipped with arrows, guns and tomahawks give youngsters the harmful message that Indians favor mayhem. Many Indian people can tell about children screaming in fear after being introduced to them.

It is time to consider how these images impede the efforts of Indian parents and communities to raise their children with positive information about their heritage. It is time to get rid of stereotypes that, whether deliberately or inadvertently, denigrate Indian cultures and people.

It is time to bury the Halloween costumes, trick arrows, bulletin board pin-ups, headdresses and mascots. It has been done before. In the 1970s, after student protests, Marquette University dropped its "Willie Wampum," Stanford University retired its mascot, "Prince Lightfoot," and Eastern Michigan University and Florida State modified their savage-looking mascots to reduce criticism.

It is time to stop playing Indians. It is time to abolish Indian images that sell merchandise. It is time to stop offending Indian people whose lives are all too often filled with economic deprivation, powerlessness, discrimination and gross injustice. This time next year, let's find more appropriate symbols for the holiday and sports seasons.

DIALOGUE

1. Why, according to the author, is it time to "stop playing Indians"? Make a list of her arguments and evaluate them. Which do you think is the strongest argument? Which is the weakest?

2. Is it practical or possible to expect that our society will ever abandon Indian images that sell merchandise? Under what conditions could this occur?
3. How is the Indian cultural heritage misrepresented or ignored in your college's curriculum and student organizations?

WRITING TOPICS

1. What images, costumes, nicknames, or stereotypical figures are associated with non-Indian ethnic groups? Has American society changed the way it treats these images and stereotypes? Are Indian images and symbols treated differently than those of other minority groups? Explore this issue in a brief essay.
2. List creative and constructive ways that your college can help fight prejudicial stereotypes.
3. Arlene B. Hirschfelder asserts that the invented images drawn from Indian culture "prevent millions of us from understanding the authentic Indian America, both long ago and today." Discuss the misunderstandings about Indian culture, life, language, values, and history that have occurred from trivialized and commercialized representations of their ways of life.

INTERACTION

Working in groups, think of racial or cultural epithets that make you angry. How would you feel if your school fielded a team with that name? Consider the following team nicknames and discuss them in your group:

Washington Redskins
Florida State Seminoles
Atlanta Braves
Kansas City Chiefs

Are these names racially or culturally offensive to the group? What about Atlanta's "tomahawk chop" or Florida State's war chant? Do these names and traditions perpetuate negative stereotypes, or are they harmless? If you are Anglo, would you be offended by team names such as the Washington Ofays or the Chicago Honkies? If you are a woman or a pacifist, how would you feel about being counted among the University of Massachusetts Minutemen or the Fighting Irish of Notre Dame?

Try to reach a consensus on which mascot names are acceptable and which should be modified or dropped altogether.

The Recoloring of Campus Life:
Student Racism, Academic Pluralism,
and the End of a Dream

Shelby Steele

PREVIEW

*Shelby Steele, who teaches English at San Jose State University, is a
minority within a minority. Despite impeccable credentials as a scholar
and civil rights activist, Steele has incurred the wrath of many
African-Americans by taking a firm stand against such popular correc-
tive measures as affirmative action hiring procedures, race-based admissions policies, and black studies programs. This essay is one of
several originally written for* Harper's *magazine that examine the
state of race relations on campus. Afro-American studies departments,
all-black fraternities, self-segregation by black students in dining halls
and classrooms, and black student unions, he argues, encourage a separatism that hinders learning by both blacks and whites. He believes
that current racial tensions are the result of group-perpetuated preconceptions of guilt and inferiority among blacks and whites alike.*

In the past few years, we have witnessed what the National Institute
Against Prejudice and Violence calls a "proliferation" of racial incidents
on college campuses around the country. Incidents of on-campus "inter-
group conflict" have occurred at more than 160 colleges in the last two
years, according to the institute. The nature of these incidents has ranged
from open racial violence—most notoriously, the October 1986 beating of
a black student at the University of Massachusetts at Amherst after an argument about the World Series turned into a racial bashing, with a crowd
of up to three thousand whites chasing twenty blacks—to the harassment
of minority students and acts of racial or ethnic insensitivity, with by far
the greatest number of episodes falling in the last two categories. At Yale
last year, a swastika and the words "white power" were painted on the

SOURCE: Shelby Steele, "The Recoloring of Campus Life: Student Racism, Academic Pluralism,
and the End of a Dream. Copyright © 1989 *Harper's Magazine*. All rights reserved. Reproduced
from the February issue by special permission.

university's Afro-American cultural center. Racist jokes were aired not long ago on a campus radio station at the University of Michigan. And at the University of Wisconsin at Madison, members of the Zeta Beta Tau fraternity held a mock slave auction in which pledges painted their faces black and wore Afro wigs. Two weeks after the president of Stanford University informed the incoming freshmen class last fall that "bigotry is out, and I mean it," two freshmen defaced a poster of Beethoven—gave the image thick lips—and hung it on a black student's door.

In response, black students around the country have rediscovered the militant protest strategies of the sixties. At the University of Massachusetts at Amherst, Williams College, Penn State University, University of California–Berkeley, UCLA, Stanford University, and countless other campuses, black students have sat in, marched, and rallied. But much of what they were marching and rallying about seemed less a response to specific racial incidents than a call for broader action on the part of the colleges and universities they were attending. Black students have demanded everything from more black faculty members and new courses on racism to the addition of "ethnic" foods in the cafeteria. There is the sense in these demands that racism runs deep. Is the campus becoming the battleground for a renewed war between the races? I don't think so, not really. But if it is not a war, the problem of campus racism does represent a new and surprising hardening of racial lines within the most traditionally liberal and tolerant of America's institutions—its universities.

As a black who has spent his entire adult life on predominantly white campuses, I found it hard to believe that the problem of campus racism was as dramatic as some of the incidents seemed to make it. The incidents I read or heard about often seemed prankish and adolescent, though not necessarily harmless. There is a meanness in them but not much menace; no one is proposing to reinstitute Jim Crow on campus. On the California campus where I now teach, there have been few signs of racial tension.

And, of course, universities are not where racial problems tend to arise. When I went to college in the mid-sixties, colleges were oases of calm and understanding in a racially tense society; campus life—with its traditions of tolerance and fairness, its very distance from the "real" world—imposed a degree of broad-mindedness on even the most provincial students. If I met whites who were not anxious to be friends with blacks, most were at least vaguely friendly to the cause of our freedom. In any case, there was no guerrilla activity against our presence, no "mine field of racism" (as one black student at Berkeley recently put it to me) to negotiate. I wouldn't say that the phrase "campus racism" is a contradiction in terms, but until recently it certainly seemed an incongruence.

But a greater incongruence is the generational timing of this new problem on the campuses. Today's undergraduates were born after the passage of the 1964 Civil Rights Act. They grew up in an age when racial equality was for the first time enforceable by law. This too was a time when blacks suddenly appeared on television, as mayors of big cities, as icons of popular culture, as teachers, and in some cases even as neighbors. Today's black and white college students, veterans of "Sesame Street" and often of integrated grammar and high schools, have had more opportunities to know each other than any previous generation in American history. Not enough opportunities, perhaps, but enough to make the notion of racial tension on campus something of a mystery, at least to me.

To look at this mystery, I left my own campus with its burden of familiarity and talked with black and white students at California schools where racial incidents had occurred: Stanford, UCLA, and Berkeley. I spoke with black and white students—not with Asians and Hispanics—because, as always, blacks and whites represent the deepest lines of division, and because I hesitate to wander onto the complex territory of other minority groups. A phrase by William H. Gass—"the hidden internality of things"—describes, with maybe a little too much grandeur, what I hoped to find. But it is what I wanted to find, for this is the kind of problem that makes a black person nervous, which is not to say that it doesn't unnerve whites as well. Once every six months or so someone yells "nigger" at me from a passing car. I don't like to think that these solo artists might soon make up a chorus, or worse, that this chorus might one day soon sing to me from the paths of my own campus.

I have long believed that the trouble between the races is seldom what it appears to be. It was not hard to see after my first talks with students that racial tension on campus is a problem that misrepresents itself. It has the same look, the archetypal pattern, of America's timeless racial conflict— white racism and black protest. And I think part of our concern over it comes from the fact that it has the feel of a relapse, illness gone and come again. But if we are seeing the same symptoms, I don't believe we are dealing with the same illness. For one thing, I think racial tension on campus is more the result of racial equality than inequality.

How to live with racial difference has been America's profound social problem. For the first hundred years or so following emancipation it was controlled by a legally sanctioned inequality that kept the races from each other. No longer is this the case. On campuses today, as throughout society, blacks enjoy equality under the law—a profound social advancement. No student may be kept out of a class or a dormitory or an extracurricular activity because of his or her race. But there is a paradox here: on a campus where members of all races are gathered, mixed together in the classroom as well as socially, differences are more exposed than ever. And this is where the trouble starts. For members of each race—young adults coming into their own, often away from home for the first time—bring to this site of freedom, exploration, and (now, today) equality, very deep fears, anxieties, inchoate feelings of racial shame, anger, and guilt. These feelings could lie dormant in the home, in familiar neighborhoods, in simpler days of childhood. But the college campus, with its structures of interaction and adult-level competition—the big exam, the dorm, the mixer—is another matter. I think campus racism is born of the rub between racial difference and a setting, the campus itself, devoted to interaction and equality. On our campuses, such concentrated micro-societies, all that remains unresolved between blacks and whites, all the old wounds and shames that have never been addressed, present themselves for attention—and present our youth with pressures they cannot always handle.

I have mentioned one paradox: racial fears and anxieties among blacks and whites, bubbling up in an era of racial equality under the law, in settings that are among the freest and fairest in society. But there is another, related paradox, stemming from the notion of—and practice of—affirmative action. Under the provisions of the Equal Employment Opportunity Act of 1972, all state governments and institutions (including universities) were forced to initiate plans to increase the proportion of minority and women employees and, in the case of universities, of students too. Affirmative action plans that establish racial quotas were ruled unconstitutional more than ten years ago in *University of California* v. *Bakke,* but such plans are still thought by some to secretly exist, and lawsuits having to do with alleged quotas are still very much with us. But quotas are only the most controversial aspect of affirmative action; the principle of affirmative action is reflected in various university programs aimed at redressing and overcoming past patterns of discrimination. Of course, to be conscious of past patterns of discrimination—the fact, say, that public schools in the black inner cities are more crowded and employ fewer top-notch teachers than a white suburban public school, and that this is a factor in student performance—is only reasonable. But in doing this we also call attention quite obviously to difference: in the case of blacks and whites, racial difference. What has emerged on campus in recent years—as a result of the new equality and of affirmative action and, in a sense, as a result of progress—is a *politics of difference*, a troubling, volatile politics in which each group justifies itself, its sense of worth and its pursuit of power, through difference alone.

In this context, racial, ethnic, and gender differences become forms of sovereignty, campuses become balkanized, and each group fights with whatever means are available. No doubt there are many factors that have contributed to the rise of racial tension on campus: What has been the role of fraternities, which have returned to campus with their inclusions and exclusions? What role has the heightened notion of college as some first step to personal, financial success played in increasing competition, and thus tension? But mostly, what I sense is that in interactive settings, fighting the fights of "difference," old ghosts are stirred and haunt again. Black and white Americans simply have the power to make each other feel shame and guilt. In most situations, we may be able to deny these feelings, keep them at bay. But these feelings are likely to surface on college campuses, where young people are groping for identity and power, and where difference is made to matter so greatly. In a way, racial tension on campus in the eighties might have been inevitable.

I would like, first, to discuss black students, their anxieties and vulnerabilities. The accusation black Americans have always lived with is that they are inferior—inferior simply because they are black—and this accusation has been too uniform, too ingrained in cultural imagery, too enforced by law, custom, and every form of power not to have left a mark. Black inferiority was a precept accepted by the founders of this nation; it was a principle of social organization that relegated blacks to the sidelines of American life. So when young black students find themselves on white campuses surrounded by those who have historically claimed superiority, they are also surrounded by the myth of their inferiority.

Of course, it is true that many young people come to college with some anxiety about not being good enough. But only blacks come wearing a color that is still, in the minds of some, a sign of inferiority. Poles, Jews, Hispanics, and other groups also endure degrading stereotypes. But two things make the myth of black inferiority a far heavier burden— the broadness of its scope and its incarnation in color. There are not only more stereotypes of blacks than of other groups, but these stereotypes are also more dehumanizing, more focused on the most despised human traits: stupidity, laziness, sexual immorality, dirtiness, and so on. In America's racial and ethnic hierarchy, blacks have clearly been relegated to the lowest level—have been burdened with an ambiguous, animalistic humanity. Moreover, this is made unavoidable for blacks by sheer visibility of black skin, a skin that evokes the myth of inferiority on sight. Today this myth is sadly reinforced for many black students by affirmative action programs, under which blacks may often enter college with lower test scores and high school grade point averages than whites. "They see me as an affirmative action case," one black student told me at UCLA. This reinforces the myth of inferiority by implying that blacks are not good enough to make it into college on their own.

So when a black student enters college, the myth of inferiority compounds the normal anxiousness over whether he or she will be good enough. This anxiety is not only personal but also racial. The families of these students will have pounded into them the fact that blacks are not inferior. And probably more than anything it is this pounding that finally leaves the mark. If I am not inferior, why the need to say so?

This myth of inferiority constitutes a very sharp and ongoing anxiety for young blacks, the nature of which is very precise: it is the terror that somehow, through one's actions or by virtue of some "proof" (a poor grade, a flubbed response in class), one's fear of inferiority—inculcated in ways large and small by society—will be confirmed as real. On a university campus where intelligence itself is the ultimate measure, this anxiety is bound to be triggered.

A black student I met at UCLA was disturbed a little when I asked him if he ever felt vulnerable—anxious about "black inferiority"—as a black student. But after a long pause, he finally said, "I think I do." The example he gave was of a large lecture class he'd taken with over three hundred students. Fifty or so black students sat in the back of the lecture hall and "acted out every stereotype in the book." They were loud, ate food, came in late—and generally got lower grades than whites in the class. "I knew I would be seen like them, and I didn't like it. I never sat by them." Seen like what, I asked, though we both knew the answer. "As lazy, ignorant, and stupid," he said sadly.

Had the group at the back been white fraternity brothers, they would not have been seen as dumb whites, of course. And a frat brother who worried about his grades would not worry had he been seen "like them." The terror in this situation for the black student I spoke with was that his own deeply buried anxiety would be given credence, that the myth would be verified, and that he would feel shame and humiliation not because of who he was but simply because he was black. In this lecture hall his race, quite apart from his performance, might subject him to four unendurable feelings—diminishment, accountability to the preconception of whites, a powerlessness to change those preconceptions, and finally, shame. These are the feelings that make up his racial anxiety, and that of all blacks on any campus. On a white campus a black is never far from these feelings, and even his unconscious knowledge that he is subject to them can undermine his self-esteem. There are blacks on any campus who are not up to doing good college-level work. Certain black students may not be happy or motivated or in the appropriate field of study—*just like whites.* (Let us not forget that many white students get poor grades, fail, drop out.) Moreover, many more blacks than whites are not quite prepared for college, may have to catch up, owing to factors beyond their control: poor previous schooling, for example. But the white who has to catch up will not be anxious that his being behind is a matter of his whiteness, of his being racially inferior. The black student may well have such a fear.

This, I believe, is one reason why black colleges in America turn out 37 percent of all black college graduates though they enroll only 16 percent of black college students. Without whites around on campus, the myth of inferiority is in abeyance and, along with it, a great reservoir of culturally imposed self-doubt. On black campuses, feelings of inferiority are personal; on campuses with a white majority, a black's problems have a way of becoming a "black" problem.

But this feeling of vulnerability a black may feel, in itself, is not as serious a problem as what he or she does with it. To admit that one is made anxious in integrated situations about the myth of racial inferiority is difficult for young blacks. It seems like admitting that one is racially inferior. And so, most often, the student will deny harboring the feelings. This is where some of the pangs of racial tension begin, because denial always involves distortion.

In order to deny a problem we must tell ourselves that the problem is something different from what it really is. A black student at Berkeley told me that he felt defensive every time he walked into a classroom of white faces. When I asked why, he said, "Because I know they're all racists. They think blacks are stupid." Of course it may be true that some whites feel this way, but the singular focus on white racism allows this student to obscure his own underlying racial anxiety. He can now say that his problem—facing a classroom of white faces, *fearing* that they think he is dumb—is entirely the result of certifiable white racism and has nothing to do with his own anxieties, or even that this particular academic subject may not be his best. Now all the terror of his anxiety, its powerful energy, is devoted to simply *seeing* racism. Whatever evidence of racism he finds—and looking this hard, he will no doubt find some—can be brought in to buttress his distorted view of the problem while his actual deep-seated anxiety goes unseen.

Denial, and the distortion that results, places the problem *outside* the self and in the world. It is not that I have any inferiority anxiety because of my race; it is that I am going to school with people who don't like blacks. This is the shift in thinking that allows black students to reenact the protest pattern of the sixties. *Denied racial anxiety-distortion-reenactment* is the process by which feelings of inferiority are transformed into an exaggerated white menace—which is then protested against with the techniques of the past. Under the sway of this process, black students believe that history is repeating itself, that it's just like the sixties, or fifties. In fact, it is not-yet-healed wounds from the past, rather than the inequality that created the wounds, that is the real problem.

This process generates an unconscious need to exaggerate the level of racism on campus—to make it a matter of the system, not just a handful of students. Racism is the avenue away from the true inner anxiety. How many students demonstrating for black theme dorms—demonstrating in the style of the sixties, when the battle was to win for blacks a place on campus—might be better off spending their time reading and studying? Black students have the highest dropout rate and the lowest grade point average of any group in American universities. This need not be so. And it is not the result of not having black theme dorms.

It was my very good fortune to go to college in 1964, when the question of black "inferiority" was openly talked about among blacks. The summer before I left for college, I heard Martin Luther King speak in Chicago, and he laid it on the line for black students everywhere: "When you are behind in a footrace, the only way to get ahead is to run faster than the man in front of you. So when your white roommate says he's tired and goes to sleep, you stay up and burn the midnight oil." His statement that we were "behind in a footrace" acknowledged that, because of history, of few opportunities, of racism, we were, in a sense, "inferior." But this had to do with what had been done to our parents and their parents, not with inherent inferiority. And because it was acknowledged, it was presented to us as a challenge rather than a mark of shame.

Of the eighteen black students (in a student body of one thousand) who were on campus in my freshman year, all graduated, though a number of us were not from the middle class. At the university where I currently teach, the dropout rate for black students is 72 percent, despite the presence of several academic support programs, a counseling center with black counselors, an Afro-American studies department, black faculty, administrators, and staff, a general education curriculum that emphasizes "cultural pluralism," an Educational Opportunities Program, a mentor program, a black faculty and staff association, and an administration and faculty that often announce the need to do more for black students.

It may be unfair to compare my generation with the current one. Parents do this compulsively and to little end but self-congratulation. But I don't congratulate my generation. I think we were advantaged. We came along at a time when racial integration was held in high esteem. And integration was a very challenging social concept for both blacks and whites. We were remaking ourselves—that's what one did at college—and making history. We had something to prove. This was a profound advantage; it gave us clarity and a challenge. Achievement in the American mainstream was the goal of integration, and the best thing about this challenge was its secondary message—that we *could* achieve.

There is much irony in the fact that black power would come along in the late sixties and change all this. Black power was a movement of uplift and pride, and yet it also delivered the weight of pride—a weight that would burden black students from then on. Black power "nationalized" the black identity, made blackness itself an object of celebration, an allegiance. But if it transformed a mark of shame into a mark of pride, it also, in the name of pride, required the denial of racial anxiety. Without a frank account of one's anxieties, there is no clear direction, no concrete challenge. Black students today do not get as clear a message from their racial identity as my generation got. They are not filled with the same urgency to prove themselves because black pride has said, *You're already proven, already equal, as good as anybody.*

The "black identity" shaped by black power most forcefully contributes to racial tensions on campuses by basing entitlement more on race than on constitutional rights and standards of merit. With integration, black entitlement derived from constitutional principles of fairness. Black power changed this by skewing the formula from rights to color—if you were black, you were entitled. Thus the United Coalition Against Racism (UCAR) at the University of Michigan could "demand" two years ago that all black professors be given immediate tenure, that there is a special pay incentive for black professors, and that money be provided for an all-black student union. In this formula, black becomes the very color of entitlement, an extra right in itself, and a very dangerous grandiosity is promoted in which blackness amounts to specialness.

Race is, by any standard, an unprincipled source of power. And on campuses the use of racial power by one group makes racial, ethnic, or gender difference a currency of power for all groups. When I make my *difference* into power, other groups must seize upon their difference to contain my power and maintain their position relative to me. Very quickly a kind of politics of difference emerges in which racial, ethnic, and gender groups are forced to assert their entitlement and vie for power based on the single quality that makes them different from one another.

On many campuses today academic departments and programs are established on the basis of difference—black studies, women's studies, Asian studies, and so on—despite the fact that there is nothing in these "difference" departments that cannot be studied within traditional academic disciplines. If their rationale is truly past exclusion from the mainstream curriculum, shouldn't the goal now be complete inclusion rather than separateness? I think this logic is overlooked because those groups are too interested in the power their difference can bring, and they insist on separate departments and programs as tribute to that power.

This politics of difference makes everyone on campus a member of a minority group. It also makes racial tension inevitable. To highlight one's difference as a source of advantage is also, indirectly, to inspire the enemies of that difference. When blackness (and femaleness) becomes power, then white maleness is also sanctioned as power. A white male student I spoke with at Stanford said, "One of my friends said the other day that we should get together and start up a white student union and come up with a list of demands."

It is certainly true that white maleness has long been an unfair source of power. But the sin of white male power is precisely its use of race and gender as a source of entitlement. When minorities and women use their race, ethnicity, and gender in the same way, they not only commit the same sin but also, indirectly, sanction the very form of power that oppressed them in the first place. The politics of difference is based on a tit-for-tat sort of logic in which every victory only calls one's enemies to arms.

This elevation of difference undermines the communal impulse by making each group foreign and inaccessible to others. When difference is celebrated rather than remarked, people must think in terms of difference, they must find meaning in difference, and this meaning comes from an endless process of contrasting one's group with other groups. Blacks use whites to define themselves as different, women use men, Hispanics use whites and blacks, and on it goes. And in the process each group mythologizes and mystifies its difference, puts it beyond the full comprehension of outsiders. Difference becomes inaccessible preciousness toward which outsiders are expected to be simply and uncomprehendingly reverential. But beware: in this world, even the insulated world of the college campus, preciousness is a balloon asking for a needle. At Smith College graffiti appears: "Niggers, spics, and chinks. Quit complaining or get out."

I think that those who run our colleges and universities are every bit as responsible for the politics of difference as are minority students. To correct the exclusions once caused by race and gender, universities—under the banner of affirmative action—have relied too heavily on race and gender as criteria. So rather than break the link between difference and power, they have reinforced it. On most campuses today, a well-to-do black student with two professional parents is qualified by his race for scholarship monies that are not available to a lower-class white student. A white female with a private school education and every form of cultural advantage comes under the affirmative action umbrella. This kind of inequity is an invitation to backlash.

What universities are quite rightly trying to do is compensate people for past discrimination and the deprivations that followed from it. But race and gender alone offer only the grossest measure of this. And the failure of universities has been their backing away from the challenge of identifying principles of fairness and merit that make finer and more equitable distinctions. The real challenge is not simply to include a certain number of blacks, but to end discrimination against all blacks and to offer special help to those with talent who have also been economically deprived.

With regard to black students, affirmative action has led universities to correlate color with poverty and disadvantage in so absolute a way as to encourage the politics of difference. But why have they gone along with this? My belief is that it is due to the specific form of racial anxiety to which whites are most subject.

Most of the white students I talked with spoke as if from under a faint cloud of accusation. There was always a ring of defensiveness in their complaints about blacks. A white student I spoke to at UCLA told me: "Most white students on this campus think the black student leadership here is made up of oversensitive crybabies who spend all their time looking for things to kick up a ruckus about." A white student at Stanford said, "Blacks do nothing but complain and ask for sympathy when everyone really knows that they don't do well because they don't try. If they worked harder, they could do as well as everyone else."

That these students felt accused was most obvious in their compulsion to assure me that they were not racist. Oblique versions of some-of-my-best-friends-are stories came ritualistically before or after critiques of black students. Some said flatly, "I am not a racist, but. . . ." Of course, we all deny being racist, but we only do this compulsively, I think, when we are working against an accusation of bias. I think it was the color of my skin itself that accused them.

This was the meta-message that surrounded these conversations like an aura, and it is, I believe, the core of white American racial anxiety. My skin not only accused them; it judged them. And this judgment was a sad gift of history that brought them to account whether they deserved such accountability or not. It said that wherever and whenever blacks were concerned, they had reason to feel guilt. And whether it was earned or unearned, I think it was guilt that set off the compulsion in these students to disclaim. I believe it is true that, in America, black people make white people feel guilty.

Guilt is the essence of white anxiety just as inferiority is the essence of black anxiety. And the terror that it carries for whites is the terror of discovering that one has reason to feel guilt where blacks are concerned— not so much because of what blacks might think but because of what guilt can say about oneself. If the darkest fear of blacks is inferiority, the darkest fear of whites is that their better lot in life is at least partially the result of their capacity for evil—their capacity to dehumanize an entire people for their own benefit and then to be indifferent to the devastation their dehumanization has wrought on successive generations of their victims. This is the terror that whites are vulnerable to regarding blacks. And the mere fact of being white is sufficient to feel it, since even whites with hearts clean of racism benefit from being white—benefit at the expense of blacks. This is a conditional guilt having nothing to do with individual intentions or actions. And it makes for a very powerful anxiety because it threatens whites with a view of themselves as inhuman, just as inferiority threatens blacks with a similar view of themselves. At the dark core of both anxieties is a suspicion of incomplete humanity.

So, the white students I met were not just meeting me; they were also meeting the possibility of their own inhumanity. And this, I think, is what explains how some young white college students in the late eighties could so frankly take part in racially insensitive and outright racist acts. They were expected to be cleaner of racism than any previous generation—they were born into the Great Society. But this expectation overlooks the fact that, for them, color is still an accusation and judgment. In black faces there is a discomforting reflection of white collective shame. Blacks remind them that their racial innocence is questionable, that they are the beneficiaries of past and present racism, and the sins of the father may well have been visited on the children.

And yet young whites tell themselves that they had nothing to do with the oppression of black people. They have a stronger belief in their racial innocence than any previous generation of whites and a natural hostility toward anyone who would challenge that innocence. So (with a great deal of individual variation) they can end up in the paradoxical position of being hostile to blacks as a way of defending their own racial innocence.

I think this is what the young white editors of the *Dartmouth Review* were doing when they harassed black music professor William Cole. Weren't they saying, in effect, I am so free of racial guilt that I can afford to attack blacks ruthlessly and still be racially innocent? The ruthlessness of these attacks was a form of denial, a badge of innocence. The more they were charged with racism, the more ugly and confrontational their harassment became (an escalation unexplained even by the serious charges against Professor Cole). Racism became a means of rejecting racial guilt, a way of showing that they were not, ultimately, racists.

The politics of difference sets up a struggle for innocence among all groups. When difference is the currency of power, each group must fight for the innocence that entitles it to power. To gain this innocence, blacks sting whites with guilt, remind them of their racial past, accuse them of new and more subtle forms of racism. One way whites retrieve their innocence is to discredit blacks and deny their difficulties, for in this denial is the denial of their own guilt. To blacks this denial looks like racism, a racism that feeds black innocence and encourages them to throw more guilt at whites. And so the cycle continues. The politics of difference leads each group to pick at the vulnerabilities of the other.

Men and women who run universities—whites, mostly—participate in the politics of difference because they handle their guilt differently than do many of their students. They don't deny it, but still they don't want to *feel* it. And to avoid this feeling of guilt they have tended to go along with whatever blacks put on the table rather than work with them to assess their real needs. University administrators have too often been afraid of guilt and have relied on negotiation and capitulation more to appease their own guilt than to help blacks and other minorities. Administrators would never give white students a racial theme dorm where they could be "more comfortable with people of their own kind," yet more and more universities are doing this for black students, thus fostering a kind of voluntary segregation. To avoid the anxieties of integrated situations blacks ask for theme dorms; to avoid guilt, white administrators give theme dorms.

When everyone is on the run from their anxieties about race, race relations on campus can be reduced to the negotiation of avoidances. A pattern of demand and concession develops in which both sides use the other to escape themselves. Black studies departments, black deans of student affairs, black counseling programs, Afro houses, black theme dorms, black homecoming dances and graduation ceremonies—black students and white administrators have slowly engineered a machinery of separatism that, in the name of sacred difference, redraws the ugly lines of segregation.

Black students have not sufficiently helped themselves, and universities, despite all their concessions, have not really done much for blacks. If both faced their anxieties, I think they would see the same thing: academic parity with all other groups should be the overriding mission of black students, and it should also be the first goal that universities have for their black students. Blacks can only *know* they are as good as others when they are, in fact, as good—when their grades are higher and their dropout rate lower. Nothing under the sun will substitute for this, and no amount of concessions will bring it about.

Universities can never be free of guilt until they truly help black students, which means leading and challenging them rather than negotiating and capitulating. It means inspiring them to achieve academic parity, nothing less, and helping them to see their own weaknesses as their greatest challenge. It also means dismantling the machinery of separatism, breaking the link between difference and power, and skewing the formula for entitlement away from race and gender and back to constitutional rights.

As for the young white students who have rediscovered swastikas and the word "nigger," I think that they suffer from an exaggerated sense of their own innocence, as if they were incapable of evil and beyond the reach of guilt. But it is also true that the politics of difference creates an environment that threatens their innocence and makes them defensive. White students are not invited to the negotiating table from which they see blacks and others walk away with concessions. The presumption is that they deserve to be there because they are white. So they can only be defensive, and the less mature among them will be aggressive. Guerrilla activity will ensue. Of course this is wrong, but it is also a reflection of an environment where difference carries power and where whites have the wrong "difference."

I think universities should emphasize commonality as a higher value than "diversity" and "pluralism"—buzzwords for the politics of difference. Difference that does not rest on a clearly delineated foundation of commonality is not only inaccessible to those who are not part of the ethnic or racial group, but also antagonistic to them. Difference can enrich only the common ground.

Integration has become an abstract term today, having to do with little more than numbers and racial balances. But it once stood for a high and admirable set of values. It made difference second to commonality, and it asked members of all races to face whatever fears they inspired in each other. I doubt the word will have a new vogue, but the values, under whatever name, are worth working for.

DIALOGUE

1. Shelby Steele asserts that there has been a recent rise in racial tension on American campuses. What factors does he say have contributed to this situation? Are these or other factors present on your campus?

2. The author suggests that academic programs based on difference (black studies, women's studies, Asian studies, and so on) should be abolished and incorporated into traditional disciplines. On what basis does he make this recommendation? Do you agree or disagree? Explain.

3. How do Steele's ideas and positions challenge the agenda of civil rights organizations and their advocates?

WRITING TOPICS

1. Define and illustrate what Steele means by a "politics of difference."

2. Survey eight to ten students from different ethnic groups on campus to determine their attitudes toward affirmative action policies and programs. Sample questions might include the following:

   - Have you benefited personally from affirmative action?
   - Should affirmative action programs primarily use the criteria of race and gender?
   - What considerations are appropriate to correct exclusions and compensate for past discrimination?
   - What principles of fairness and merit should be considered?

   Record responses and draw conclusions.

3. In an essay, argue for or against the following proposition:

   Black students would be more successful academically and socially if they attended black colleges.

INTERACTION

Working in groups, discuss the nature and intensity of racism on your campus. Is there observable racial tension? If so, what is the source of that tension, and how is it expressed? Suggest specific ways to reduce or eliminate racial tension on your campus. Then share your group's ideas with the other groups.

Don't Just Stand There
Diane Cole

PREVIEW

People who are sensitive to cultural differences and have learned to treat others as individuals rather than stereotypes are often uncomfortable when they hear ethnic jokes and prejudicial remarks from those they know and respect. It is difficult to challenge such remarks without appearing holier-than-thou and offending the person who made them.

In "Don't Just Stand There," Diane Cole, a contributing editor of Psychology Today, *offers some practical advice. It's important to take a stand, she insists, whenever and wherever we encounter prejudice. By focusing on one's own feelings instead of lashing out at the offender, one can do this in a way that is most likely to bring about a change of attitude.*

It was my office farewell party, and colleagues at the job I was about to leave were wishing me well. My mood was one of ebullience tinged with regret, and it was in this spirit that I spoke to the office neighbor to whom I had waved hello every morning for the past two years. He smiled broadly as he launched into a long, rambling story, pausing only after he delivered the punch line. It was a very long pause because, although he laughed, I did not: This joke was unmistakably anti-Semitic.

I froze. Everyone in the office knew I was Jewish; what could he have possibly meant? Shaken and hurt, not knowing what else to do, I turned in stunned silence to the next well-wisher. Later, still angry, I wondered, what else should I—could I—have done?

Prejudice can make its presence felt in any setting, but hearing its nasty voice in this way can be particularly unnerving. We do not know what to do and often we feel another form of paralysis as well: We think, "Nothing I say or do will change this person's attitude, so why bother?"

But left unchecked, racial slurs and offensive ethnic jokes "can poison the atmosphere," says Michael McQuillan, adviser for racial/ethnic af-

SOURCE: From *"A World of Difference,"* special supplement to *The New York Times,* sponsored by B'nai B'rith, April 16, 1989, pp. 20–21. Reprinted by permission of the author.

fairs for the Brooklyn borough president's office. "Hearing these remarks conditions us to accept them; and if we accept these, we can become accepting of other acts."

Speaking up may not magically change a biased attitude, but it can change a person's behavior by putting a strong message across. And the more messages there are, the more likely a person is to change that behavior, says Arnold Kahn, professor of psychology at James Madison University, Harrisonburg, Va., who makes this analogy: "You can't keep people from smoking in *their* house, but you can ask them not to smoke in *your* house."

At the same time, "Even if the other party ignores or discounts what you say, people always reflect on how others perceive them. Speaking up always counts," says LeNorman Strong, director of campus life at George Washington University, Washington, D.C.

Finally, learning to respond effectively also helps people feel better about themselves, asserts Cherie Brown, executive director of the National Coalition Building Institute, a Boston-based training organization. "We've found that, when people felt they could at least in this small way make a difference, that made them more eager to take on other activities on a larger scale," she says. Although there is no "cookbook approach" to confronting such remarks—every situation is different, experts stress—these are some effective strategies.

When the "joke" turns on who you are—as a member of an ethnic or religious group, a person of color, a woman, a gay or lesbian, an elderly person, or someone with a physical handicap—shocked paralysis is often the first response. Then, wounded and vulnerable, on some level you want to strike back.

Lashing out or responding in kind is seldom the most effective response, however. "That can give you momentary satisfaction, but you also feel as if you've lowered yourself to that other person's level," Mr. McQuillan explains. Such a response may further label you in the speaker's mind as thin-skinned, someone not to be taken seriously. Or it may up the ante, making the speaker, and then you, reach for new insults—or physical blows.

"If you don't laugh at the joke, or fight, or respond in kind to the slur," says Mr. McQuillan, "that will take the person by surprise, and that can give you more control over the situation." Therefore, in situations like the one in which I found myself—a private conversation in which I knew the person making the remark—he suggests voicing your anger calmly but pointedly: "I don't know if you realize what that sounded like to me. If that's what you meant, it really hurt me."

State how *you* feel, rather than making an abstract statement like, "Not everyone who hears that joke might find it funny." Counsels Mr. Strong: "Personalize the sense of 'this is how I feel when you say this.' That makes it very concrete"—and harder to dismiss.

Make sure you heard the words and their intent correctly by repeating or rephrasing the statement: "This is what I heard you say. Is that what you meant?" It's important to give the other person the benefit of the doubt because, in fact, he may *not* have realized that the comment was offensive and, if you had not spoken up, would have had no idea of its impact on you.

For instance, Professor Kahn relates that he used to include in his exams multiple-choice questions that occasionally contained "incorrect funny answers." After one exam, a student came up to him in private and said, "I don't think you intended this, but I found a number of those jokes offensive to me as a woman." She explained why. "What she said made immediate sense to me," he says. "I apologized at the next class, and I never did it again."

But what if the speaker dismisses your objection, saying, "Oh, you're just being sensitive. Can't you take a joke?" In that case, you might say, "I'm not so sure about that, let's talk about that a little more." The key, Mr. Strong says, is to continue the dialogue, hear the other person's concerns, and point out your own. "There are times when you're just going to have to admit defeat and end it," he adds, "but I have to feel that I did the best I could."

When the offending remark is made in the presence of others—at a staff meeting, for example—it can be even more distressing than an insult made privately.

"You have two options," says William Newlin, director of field services for the Community Relations division of the New York City Commission on Human Rights. "You can respond immediately at the meeting, or you can delay your response until afterward in private. But a response has to come."

Some remarks or actions may be so outrageous that they cannot go unnoted at the moment, regardless of the speaker or the setting. But in general, psychologists say, shaming a person in public may have the opposite effect of the one you want: The speaker will deny his offense all the more strongly in order to save face. Further, few people enjoy being put on the spot, and if the remark really was not intended to be offensive, publicly embarrassing the person who made it may cause an unnecessary rift or further misunderstanding. Finally, most people just don't react as well or thoughtfully under a public spotlight as they would in private.

Keeping that in mind, an excellent alternative is to take the offender aside afterward: "Could we talk for a minute in private?" Then use the strategies suggested above for calmly stating how you feel, giving the speaker the benefit of the doubt, and proceeding from there.

At a large meeting or public talk, you might consider passing the speaker a note, says David Wertheimer, executive director of the New York City Gay and Lesbian Anti-Violence Project: You could write, "You may not realize it, but your remarks were offensive because. . . ."

"Think of your role as that of an educator," suggests James M. Jones, Ph.D., executive director for public interest at the American Psychological Association. "You have to be controlled."

Regardless of the setting or situation, speaking up always raises the risk of rocking the boat. If the person who made the offending remark is your boss, there may be an even bigger risk to consider: How will this affect my job? Several things can help minimize the risk, however. First, know what other resources you may have at work, suggests Caryl Stern, director of the A World of Difference–New York City campaign: Does your personnel office handle discrimination complaints? Are other grievance procedures in place?

You won't necessarily need to use any of these procedures, Ms. Stern stresses. In fact, she advises, "It's usually better to try a one-on-one approach first." But simply knowing a formal system exists can make you feel secure enough to set up that meeting.

You can also raise the issue with other colleagues who heard the remark: Did they feel the same way you did? The more support you have, the less alone you will feel. Your point will also carry more validity and be more difficult to shrug off. Finally, give your boss credit—and the benefit of the doubt: "I know you've worked hard for the company's affirmative action programs, so I'm sure you didn't realize what those remarks sounded like to me as well as the others at the meeting last week. . . ."

If, even after this discussion, the problem persists, go back for another meeting, Ms. Stern advises. And if that, too, fails, you'll know what other options are available to you.

> *It's a spirited dinner party, and everyone's having a good time, until one guest starts reciting a racist joke. Everyone at the table is white, including you. The others are still laughing, as you wonder what to say or do.*

No one likes being seen as a party-pooper, but before deciding that you'd prefer not to take on this role, you might remember that the person who told the offensive joke has already ruined your good time.

If it's a group that you feel comfortable in—a family gathering, for instance—you will feel freer to speak up. Still, shaming the person by shouting "You're wrong!" or "That's not funny!" probably won't get your point across as effectively as other strategies. "If you interrupt people to condemn them, it just makes it harder," says Cherie Brown. She suggests trying instead to get at the resentments that lie beneath the joke by asking open-ended questions: "Grandpa, I know you always treat everyone with such respect. Why do people in our family talk that way about black people?" The key, Ms. Brown says, "is to listen to them first, so they will be more likely to listen to you."

"If you don't know your fellow guests well, before speaking up you could turn discreetly to your neighbors (or excuse yourself to help the host or hostess in the kitchen) to get a reading on how they felt, and whether or not you'll find support for speaking up. The less alone you feel, the more comfortable you'll be speaking up: "I know you probably didn't mean anything by that joke, Jim, but it really offended me. . . ." It's important to say that *you* were offended—not state how the group that is the butt of the joke would feel. "Otherwise," LeNorman Strong says, "you risk coming off as a goody two-shoes."

If you yourself are the host, you can exercise more control; you are, after all, the one who sets the rules and the tone of behavior in your home. Once, when Professor Kahn's party guests began singing offensive, racist songs, for instance, he kicked them all out, saying, "You don't sing songs like that in my house!" And, he adds, "they never did again."

At school one day, a friend comes over and says, "Who do you think you are, hanging out with Joe? If you can be friends with those people, I'm through with you!"

Peer pressure can weigh heavily on kids. They feel vulnerable and, because they are kids, they aren't as able to control the urge to fight. "But if you learn to handle these situations as kids, you'll be better able to handle them as an adult," William Newlin points out.

Begin by redefining to yourself what a friend is and examining what friendship means, advises Amy Lee, a human relations specialist at Panel of Americans, an intergroup-relations training and educational organization. If that person from a different group fits your requirement for a friend, ask, "Why shouldn't I be friends with Joe? We have a lot in common." Try to get more information about whatever stereotypes or resentments lie beneath your friend's statement. Ms. Lee suggests: "What makes you think they're so different from us? Where did you get that information?" She explains: "People are learning these stereotypes from somewhere, and they cannot be blamed for that. So examine where these ideas came from." Then talk about how your own experience rebuts them.

Kids, like adults, should also be aware of other resources to back them up: Does the school offer special programs for fighting prejudice? How supportive will the principal, the teachers, or other students be? If the school atmosphere is volatile, experts warn, make sure that taking a stand at that moment won't put you in physical danger. If that is the case, it's better to look for other alternatives.

These can include programs or organizations that bring kids from different backgrounds together. "When kids work together across race lines, that is how you break down the barriers and see that the stereotypes are not true," says Laurie Meadoff, president of CityKids Foundation, a nonprofit group whose programs attempt to do just that. Such programs can also provide what Cherie Brown calls a "safe place" to express the anger and pain that slurs and other offenses cause, whether the bigotry is directed against you or others.

In learning to speak up, everyone will develop a different style and a slightly different message to get across, experts agree. But it would be hard to do better than these two messages suggested by teenagers at City-Kids: "Everyone on the face of the earth has the same intestines," said one. Another added, "Cross over the bridge. There's a lot of love on the streets."

DIALOGUE

1. What responses to an ethnic slur or joke does the author consider to be inappropriate? Why are they inappropriate?
2. If racially insensitive remarks and bigoted statements are as prevalent in our society as the author suggests, what are the contributing causes? Do all cultures with diverse ethnic populations have the same problem?
3. Why does Diane Cole say that an offensive remark made "in the presence of others . . . can be even more distressing than an insult made privately"? Is this statement always true? If not, when isn't it true?

WRITING TOPICS

1. Describe how you respond to a racist joke or ethnic slur. Are you uncomfortable? Do you sometimes find these remarks amusing? If offended, do you respond? Explain.

2. Is a racist or ethnic joke acceptable if it is directed at one's own race or group? Explain why or why not.
3. Suggest specific ways that students can fight prejudice and bigotry on campus. What resources should be provided? How should the issue be presented to students to ensure a positive outcome?

INTERACTION

In small groups, list Cole's strategies for responding to offensive remarks. Discuss the effectiveness of each strategy.

Part V Reflections

Review the ideas you expressed at the beginning of this part in "Write Before You Read." How have your ideas changed as a result of reading the articles in this part? Explain in the space below.

1. Self-segregation on your campus _____

_____

_____

_____

_____

_____

2. Difficulties you have had understanding or accepting another

   culture _____

_____

_____

_____

_____

_____

3. Difficulties you have had being accepted by others _____

_____

_____

_____

_____

Part V Writing Assignment

In the early 1970s, William B. Shockley, an electrical engineer from Stanford University who was awarded the Nobel Prize for his invention of the junction transistor, stirred emotional controversy by presenting research "proving" that blacks are genetically less intelligent than whites. Despite the outrage provoked by his claim, he proposed that the U.S. government offer cash incentives for people with genetic deficiencies to undergo voluntary sterilization.

The controversy over race and intelligence resurfaced in 1994 with the publication of *The Bell Curve: Intelligence and Class Structure in American Life* by Charles Murray, a conservative policy analyst, and Richard J. Herrnstein, a Harvard psychologist, who argued that intelligence is hereditary and that the average IQ of blacks is fifteen points lower than that of whites.

This work, too, was greeted with a storm of protest, typified by the remarks of Alvin Poussaint, professor of psychiatry at Harvard Medical School, who called it "simplistic pseudoscience, bogus, false, stupid," and "a self-fulfilling prophecy." Poussaint, who is African American, said, "We were not enslaved because of low I.Q."

Prepare a short history of the controversy over intelligence and race. What social and political conditions caused this controversy to surface in the 1970s and again, a generation later, in the 1990s? Evaluate the conflicting claims of people on both sides of the argument.

LD
3930.2
.B9452